Learning the Language of Addiction Counseling

Geraldine A. Miller

Appalachian State University

Allyn and Bacon

Boston ■ London ■ Toronto ■ Sydney ■ Tokyo ■ Singapore

Senior Editor: Ray Short
Editorial Assistant: Karin Huang
Marketing Manager: Susan E. Ogar
Editorial-Production Administrator: Annette Joseph
Editorial-Production Coordinator: Holly Crawford
Editorial-Production Service: Lynda Griffiths, TKM Productions
Composition Buyer: Linda Cox
Manufacturing Buyer: Dave Repetto
Cover Administrator: Jenny Hart
Cover Designer: Brian Gogolin

Copyright © 1999 by Allyn & Bacon
A Viacom Company
160 Gould Street
Needham Heights, MA 02494

Internet: www.abacon.com

Library of Congress Cataloging-in-Publication Data

Miller, Geraldine A.
    Learning the language of addiction counseling / Geraldine A.
    Miller
        p.   cm.
    Includes bibliographical references and index.
    ISBN 0-205-26318-6
    1. Drug abuse counseling.   2. Substance abuse—Patients—
Counseling of. 3. Narcotic addicts—Patients—Counseling of.
I. Title.
RC564.M536   1998
616.86'06—dc21   98-29190
                                                        CIP

Printed in the United States of America

10 9 8 7 6 5 4 3 2   03 02 01 00

This book is dedicated to

Ron Hood, my husband and friend,
who was there through it all,

Gale, Abby, Jason, and Laura Miller,
my family,

the women who were with me from the beginning,
Donna Dale, Kathleen Kasprick, Pat Mitchell,
Judy Retterath, and Sharon Woods,

and the addicted clients and their loved ones
who I had the honor of counseling.

CONTENTS

PREFACE

Learning the Language of Addiction Counseling emerged from a desire to summarize the clinical, theoretical, and research work in the addiction counseling field from a practitioner's point of view. I have been lucky in my life to have been trained by numerous addiction counseling professionals who are deeply committed to the field, to helping people who are caught in a destructive cycle and who face horrific odds in life. Throughout my years of work in the addictions field, I have watched these professionals respect and care for individuals who have experienced, at a piercing level, a lack of self-respect and a lack of love both within themselves and from others. Their compassion for the suffering of both addicts and their loved ones led me to this field and has kept me in it all of these years.

This book provides a summary of addiction counseling based on practical application of both theory and research to counseling. It will serve as a reference that can be used by two groups: (1) undergraduate and graduate students who are training to be direct service workers with addicted individuals and (2) clinicians who are new to the field of addiction counseling or who would like to review some addiction counseling basics. Although the book discusses techniques and approaches that are grounded in research, it is considered more of a practitioner's than researcher's text.

Throughout the text, interactive exercises, such as case studies and discussion exercises, are provided to assist the reader in applying the information and to assist the teacher in integrating the material into classroom discussion. Because of the different avenues in the addictions field, there are often controversies regarding theory and practice. This book does not reconcile these differences, but it does fuse theoretical and practitioner concerns into a pragmatic counseling framework, resulting in a helpful manual for counselors who work with addicts. *Learning the Language of Addiction Counseling* is a text that a practitioner can turn to for fundamental, practical, clinical guidelines.

Chapter 1, Introduction, is a brief overview of addiction counseling and this book. It also examines past and current influences on addiction counseling.

Chapter 2, Assessment and Diagnosis of Addiction, examines the assessment process with clients. Interviews, behavioral observations, physiological instruments, and psychometric instruments are discussed.

Chapter 3, Assessment and Diagnosis of Dual Disorders, explores the assessment process within the context of dual disorders. Specifically, principles of diagnosis and treatment, general guidelines, types of diagnosis, and treatment modifications are presented.

Chapter 4, The Treatment Process for Addictions, provides an overview of addiction treatment. Four specific forms of addiction counseling are discussed: crisis intervention, individual, group, and family.

Chapter 5, Treatment-Related Issues, explores issues that may arise in relation to addiction counseling. The chapter addresses the specific topics of sexual abuse, sexual orientation, and HIV/AIDS; domestic violence; and eating disorders. Recommendations for counseling in these related areas are provided.

Chapter 6, Relapse Prevention, provides an overview of relapse prevention issues. Counselor approaches, models, and techniques are explored.

Chapter 7, Self-Help Groups, addresses the national, abstinence-based self-help groups in the United States. Five specific groups are presented in terms of their historical development, basic concepts, use in counseling, and strengths and weaknesses.

Chapter 8, Brief Therapy and Addiction Counseling, presents information on brief therapy, one of the most current addiction treatment modalities, as it relates to addiction counseling. Counselor attitudes, screening and interviewing, theoretical orientations and interventions, possible clinical issues, and treatment effectiveness are examined.

Chapter 9, Treatment of Addiction: Special Issues, examines issues that have an impact on addiction counseling. These issues include multicultural counseling as it relates to gender, race, disability, adolescents, the elderly, and the homeless.

Chapter 10, Professional Development of the Counselor, explores areas of professional development concern for the counselor. Ethical issues, court testimony, working with difficult others, self-care, and issues related to working with addicts are discussed.

Acknowledgments

I cannot possibly name the many professional role models I have encountered in the field but I do acknowledge each and every one of you. You know who you are. You spent time explaining basic concepts of working in this field to me, you challenged me to be the best therapist and person I could be, and you never settled for less in me or gave up on me. Thank you from the core of my being.

I also gratefully acknowledge the addicted clients and their loved ones who taught me through their amazing life stories about the destructive nature of addiction and the amazing capacity of the human spirit to survive and change. I thank these many people for showing me how to work in this field and how to live in this world. The courage and integrity of watching individuals struggle to break out of the pain of the addictive cycle is a powerful experience. To these people, I simply say, Thank you.

My gratitude is offered to the following reviewers for their comments and suggestions: William V. Fassbender (College of New Jersey), Edlyn N. Jones (Indiana University–Purdue University at Ft. Wayne), Patricia A. Markos (University of Nevada–Las Vegas), and Anne Helene Skinstad (The University of Iowa).

Additionally, I want to thank the people who believed I could write such a book and supported me on the journey. Ray Short, Senior Editor at Allyn and Bacon, gave me support, challenged me, and added humor along the way. His early words of encouragement to me, "I want this to be a good experience for you," stayed with me throughout the writing of the book. Lee Baruth, Chairperson of my department, Human Development and Psychological Counseling, encouraged me to "try and see what happens" and provided me with practical manuscript writing suggestions throughout the process. Finally, Ron Hood, my husband and friend, painstakingly read every word in this book and always said, "I believe in you." To Ray, Lee, and Ron: Thank you for walking this journey with me.

1 Introduction

PRETEST

1. What factors increased mental health workers' interest in working with addicted individuals?
2. What are three main influences in addiction counseling?
3. Which addiction theory served as a bridge between the research community and the grassroots network?
4. How have these influences affected addiction treatment?
5. What is an example of a controversial topic in the addictions field?
6. What are four common components of theories of addiction?
7. What are the four main theoretical models of addiction?
8. Which addiction models seem most amenable to managed health care?

Mental health workers, both historically and currently, have not always liked working with alcoholics and addicts for at least two reasons: (1) the difficulty in treating them due to factors such as relapses, poor impulse control, emotional reactivity, and/or lying to protect their addiction; and (2) the lack of knowledge (techniques) on how best to treat them. However, an openness to treating addicts grew as information on how to treat addicts emerged and as additional funding for treatment became available. For example, addicts commonly deny the consequences of their usage to themselves and others (Levinthal, 1996). It became easier for counselors to deal with denial when the technique of intervention was introduced (Fields, 1995).

Changes in public policy also affected the work of counselors. In 1970, the National Institute on Alcohol Abuse and Alcoholism (NIAAA) was established to provide funding for alcoholism treatment and research, and in the 1970s, insurance companies began to reimburse agencies for providing addiction treatment (O'Dwyer, 1993). It was the Hughes Act (Public Law 91-616) in 1970 that established NIAAA, funded states that established alcoholism divisions, and started and maintained alcohol treatment programs for federal employees (Fisher & Harrison, 1997). This policy change expanded the field of addiction counseling.

Due to this expansion, in the 1980s, states started to create credentialing and licensing bodies to ensure quality addiction counseling (O'Dwyer, 1993); being a recovering addict no longer meant immediate entry into the addiction counseling field. Instead, addiction professionals needed to document a combination of credentials regarding both counseling experience and training. In 1993–94, the Commission on Rehabilitation Counselor Certification (CRCC) developed another certification to compliment the Certified Rehabilitation Counselor (CRC) certification: Certified Rehabilitation Counselor-Substance Abuse Counselor (CRC-SAC). Certification of addiction professionals expanded in 1995 when the National Board of Certified Counselors (NBCC) established an addiction certification specialty for mental health counselors, and in 1996, the American Psychological Association established a proficiency certification for licensed psychologists. As of January 1, 1997, counselors who are certified as addiction counselors by the CRCC, the NBCC, or the National Association of Alcoholism and Drug Abuse Counselors (NAADAC) can apply for the Master's in Addictions Counseling (MAC) certification ("New Credential for Addictions Counselors," 1996). For example, prior to January 1, 1997, CRC-SAC counselors could be grandfathered in to the credential of CRC-MAC.

With the growth of the addictions field in terms of research and treatment, there are now many routes of entry into addiction counseling. One may enter the field through a primarily research-based avenue, a grassroots network avenue, or a certification/licensure process. As a result, there are numerous disagreements in the field of addictions regarding applicable theoretical models and effective treatment approaches based on the individual's personal and/or professional biases. For example, some addiction experts emphasize the strengths of the disease model of addiction and Alcoholics Anonymous (AA) (Gragg, 1995), whereas other experts point out the weaknesses of the disease model and AA (Marlatt, 1985a).

Addiction Counseling Influences

Currently, there are three main influences in addiction counseling. One influence is the traditional addiction counseling approach of the *disease model,* which asks: Is this approach healing for the addict within the scope of the disease model of addiction? A second influence is from the *addiction research,* which presents counselors with the question: Which addiction counseling approaches are supported in research findings? A final, and more recent, influence stems from *managed care organizations,* which confront counselors with the question: What counseling approaches provide the greatest benefit for the least cost?

Because each of these influences has an important impact on addiction counseling, there are numerous areas of conflict in the addictions field. For example, disease model counselors may advocate use of the term *codependency* for the partners and family members of addicts, but the research community may respond by stating that there is not enough research to warrant the use of such a diagnostic term, and the managed care organizations may not be willing to pay for codependency treatment because of the disagreement among the professionals. It is important to understand the historical influences of both the addiction treatment disease model and addiction research.

Disease Model of Addiction Treatment

The addiction counseling field has two main root systems: a grassroots addiction recovery network and a research community base. In 1935, the grassroots recovery network began with the formation of the self-help group, Alcoholics Anonymous (AA). AA looked at alcoholics as having an allergy to alcohol, which results in a craving and a loss of control (Alcoholics Anonymous, 1939). Other than Thomas Trotter and Benjamin Rush, who, at the end of the eighteenth century, viewed alcoholism as a disease, alcoholism was typically viewed as a moral weakness (O'Dwyer, 1993). AA's view of alcoholism as an allergic reaction helped shift alcoholism from a moral problem to a physical or medical problem: The alcoholic was no longer blamed for developing the addiction (Marlatt, 1985a).

The AA view of alcoholism as an allergic reaction affected treatment in a number of ways. First, defining addiction as a physical reaction (allergy, craving) allowed the addicted individual to feel not like a "bad person," but a "sick person," which preserved or restored self-esteem and self-respect. Second, viewing addicts as having an allergic reaction to mood-altering substances provided a simple, straightforward definition of their struggle that most people can readily grasp. Third, this grassroots model encouraged the use of self-help groups, thereby helping addicts develop a sense of community.

Addiction Research

While the self-help group movement was growing, so was the research on addiction. About the same time as AA's development, the federal government began two drug treatment programs for prisoners, which facilitated research opportunities on addictions (O'Dwyer, 1993). Through his alcoholism research and the creation of the Yale School of Alcohol Studies in 1942, Jellinek developed the disease model of alcoholism (Bowman & Jellinek, 1941; Gragg, 1995; Jellinek, 1960). The disease model of alcoholism fit well with AA's model of an allergy, and a significant bridge developed between the self-help group movement and the research community. In 1956, the American Medical Association agreed that alcoholism was a disease (Marlatt, 1985a). Through the development of the disease model of alcoholism, both the self-help group movement and the research community guided mental health professionals in their work with addicts (Gragg, 1995).

In a manner similar to AA's view of addiction as an allergy, the disease model of addiction had an impact on treatment. The addict's self-esteem and respect is preserved or restored because the problem is framed as physically, not morally, based. Also, the disease model provided information regarding the stages of the disease's development, thereby enhancing the diagnostic process. Finally, the model provided counselors with a framework and terminology to provide clients with information about the current and eventual progression of the disease.

Managed Care Organizations

Significant concerns regarding the third influence, managed care organizations, abound in the addictions field. Armstrong (1997) summarizes three common areas of focus in managed care: accessing care, containing costs, and assuring quality. The primary impact of managed care on addictions treatment is a shortened length of treatment. Due to limited funding, counselors increasingly need to use briefer therapy models as well as assist clients in accessing community supports, such as self-help groups, to provide effective, comprehensive care. Although counselors may experience negative reactions to the treatment control of managed care, they must work with the economic realities of the managed care philosophy (Hood & Miller, 1997).

As a result of the increasing emphasis on cost containment by these health organizations, Chapter 8 will focus on brief therapy as it applies to addiction counseling. Also, counseling approaches presented in the text are suggested, in part, because of their fit with managed care philosophy. For example, Chapter 6 focuses on relapse prevention. For clinicians to work with clients who have addiction problems within a managed care framework, clinicians need to include relapse prevention information early in treatment because of a limited number of treatment sessions. Also, because managed care funding may encourage counselors to make use of community services for their clients to augment the limited number of therapy sessions, this text will emphasize community counseling approaches. For example, Chapter 7 focuses on self-help groups. It provides counselors with an opportunity both to learn about the philosophy of some of the national self-help groups and to assist their clients in making the best use of them.

Theories of Addiction

In the face of these many changes in the addictions field, theories of addiction have also changed. Some theories may be more popular in one area of the country than another. A counselor working with addicted individuals should find and become familiar with a model he or she is comfortable using for the assessment and treatment process. Also important are the theories of addiction advocated by the counselor's employer, the client's funding organization, and the state's addiction credentialing and licensing board. The theoretical models advocated by these organizations can have an impact on the counselor's employment, the client's treatment, and the counselor's liability, especially with regard to court testimony. Although theoretical models vary, there is a standard classification of addiction found in the *Diagnostic and Statistical Manual of Mental Disorders (DSM-IV)* frequently used by professionals.

The *DSM-IV* (APA, 1994) classifies mood-altering substances into 11 substance-related disorders: alcohol, amphetamine, caffeine, cannabis, cocaine, hallucinogens, inhalants, nicotine, opiods, phencyclidine (PCP), and sedatives, hypnotics, and anxiolytics. Substance-Related Disorders in the *DSM-IV* are divided into two categories: Substance Use (Dependence and Abuse) and Substance-Induced (intoxication, withdrawal, delirium, dementia, amnestic, psychotic, mood disorder, anxiety, sexual dysfunction, and sleep disorder).

To meet the criteria for dependence, the client must have a maladaptive use pattern causing some type of impairment with at least three of the following occurring within one year: tolerance; withdrawal; more or longer use than planned; desire without ability to cut down or control usage; time spent on obtaining, using, or recovering from the substance; impact on activities that are social, occupational, or recreational (do less or not at all); and continued use in spite of physical or psychological problems related to use. Counselors need to refer to the *DSM-IV* to understand more thoroughly the complexities of a dependence diagnosis.

McHugh, Beckman, and Frieze (1979) provide a four-part framework (moral, psychological, sociocultural, and medical) that helps link theoretical models of addiction to the diagnosis of dependence. Each theoretical model includes a view of alcoholism, cause of alcoholism, and form of treatment, yet each emphasizes different addiction components. Some of these components are (Leigh, 1985):

1. *Cultural factors,* which influence how a person decides to take a drug, attitudes toward taking the drug, the practices of a group/subculture, and the drug's availability
2. *Environmental factors,* which include conditioning and reinforcement principles (drugs are taken to experience pleasure and reduce discomfort), learning factors (modeling, imitation, identification, etc.), and life events
3. *Interpersonal factors,* which include social influences (life-style choice, peer pressure, expectations of drug use, etc.) and family factors (system maintenance, genetic influences, etc.)
4. *Intrapersonal factors,* which include human development, personality, affect/ cognition, and sex differences

The following four models incorporate different aspects of these factors. One of the main concerns in managed health care is cost containment, which has an impact on developing specific therapeutic interventions (Austad & Berman, 1995). Some addiction theories are more amenable to this type of therapeutic framework than others and will be highlighted in the following theoretical discussion.

Moral Model

The moral model views the alcoholic as a degenerate and sees alcoholism as a moral weakness (Keller, 1976). Punishment is preferred over treatment because a cure is not envisioned (McHugh, Beckman, & Frieze, 1979).

Psychological Models

There are three main psychological theories: psychodynamic, personality trait, and behavior learning. Although each theory views the specific cause of alcoholism differently, they all share a similar outlook: The causal factors must be changed in order for treatment to be effective.

Psychodynamic theory focuses on the personal pathology of alcoholics. The goal in treatment is to uncover the unconscious conflicts. Because the conflicts are seen as fairly unchanging, treatment is not viewed as very effective. An example of such a conflict is parental rejection that results in dependency needs that cannot be met in reality (Zimberg, 1985).

The focus in personality trait theory is on changing the personality traits of the alcoholic—for example, treating high anxiety (Barry, 1974). However, treatment is not very effective because of the stability of personality traits (McHugh, Beckman, & Frieze, 1979).

The behavior-learning theorists emphasize the changing of reinforcements, since alcohol is reinforcing for alcoholics. For instance, a change in reinforcers may occur by changing environments (Wallace, 1985). This theory offers the best prognosis of the three psychological theories, for reinforcers can be readily changed.

Because the behavioral-learning theorists emphasize the reinforcements involved in alcohol/drug addiction, the counselor working within the framework of a managed care organization can use this theory in the treatment and recovery process (Tulkin & Frank, 1985). The counselor can develop a plan with the client that examines how the client is specifically reinforced by abusing alcohol/drugs. For example, if a client is psychologically addicted to marijuana because it helps him or her relax, the counselor can use this information to help the client develop a treatment and recovery maintenance plan that includes relaxation coping skills.

Sociocultural Models

The sociocultural model emphasizes social forces and contexts that give birth to and feed alcoholism. Cultural attitudes (Marlatt, 1985b), family structure (Bowen, 1978), and crisis times (Bratter, 1985) need to be addressed in order to have an impact on alcoholism. Treatment focuses on changing the environmental contexts for the alcoholic.

One example of a sociocultural model is Cushman's (1990) Empty Self Theory. In this model, industrialization, urbanization, and secularism are societal aspects that have resulted in the increasing loss of family, community, and tradition—those things that offer people shared meaning in their lives. The loss of these aspects results in an empty self, which views psychological boundaries as specific ("My mental health depends on me"), a locus of control as internal ("I am in charge of my life"), and a wish to manipulate the external world for personal ends ("I will be happy if I manage well"). Cushman (1990) states that the active addict, then, is using drugs to fight off feelings of alienation, fragmentation, worthlessness, and confusion (particularly around values). This theory can be readily applied in addiction counseling by assisting the client in developing a recovery life-style that involves a sense of family, community, and tradition, all supportive of the addiction recovery.

Medical Model

The medical model looks at specific physiological dysfunctions such as endocrine dysfunction (Gross, 1945). Although theories in the medical model may assist in defining and describing alcoholism, they fail to promote any specific treatments. The disease model of alcoholism is related to this category because of its basis in physiology (i.e., genetic predisposition, allergic reaction); however, it has a slightly different twist to it because of the individual's responsibility for future behavior and the need for spiritual help in recovery.

The disease model views alcoholism as a progressive disease with symptoms. The two key elements in this model are loss of control over drinking and progression of the disease, which ends in death. This view is partially accepted by Alcoholics Anonymous (McHugh, Beckman, & Frieze, 1979): Alcoholism is an illness that is physical, mental, and spiritual in nature, and the alcoholic is not responsible for his or her addiction, but is responsible for future behavior. In AA, the alcoholic enters into recovery from addiction by admitting a powerlessness over alcohol as well as wrongs done to others, and receiving the help of a Higher Power (McHugh, Beckman, & Frieze, 1979)—what might be called a spiritual solution. This theory of addiction, according to Alcoholics Anonymous, has been implemented in what has been called the *Minnesota Model* of treatment: Professional services are combined with the 12 Steps of AA, using counselors who are often in addiction recovery themselves (O'Dwyer, 1993). Gragg (1995) highlights the benefits of using the disease model of alcoholism/addiction within a health maintenance organization (HMO) framework: It reduces the client's guilt over the addiction and it encourages community involvement (AA) to supplement managed care therapy.

More recently, models of addiction have been presented as biopsychosocial (Perkinson, 1997). In this type of model, biogenetic traits and psychosocial factors are combined when addressing addiction in an attempt to provide an integrated, comprehensive model.

Summary

Theories of addiction play a critical part in the assessment and treatment process for the client. The counselor working with addicts needs to be aware of the biases of his or her theoretical orientation in order to determine exactly what aspects will be addressed as well as overlooked by the theoretical approach. An awareness of one's theory at this level can result in a holistic therapeutic approach.

This chapter has established a baseline for examining addiction by addressing different theories in the field. The remaining chapters will focus on assessment and diagnosis, treatment, relapse prevention, self-help groups, brief therapy, special issues in treatment, and personal and professional development of the counselor.

CASE STUDY: JACOB

Jacob is a 30-year-old male who came to your agency for an addiction assessment. At his first session, he was diagnosed as addicted (according to *DSM-IV* criteria) to cocaine, his drug of choice. Jacob's HMO insurance coverage is limited to 5 days of inpatient treatment and 10 outpatient sessions with you. This is his first treatment for addiction. He tells you that all of his friends use cocaine and that his roommate started him on it. He says he likes cocaine because he does not feel depressed when he takes it. He also states that he feels like a failure because he became a drug addict like his father.

1. How would you use behavioral theories in terms of Jacob's recovery?
2. How would his culture be important to his recovery process?
3. What aspect of the disease model might be helpful to him?

SUGGESTED READINGS

Cushman, P. (1990). Why the self is empty. *American Psychologist, 45,* 599–611.

Gragg, D. M. (1995). Managed health care systems: Chemical dependency treatment. In C. S. Austad & W. H. Berman (Eds.), *Psychotherapy in managed health care* (pp. 202–219). Washington, DC: American Psychological Association.

Jellinek, E. M. (1960). *The disease concept of alcoholism.* New York: College and University Press.

Marlatt, G. A. (1985a). Relapse prevention: Theoretical rationale and overview of the model. In G. A. Marlatt & J. R. Gordon (Eds.), *Relapse prevention: Maintenance strategies in the treatment of addictive behaviors* (pp. 3–70). New York: Guilford.

McHugh, M., Beckman, L., & Frieze, I. H. (1979). Analyzing alcoholism. In I. H. Frieze, D. Bar-Tal, & J. S. Carroll (Eds.), *New approaches to social problems* (pp. 168–208). San Francisco: Jossey-Bass.

O'Dwyer, P. (1993). Alcoholism treatment facilities. In S. L. A. Straussner (Ed.), *Clinical work with substance-abusing clients* (pp. 119–134). New York: Guilford.

REFERENCES

Alcoholics Anonymous. (1939). *Alcoholics anonymous* (1st ed.). New York: Author.

American Psychiatric Association. (1994). *Diagnostic and statistical manual of mental disorders* (4th ed.). Washington, DC: Author.

Armstrong, G. (1997). Managed care. In J. H. Lowinson, P. Ruiz, R. B. Millman, & J. G. Langrod (Eds.), *Substance abuse: A comprehensive textbook* (3rd ed.) (pp. 911–920). Baltimore: Williams & Wilkins.

Austad, C. S., & Berman, W. H. (1995). Managed health care and the evolution of psychotherapy. In C. S. Austad & W. H. Berman (Eds.), *Psychotherapy in managed health care* (pp. 3–18). Washington, DC: American Psychological Association.

Barry, H., III. (1974). Psychological factors in alcoholism. In B. Kissin & H. Begleiter (Eds.), *The biology of alcoholism. Volume 3: Clinical pathology* (pp. 53–108). New York: Plenum.

Bowen, M. (1978). *Family therapy in clinical practice.* New York: Jason Aronson.

Bowman, K., & Jellinek, E. M. (1941). Alcohol addiction and its treatment. *Quarterly Journal of Studies on Alcohol, 2,* 18–176.

Bratter, T. E. (1985). Special clinical psychotherapeutic concerns for alcoholic and drug-addicted individuals. In T. E. Bratter & G. G. Forrest (Eds.), *Alcoholism and substance abuse strategies for clinical intervention* (pp. 523–574). New York: Free Press.

Cushman, P. (1990). Why the self is empty. *American Psychologist, 45,* 599–611.

Fields, R. (1995). *Drugs in perspective* (2nd ed.). Madison, WI: Brown & Benchmark.

Fisher, G. L., & Harrison, T. C. (1997). *Substance abuse: Information for school counselors, social workers, therapists, and counselors.* Boston: Allyn and Bacon.

Gragg, D. M. (1995). Managed health care systems: Chemical dependency treatment. In C. S. Austad & W. H. Berman (Eds.), *Psychotherapy in managed health care* (pp. 202–219). Washington, DC: American Psychological Association.

Gross, M. (1945). The relation of the pituitary gland to some symptoms of alcohol intoxication and chronic alcoholism. *Quarterly Journal of Studies on Alcohol, 6,* 25–35.

Hood, R., & Miller, G. (1997). Maintaining compassion in an era of health care management technology. *Proceedings of the Sixth International Counseling Conference.* Beijing, China.

Jellinek, E. M. (1960). *The disease concept of alcoholism.* New York: College and University Press.

Keller, M. (1976). The disease concept of alcoholism revisited. *Journal of Studies on Alcohol, 11,* 1701.

Leigh, G. (1985). Psychosocial factors in the etiology of substance abuse. In T. E. Bratter & G. G. Forrest (Eds.), *Alcoholism and substance abuse: Strategies for clinical intervention* (pp. 3–48). New York: Free Press.

Levinthal, C. F. (1996). *Drugs, behavior, and modern society.* Boston: Allyn and Bacon.

Marlatt, G. A. (1985a). Relapse prevention: Theoretical rationale and overview of the model. In G. A. Marlatt & J. R. Gordon (Eds.), *Relapse prevention: Maintenance strategies in the treatment of addictive behaviors* (pp. 3–70). New York: Guilford.

Marlatt, G. A. (1985b). Cognitive factors in the relapse process. In G. A. Marlatt & J. R. Gordon (Eds.), *Relapse prevention: Maintenance strategies in the treatment of addictive behaviors* (pp. 128–200). New York: Guilford.

McHugh, M., Beckman, L., & Frieze, I. H. (1979). Analyzing alcoholism. In I. H. Frieze, D. Bar-Tal, & J. S. Carroll (Eds.), *New approaches to social problems* (pp. 168–208). San Francisco: Jossey-Bass.

New credential for addictions counselors. (1996). *Counseling Today, 39,* 42.

O'Dwyer, P. (1993). Alcoholism treatment facilities. In S. L. A. Straussner (Ed.), *Clinical work with substance-abusing clients* (pp. 119–134). New York: Guilford.

Perkinson, R. R. (1997). *Chemical dependency counseling: A practical guide.* Thousand Oaks, CA: Sage.

Spiegel, B. R. (1993). 12-Step programs as a treatment modality. In S. L. A. Straussner (Ed.), *Clinical work with substance-abusing clients* (pp. 153–168). New York: Guilford.

Tulkin, S., & Frank, G. W. (1985). The changing role of psychologists in health maintenance organizations. *American Psychologist, 40,* 1125–1129.

Wallace, J. (1985). Behavioral modification methods as adjuncts to psychotherapy. In S. Zimberg, J. Wallace, & S. Blume (Eds.), *Practical approaches to alcoholism psychotherapy* (pp. 109–129). New York: Plenum.

Zimberg, S. (1985). Principles of alcoholism psychotherapy. In S. Zimberg, J. Wallace, & S. B. Blume (Eds.), *Practical approaches to alcoholism psychotherapy* (pp. 3–21). New York: Plenum.

CHAPTER

2 Assessment and Diagnosis of Addiction

PRETEST

1. How can a counselor obtain accurate information yet also be respectful of clients?

2. Which instruments are helpful in a broad, general screening of alcohol/drug use?

3. What aspects of a chemical use history are important for a counselor to know?

4. How may it be helpful, clinically, to know about a client's previous treatments?

5. What areas of life need to be examined for consequences of alcohol/drug use?

6. Why is interviewing significant others important?

7. What is a limited use contract and how is it helpful to an assessment?

8. How might physiological instruments help an assessment?

9. What are some examples of psychometric instruments that can be used for adults? Adolescents?

10. How is the *DSM-IV* used in the assessment and diagnosis process?

Assessment of alcohol/drug use requires a counselor to be thorough in terms of both depth and breadth. Shaffer and Kauffman (1985) suggest using many different sources in order to make a quality assessment. These sources include interviews with clients (along with case histories) and significant others, behavioral observations, physiological instruments, and psychometric instruments.

Interviews

Interviewing Clients

As Straussner (1993) indicates, the first priority of an assessment is not to stereotype the individual who is being assessed. In order to accomplish this openness, the counselor must be able to hear the individual's story as well as obtain verification that the client's story is accurate. Hearing the individual's story means that the clinician must establish an atmosphere where the client feels invited to tell his or her story of alcohol/drug usage. Treating clients with respect can facilitate any evaluation, including those of clients who are involuntarily present for an assessment.

Because individuals who are addicted may use defense mechanisms (e.g., denial) when asked about their usage (Griffin, 1991), a counselor may be drawn to using a confrontational approach in the interview process. However, the style of the interview (i.e., focusing on labeling the problem and insisting the client accept this label) may encourage resistance and defensiveness in the client (Lewis, Dana, & Blevins, 1994). The counselor, then, walks a fine line between a commitment to obtaining accurate information in order to maintain a quality assessment and being aware that individuals who are addicted may distort their usage in order to prevent their addiction from being discovered by the counselor.

One way to approach an assessment process fairly is to tell the client that information will be drawn from numerous sources and that a pattern of behaviors will be looked for throughout the assessment process. The client will have an awareness from the beginning, then, that not only will his or her story be a source of information, but other avenues of information will be sought.

Initially, a counselor may want to use a broad general assessment instrument, such as the CAGE, MAC/MAC-R, or MAST (see Psychometric Instruments section). The use of one of these instruments may determine if additional evaluation is required.

In the interview process, the counselor needs to ask the client what he or she sees as the presenting problem. Although this may be a different answer than the referral source (if the referral source is different from the client), it may assist the counselor in determining the client's level of concern with his or her alcohol/drug use. In addition, gathering information regarding the client's family of origin, particularly around history of addiction, may be beneficial to the assessment process. Finally, knowledge of the client's living situation may underscore some environmental factors (e.g., roommate's usage) that are influencing client use and may be possible sources for relapse if the client is determined to have an alcohol/drug problem. With regard to chemical use history, a counselor wants to find out the date of the client's last use, his or her drug of choice, drugs that have been used, prior treatments for abuse and addiction problems, and any consequences for using drugs (legal; family, significant others, friends; job, school, military; medical; financial; etc.). Senay (1997) suggests the counselor ask about frequency and amount with regard to alcohol, cannabis, central nervous system (CNS) depressants (barbiturates, benzodiazipines), CNS stimulants (amphetamines, crack, cocaine), opiods, hallucinogens, PCP, inhalants, nicotine, caffeine, and over-the-counter drugs. The date of the client's last chemical usage is important in determining the presence of a life-threatening process of withdrawal. The reported date of last use can provide the counselor with helpful baseline information for possible confrontation later in the interview. For example, the client may say he drinks only a couple beers once a week on Fridays, yet may say he had four mixed drinks on Tuesday.

The assessment may reveal that the client may or may not have a drug of choice—that is, the drug the client most frequently uses or prefers. If there is a drug of choice, it is important to determine the pattern of usage with this drug and the life consequences that it has brought the client. It may also indicate the focus of treatment in terms of any denial process; for example, a client may realize he or she has a problem with the drug of choice, but be able to rationalize the usage of other drugs.

When taking drug history information, the age of the client's first use and the age of last use for each drug reported should be noted. Then, during that time for each drug, the counselor should examine the typical use pattern and the most recent typical use pattern (including how much, how often, use setting, and administration route). For example, a woman may have increased her marijuana usage to daily at the time of a divorce for about two years, even though she had been smoking marijuana once a week for ten years, and in the last one year (three years since her divorce) she has only smoked it once a month. This provides an indication that she probably used the marijuana as a way to cope with the stress of her divorce. It may be frustrating for a client to be asked such specific questions regarding each drug ever used. Prefacing and restating through the information gathering that the client make his or her best guess regarding dates will help alleviate this problem. Throughout the assessment, the client may need to be reminded that accurate information requires very specific questioning and the counselor is not intending to upset him or her by asking such detailed questions.

Asking the client about prior treatment for substance abuse or dependency is important for a number of reasons. First, previous treatment is indicative of an abuse problem with alcohol/drugs. Second, previous treatment experiences may affect the view of the client in terms of his or her approach to this assessment. Third, previous treatment means that there are records that can be obtained, with the client's consent, for corroborating information. Fourth, previous treatment information may be able to guide the treatment planning to make it more effective for the client.

The counselor also wants to know of any consequences experienced due to the use of alcohol/drugs. Specific areas to examine include legal; family, significant others, and friends; job, school, and military; medical; and financial. One way to ask about consequences is to ask the client if there have ever been any problems in these areas where alcohol/drugs have been involved. Asking the question in such a manner does not imply causality, but does get at the overlap of using alcohol/drugs and behavior. The consequences are an important source of corroborating information by the counselor. If the client agrees, releases of information can be obtained for each area that seems pertinent in order to receive information regarding the level of the alcohol/drug problem. If the client does not agree to signing releases of information, the counselor needs to document on the chart that the assessment is limited in scope and possibly in terms of accuracy because the client refused to allow information to be gathered from specific, relevant sources. This refusal also needs to be shared with any referral agent for the client's evaluation.

Some sample questions that may be used in an interview process follow:

1. What happened in your life that caused you to come in for an assessment of your alcohol/drug usage?
2. Is there any history of addiction (chemical or other) in your family of origin?
3. Where do you currently live? Who do you currently live with? What is that person's (persons') use of alcohol/drugs like?
4. When is the last time you used alcohol or drugs?
5. What is your favorite drug and how do you like to take it (smoking, inhaling, injecting, ingesting)?
6. Tell me all the drugs you have ever tried.
7. (For each drug reported) When did you first take this drug? When did you last take this drug? What was your typical use pattern with this drug? Within the last few months (or years, depending on the person's length of use history), how have you typically used this drug?
8. Have you ever been treated previously for addiction? If so, where, when, how long, and what type of treatment (inpatient, outpatient, detox)? How long did you stay sober after each treatment and what helped you stay sober that long?
9. (If the client had previous treatment) What was most helpful to you in that treatment? What was least helpful to you?
10. Have you ever experienced any problems in the ____ area connected with your alcohol and drug use? (Put in one area each time this question is asked: legal; family, significant others, friends; job, school, military; medical; financial.)

Finally, the counselor needs to use a mental status examination throughout the interview process. Buelow and Buelow (1998) suggest that the exam cover the client's functioning in terms of appearance, orientation, behavior, speech, cooperation, mood, perception, thinking process, intellectual abilities, and insight/judgment.

Interviewing Significant Others

Interviews with significant others are similar to those with the client. Significant others include those individuals who are close to the client and know him or her well. For example, this may include parents, children, intimate partner, and co-workers. When interviewing significant others, it is necessary for the counselor to remember that the significant other may have a hidden agenda (e.g., a lot of pent-up anger) that slants his or her viewpoint, or may have his or her own denial about the alcohol/drug problem, or may be unable to tell the truth about his or her concerns due to some dynamics of the relationship (e.g., a domestic violence situation). Keeping in mind these possible limitations, the counselor can begin to obtain information from the significant other.

The client needs to sign a release that allows the counselor to talk with the significant other. The significant other needs to understand that the client is aware of and has agreed to a discussion of his or her alcohol/drug-taking behavior. Once the parameters of the situation are understood, the counselor needs to obtain a brief history of the relationship between the client and the significant other. This will provide the counselor with a context for understanding the information given. It is also important for the counselor to determine if the significant other may also have a drinking and drug problem by asking such questions as: Do you often drink with_____? How often and how much do the two of you drink in a week? Even though the significant other is not being evaluated for a drinking/drug problem, the counselor needs to know if there is a possibility of such a problem in the significant other, because it could affect the assessment and, if appropriate, treatment and aftercare process.

The significant other needs to be asked similar questions regarding the client's alcohol/drug usage as the client was asked. Finding out what the significant other views as the presenting problem may provide the counselor with valuable information. Also, hearing from the significant other about the client's family of origin, living situation, drug of choice, drug use history, previous treatment, and consequences of his or her usage may provide additional, clarifying information that can be used in the assessment process. The significant other may involve more than one individual. For example, the counselor may want to talk with an entire family about the information they have regarding the client's use. Once again, the counselor needs to remember that individuals may differ in their perceptions, but what is being sought are patterns of behavior that emerge in different areas of the client's life.

Behavioral Observations

Involving the client in observing his or her own alcohol/drug-using behavior can work to educate the client and the counselor about the client's usage. One example of such a behavioral observation is to have the client agree to a limited use contract. In this type of contract, the counselor asks the client to set a limit on his or her usage with one drug (and not using other drugs at all), preferably the client's drug of choice or most frequently used drug. This limit is set for less than the typical amount used and for a specific time. For instance, the client may normally drink six beers three times a week and use small amounts of marijuana and speed. The contract may read that the client will not drink more than three beers at a sitting for one month (and will not use marijuana, speed, or any other drug at all). The counselor would ask the client to keep a log of his or her use. If the amount is exceeded, the counselor would then ask the client to note the situation and why the amount was exceeded. The client needs to understand that an inability to follow the agreed-upon limit indicates a problem with alcohol/drugs.

The client may be in denial and return to the counselor with notations made as to when the agreement was violated and why. This is an excellent opportunity for the counselor to confront the client regarding his or her possible drug problem. The client also may not tell the counselor the truth about his or her usage. Even if the information about breaking the limit does not get back to the session, that does not mean that the client did not learn from the experience. The client may have learned that he or she has an alcohol/drug problem because of the inability to limit usage. If the client was able to follow the use limit, this information can also be used in the diagnostic process as an indication of control over chemical use.

Other behavioral observations may occur more formally or informally. That information can be supplied through chart notations made at institutions and through conversations with individuals in different aspects of the client's life.

Physiological Instruments

One way to obtain information regarding a client's chemical usage is through medical examinations and diagnostic tests. Physicians may be able to document the irrefutable impact of alcohol/drugs on the client's body. Also, when high or in withdrawal, an addicted client may appear to have physical or psychiatric problems that are present only because of their relationship with the drug(s) (Vereby & Buchan, 1997). Therefore, a summary of medical history and concerns may assist the assessing counselor in determining if a problem is present by providing factual information about the client's body that can be readily linked to problems with alcohol/drugs.

Another avenue for determining if a client has been free of alcohol/drugs is through drug testing. A counselor may check on a drug testing referral process by contacting a local alcohol/drug treatment center to determine how it does drug testing. Inaba and Cohen (1989) report that there are numerous forms of drug testing that can be done with samples of tissue, hair, blood, saliva, and urine. If a counselor uses a form of drug testing, the counselor needs to receive informed consent from the client, carefully choose the laboratory that will do the testing, and know both the limitations and strengths of the methods used (Miller & Kaplan, 1996). An obvious drawback to such an approach in an assessment process is that it may cause the client to feel untrusted by the counselor in terms of his or her self-report. Using drug testing in the assessment process needs to be carefully weighed by the counselor in terms of this potential mistrust. The counselor may decrease the anxiety and/or defensiveness of the client by reframing the purpose of the drug testing. For example, it may help clients to be reminded that people who are addicted tend to have a sense of denial about their addiction and that during their assessment and treatment process they may need to have some validation of their sobriety by taking a test. This process does not need to occur throughout their recovery, but sometimes, especially early in the process, it may prevent the client and counselor from conflicting views around usage by having an outside, objective view (test results) incorporated into the counseling. Also, a matter-of-fact attitude by the counselor can communicate this testing as a routine process done with clients.

The same approaches can be used when the client is court-ordered for testing. Within this context, the counselor needs to talk openly with the client about the requirement for the testing and the impact of this testing on the counseling relationship.

Psychometric Instruments

The National Institute on Alcohol Abuse and Alcoholism (1995) lists nine factors that a counselor needs to consider when selecting an assessment instrument:

1. The use of the instrument
2. The alcohol use time frame being assessed
3. The population for which the instrument was developed
4. The groups used in determining the evaluative capacity of the instrument
5. The comparison norms available
6. The options for administration
7. The administration training required
8. The availability of computerized scoring
9. The cost

Each counselor may not have access to all of the tests discussed next, so he or she should choose one or two from each section (broad/overview, adult, adolescent) based on these nine criteria. The counselor may then become familiar with the instrument he or she anticipates using most often. The NIAAA (1995) provides a thorough review of alcohol assessment instruments. The following review is a select one, emphasizing a few instruments that may be used in a broad fashion, and more extensive assessment instruments that may be used with adults and adolescents.

When choosing and using tests, the counselor needs to be familiar with the reliability and validity of the tests in order to choose and use them appropriately. *Reliability* reflects the consistency of the instrument (the stability of the instrument) and *validity* reflects if the test meets its intended purpose (it measures what it is intending to measure). There are different types of reliability (test-retest, alternate form, internal consistency, Kuder-Richardson formula 20 coefficient, and Cronbach's coefficient alpha) and validity (content, construct, criterion-related, and predictive) (Sattler, 1992). Typically, reliability coefficients of .80 or greater reflect adequate reliability. For example, a reliability coefficient of .80 means that 80 percent of the score is true and 20 percent is due to error.

Broad Overview

The following three instruments (CAGE, MAC/MAC-R, MAST) can be used by a clinician to obtain a general overview of the client's alcohol/drug usage. Positive indicators of an alcohol/drug problem can be more extensively evaluated by applicable instruments in the next two sections on adults and adolescents.

CAGE

The CAGE (Ewing, 1984) has been used to determine if there is a problem with alcohol. It can be given verbally or in a paper-and-pencil format. The first letter of each of the capitalized phrases spells out the acronym (see Figure 2.1). The instrument can be used

FIGURE 2.1   The CAGE Questionnaire

1. Have you ever felt that you ought to CUT DOWN on your drinking?
2. Have people ANNOYED you by criticizing your drinking?
3. Have you ever felt bad or GUILTY about your drinking?
4. Have you ever had a drink first thing in the morning? (EYE OPENER) to steady your nerves or get rid of a hangover?

Note: Scoring is either a 0 or a 1 for each item and clinical significance is noted at total scores of 2 or greater.

Source: "Detecting Alcoholism: The CAGE Questionnaire" by J. A. Ewing, 1984, *Journal of the American Medical Association, 252,* pages 1905–1907. Copyright 1984, American Medical Association. Reprinted by permission.

with individuals age 16 or older and appears to have internal consistency reliability and criterion validity (NIAAA, 1995).

MAC and MAC-R

The MacAndrew Alcoholism Scale (MAC) and the MacAndrew Alcoholism Scale-Revised (MAC-R) are also measurements of alcohol/drug use (Duckworth & Anderson, 1986; Graham, 1990). The MAC consists of 49 objective true/false statements included in the 566-item Minnesota Multiphasic Personality Inventory (MMPI), which was developed in the 1930s and 1940s. The MAC-R was created in the MMPI-2 (1989; 567 items) by deleting four objectionable items from the MAC and adding four additional items, resulting in the same number of true/false statements (49). Both the MAC and the MAC-R are self-administered tests, work as well for drugs as alcohol, and are easily scored by clerical personnel. It takes approximately 90 minutes to administer the tests and it takes about 2 to 3 minutes each to score by hand, although typically the instrument is computer scored. Both the MAC and the MAC-R measure the *potential* for addiction to alcohol/drugs. Both have adequate test-retest reliability (MAC-R has .82 for males and .75 for females over a six-week interval). Because they measure more than one dimension, the construct validity is questionable. Graham (1990) recommends no clinical decisions should be based on the MAC or the MAC-R scores alone, due to problems with the accuracy of classification.

MAST

The purpose of the Michigan Alcohol Screening Test (MAST) (Selzer, 1971) is to detect the presence and extent of drinking in adults. This paper-and-pencil test (see Figure 2.2) is a convenient, efficient screening (not diagnostic) measure of drinking problems. It uses a yes/no format and has 25 items. It can be completed in approximately 10 minutes. The most popular scoring procedure assigns scores of 2 or 1 for each of the questions (0 if the response is nondrinking), except item number 7, which does not receive a score. Because item 7 ("Do you ever try to limit your drinking to certain times of the day or to certain places?") does not receive a score of 1 or 2, this

FIGURE 2.2   Michigan Alcoholism Screening Test (MAST)

1. Do you feel you are a normal drinker?	Yes	No
2. Have you awakened in the morning after some drinking the night before and found that you could not remember a part of the evening before?	Yes	No
3. Does your wife (or parents) ever worry or complain about your drinking?	Yes	No
4. Can you stop drinking without a struggle after one or two drinks?	Yes	No
5. Do you ever feel bad about your drinking?	Yes	No
6. Do your friends or relatives think you are a normal drinker?	Yes	No
7. Do you ever try to limit your drinking to certain times of the day or to certain places?	Yes	No
8. Are you always able to stop drinking when you want to?	Yes	No
9. Have you ever attended a meeting for Alcoholics Anonymous (AA)?	Yes	No
10. Have you ever gotten into fights when drinking?	Yes	No
11. Has drinking ever created problems with you and your wife?	Yes	No
12. Has your wife (or other family member) ever gone to anyone for help about your drinking?	Yes	No
13. Have you ever lost friends or girlfriends/boyfriends because of your drinking?	Yes	No
14. Have you ever gotten into trouble at work because of drinking?	Yes	No
15. Have you ever lost a job because of drinking?	Yes	No
16. Have you ever neglected your obligations, your family, or your work for two or more days in a row because you were drinking?	Yes	No
17. Do you ever drink before noon?	Yes	No
18. Have you ever been told you have liver trouble? Cirrhosis?	Yes	No
19. Have you had delirium tremens (DTs), severe shaking, heard voices, or seen things that weren't there after heavy drinking?	Yes	No
20. Have you ever gone to anyone for help about your drinking?	Yes	No
21. Have you ever been in a hospital because of drinking?	Yes	No
22. Have you ever been a patient in a psychiatric hospital or on a psychiatric ward of a general hospital where drinking was part of the problem?	Yes	No
23. Have you ever been seen at a psychiatric or mental health clinic, or gone to a doctor, social worker, or clergyman for help with an emotional problem in which drinking had played a part?	Yes	No
24. Have you ever been arrested, even for a few hours, because of drunk behavior?	Yes	No
25. Have you ever been arrested for drunk driving after drinking?	Yes	No

Source: American Journal of Psychiatry, 127, pages 1653–1658, 1971. Copyright 1971, the American Psychiatric Association. Reprinted by permission.

item is sometimes eliminated in the test taking (Selzer, 1985). To control for clients appearing to have alcohol problems when they actually do not, the counselor may need to gather more clinical information or modify the scoring system to make it more stringent. (The more conservative scoring system makes a score of 5 indicative of alcoholism.) The instrument appears valid; a number of studies show high agreement between MAST scores and previous alcohol-related problems. Studies report high internal consistency reliabilities of .83 to .95 and test-retest reliability over one to three days is .86 (Connors & Tarbox, 1985).

A shortened version of the MAST is called the SMAST (Short MAST) (Selzer, Vinokur, & vanRooijen, 1975), seen in Figure 2.3. Using stepwise multiple regression, 13 MAST items (1, 3, 5, 6, 8, 9, 11, 14, 16, 20, 21, 24, 25) were retained because they distinguished especially well between alcoholics and nonalcoholics; and 1 MAST item (24) was expanded to alcohol-related arrests. All items are scored 1 point if the answer indicates alcoholism. A total of 3 or more points mean alcoholism is probable, 2 or more points mean it is possible, and less than 2 points means it is unlikely.

Adults

These instruments can be used for a more in-depth evaluation of adults if there are positive indicators of an alcohol/drug problem based on broad overview instrument results or otherwise obtained client information.

DRI

The Driver Risk Inventory (DRI) (Behavior Data Systems, 1987) is a self-report test that has 139 items and takes about 25 to 30 minutes to administer and score. It results in risk-level classifications and recommendations based on those classifications. The

---

FIGURE 2.3   The Short Michigan Alcoholism Screening Test (SMAST)

---

1. Do you feel you are a normal drinker? (By *normal* we mean you drink less than or as much as most other people?) (No)
2. Does your wife, husband, a parent, or other near relative ever worry or complain about your drinking? (Yes)
3. Do you ever feel guilty about your drinking? (Yes)
4. Do friends or relatives think you are a normal drinker? (No)
5. Are you able to stop drinking when you want to? (No)
6. Have you ever attended a meeting of Alcoholics Anonymous? (Yes)
7. Has drinking ever created problems between you and your wife, husband, a parent or other near relative? (Yes)
8. Have you ever gotten into trouble at work because of your drinking? (Yes)
9. Have you ever neglected your obligations, your family, or your work for 2 or more days in a row because you were drinking? (Yes)
10. Have you ever gone to anyone for help about your drinking? (Yes)
11. Have you ever been in a hospital because of drinking? (Yes)
12. Have you ever been arrested for drunken driving, driving while intoxicated, or driving under the influence of alcoholic beverages? (Yes)
13. Have you ever been arrested, even for a few hours, because of other drunken behavior? (Yes)

Note: Answers related to alcoholism are given in parentheses after each question. Three or more of these answers indicate probable alcoholism; two answers indicate the possibility of alcoholism; less than two answers indicate that alcoholism is not likely.

Source: Reprinted with permission from *Journal of Studies on Alchohol,* vol. 36, pp. 117–126, 1975. Copyright by Journal of Studies on Alcohol Inc., Rutgers Center of Alcohol Studies, Piscataway, NJ 08855.

test uses five behavioral pattern scales (truthfulness, alcohol, drugs, driver risk, and stress coping ability) and it can be given in either a paper-and-pencil or computer format. The DRI was researched and normed on a driving while intoxicated (DWI) population. It was validated in comparison with screener and evaluator ratings, and its internal consistency reliabilities for the five scales range from .83 to .93.

MACH

The Minnesota Assessment of Chemical Health (MACH) (Kincannon, 1984) is a computer-based, interactive chemical health assessment instrument. The instrument has standard questions, but through "branching," the answers of the client direct the next part of the program. The test takes less than 30 minutes to administer. Its construct validity was determined through a comparison with clinicians' judgments. Factor analysis found one diagnostic variable that correlated highly with the MAST, the Mortimer-Filkins Court Procedure for Identifying Problem Drinkers, and the MACH Drug Involvement Scale (Kincannon, 1989).

SALCE

The Substance Abuse/Life Circumstance Evaluation (SALCE) (ADE, 1991) has 98 items, takes about 20 minutes to administer, and is computer based. It evaluates alcohol and drug use and locates the current stressors in the client's life. It has construct validity with professional interviews (94 percent) and a one-month interval test-retest reliability of .91.

SASSI

The Substance Abuse Subtle Screening Inventory (SASSI) (Miller, 1985) consists of 52 items in a true/false format (adult). It can be used with ages 12 to adult. There are four scales: Obvious Attributes Scale (OAT) (openness to admit to problems), Subtle Attributes Scale (SAT) (chemical dependency predisposition), Defensiveness (DEF) (defensiveness in test taking), and Defensive Abuser vs. Defensive Non-Abuser (DEF2) (compares defensiveness between these two populations) (Fisher & Harrison, 1997). This paper-and-pencil test takes about 5 to 10 minutes to complete and 1 to 2 minutes to score, unless combined with "Face Valid Alcohol" and "Face Valid Other Drugs" Scales, which increase the completion and scoring time to 10 to 15 minutes. The two other adult scales are the Alcohol vs. Drug (ALD), which indicates whether the preference is for alcohol or drugs, and the Family vs. Controls (FAM), which measures codependency (Fisher & Harrison, 1997). Validation studies found 85 to 90 percent accuracy in differentiating residential abusers from nonabusers.

Adolescents

These adolescent assessment instruments can further evaluate the presence of an alcohol/drug problem as evidenced in the results of a broad overview assessment instrument or other sources of clinical information.

JASAE

The Juvenile Automated Substance Abuse Evaluation (JASAE) (ADE, 1988) has a format and administration procedure similar to the SALCE instruments for adults; however, it has been normed with adolescents. It examines the individual (use of alcohol and drugs, attitudes, and life stresses) and provides recommendations for interventions. The computer-based JASAE has 102 items and is designed for 12- to 18-year-olds. It takes about 20 minutes to administer and process. There is construct validity with professional interview results of 85 percent and the one-month interval test-retest reliability is .93.

PESQ

The Personal Experience Screen Questionnaire (PESQ) (Winters, 1991) has 40 items and is designed for 12- to 18-year-olds. The paper-and-pencil test takes about 10 minutes and is written at a fourth-grade reading level. It is a screening instrument that examines the severity of the problem with alcohol/drugs (psychological and behavioral involvement), the psychological risks (personal and environmental problems) related to substance abuse, and drug use history (beginning use, frequency of use of 12 substances over 12 months). There are also two validity scales that help determine if the client is lying in his or her responses. Problem severity has construct validity with treatment history, treatment referral decisions, diagnosis, and group status, and alpha reliability coefficients range from .90 to .95.

SASSI

Because the Substance Abuse Subtle Screening Inventory (SASSI) can be used with individuals ranging in age from 12 to adult, it was reviewed under the Adults section. It has 55 items in the adolescent form. In addition to the OAT, SAT, DEF, and DEF2 scales, it has the Correctional (COR) scale, which examines the level of acting-out behavior, and the Random Answering Pattern (RAP) scale, which determines if the client is answering questions randomly (Fisher & Harrison, 1997).

Diagnosis

The diagnosis of use, abuse, and addiction to alcohol/drugs is both an art and a science. Working with addicted individuals and problem drinkers over time provides a counselor with a "sixth sense" of the type of problem that is being presented. Nonetheless, both experienced and novice counselors in the addictions field need to have their senses supported by clinical data. Such a grounding of assessment will assist the counselor in situations such as testifying in court (Miller & Kaplan, 1996). The counselor assessing addiction level, then, needs to have as much information as possible from as many sources as possible.

A thorough addiction assessment requires time, energy, and a commitment to thoroughness by the counselor. The counselor needs to look for a pattern of problems related to alcohol/drug usage that does not seem to respond significantly to environmental changes. This pattern is strengthened if it appears in more than one area of consequences (legal; family, significant others, friends; job, school, military; medical; financial) and occurs in different contexts over time. The pattern is stronger if it is broader and longer in terms of its consequences. Data from numerous sources can indicate conflictual areas where more information is needed to make a diagnosis as well as provide support for clinical decisions.

The Diagnostic and Statistical Manual of Mental Disorders (DSM-IV) (APA, 1994) provides a chapter titled Substance-Related Disorders. The first major section of that chapter is Substance Use Disorders, which includes Substance Dependence and Substance Abuse. Criteria are listed for each that must be met in order to make a diagnosis. If the diagnostic criteria are met for substance dependence, then the counselor must determine if it is with or without physiological dependence and must choose one of six course specifiers (early full remission, early partial remission, sustained full remission, sustained partial remission, on agonist therapy, in a controlled environment).

The second section of the *DSM-IV* is chapter Substance-Induced Disorders. This section lists the criteria that must be met for diagnosis of substance intoxication and substance withdrawal. The remaining sections of that chapter cover disorders related to alcohol, amphetamines, caffeine, cannabis, cocaine, hallucinogens, inhalants, nicotine, opioids, phencyclidine, sedative/hypnotics/anxiolytics, polysubstances, and others (or unknown).

The counselor assessing the level of usage of a client needs to be familiar with these different *DSM-IV* categories of use, abuse, and addiction related to alcohol/drugs. Awareness of the different categories will facilitate a continuum of care, the referral process, treatment planning, outcome measures, and work with other professionals to assure client change. For a counselor new to the addictions field, it is important to have supervision with a qualified professional in the addictions field when initially giving diagnoses based on the *DSM-IV* criteria.

Finally, when providing the client with the diagnosis of his or her alcohol/drug usage, it is important to do so with the utmost respect of the individual; particularly when the diagnosis is one of addiction. No one ever sets out to achieve alcohol/drug addiction as a life goal. Clients who are diagnosed as *addicted* need to be given the diagnosis with compassion. Clients who are diagnosed as *abusing* alcohol/drugs need to be given the diagnosis with a warning of what further abuse of these chemicals may do to their lives.

Summary

This chapter reviewed the types of interviews, behavioral observations, physiological instruments, and psychometric instruments that may be used in the assessment process as well as how they may be used by the clinician. The diagnostic process was presented with specific suggestions for clinical use.

CASE STUDY: JAY

Jay is a 45-year-old male who has been referred for an assessment of his alcohol/drug usage. He recently received his first DUI charge. He divorced in the last year and reports that he has had a difficult time adjusting to living away from his ex-wife and their three children, which is why he is drinking more than normal. He says his ex-wife left him because of his drinking, but also said she has a "history of mental problems and always exaggerates everything." He denies any job or social problems related to his alcohol use. He says he mostly uses alcohol, although he has "tried a few other things along the way."

1. Does Jay have any significant others you would want to interview? If so, who?
2. Would you use a limited use contract or any physiological instruments in the assessment? Why or why not?
3. Which broad overview psychometric instrument would you use? Why did you choose that one?
4. Which adult psychometric instrument would you use if you discovered Jay was positive for alcohol abuse on the broad overview psychometric instrument? Why?
5. If you discovered this client was alcoholic, how would you tell him his diagnosis?
6. If you determined this client was not alcoholic, what warnings might you give him about his usage?

SUGGESTED READINGS

National Institute on Alcohol Abuse and Alcoholism (U.S. Department of Health and Human Services). (1995). *Assessing alcohol problems: A guide for clinicians and researchers.* (NIH Publication No. 95-3745). Bethesda, MD: Author.

Senay, E. C. (1997). Diagnostic interview and mental status examination. In J. N. Lowinson, P. Ruiz, R. B. Millman, & J. G.

Langrod (Eds.), *Substance abuse: A comprehensive textbook* (3rd ed.) (pp. 364–369). Baltimore: Williams & Wilkins.

Straussner, S. L. A. (1993). Assessment and treatment of clients with alcohol and other drug abuse problems: An overview. In S. L. A. Straussner (Ed.), *Clinical work with substance-abusing clients* (pp. 3–30). New York: Guilford.

REFERENCES

ADE Incorporated. (1988). *Juvenile Automated Substance Abuse Evaluation (JASAE).* Clarkston, MI: Author.

ADE Incorporated. (1991). *Substance Abuse Life Circumstances Evaluation (SALCE).* Clarkston, MI: Author.

American Psychiatric Association. (1994). *Diagnostic and statistical manual of mental*

disorders (4th ed.). Washington, DC: Author.

Behavior Data Systems. (1987). *Driver Risk Inventory.* Phoenix, AZ: Author.

Buelow, G. D., & Buelow, S. A. (1998). *Psychotherapy in chemical dependence treatment: A practical and integrative approach.* Pacific Grove, CA: Brooks/Cole.

Connors, G. J., & Tarbox, A. R. (1985). Michigan alcoholism screening test. In D. J. Keyer & R. C. Sweetland (Eds.), *Test critiques: Volume III* (pp. 439–446). Kansas City, MO: Westport.

Duckworth, J., & Anderson, W. (1986). *MMPI interpretation manual for counselors and clinicians* (3rd ed.). Muncie, IN: Accelerated Development.

Ewing, J. A. (1984). Detecting alcoholism: The CAGE questionnaire. *Journal of the American Medical Association, 252,* 1905–1907.

Fisher, G. L., & Harrison, T. C. (1997). *Substance abuse: Information for school counselors, social workers, therapists, and counselors.* Boston: Allyn and Bacon.

Graham, J. R. (1990). *MMPI-2: Assessing personality and psychopathology.* New York: Oxford.

Griffin, R. E. (1991). Assessing the drug involved client. *Families in Society: Journal of Contemporary Human Services, 72,* 87–94.

Inaba, D. S., & Cohen, W. E. (1989). *Uppers, downers, all arounders.* Ashland, OR: CNS Productions.

Kincannon, J. (1984). *Minnesota assessment of chemical health.* Chaska, MN: Author.

Kincannon, J. (1989). *Assessment by computer-assisted interview: Analysis of 2000 cases.* Paper presented at the National Convention on Alcohol & Drug Problems, Washington, DC.

Lewis, J. A., Dana, R. Q., & Blevins, G. A. (1994). *Substance abuse counseling: An individualized approach* (2nd ed.). Pacific Grove, CA: Brooks/Cole.

Miller, G. A. (1985). *The Substance Abuse Subtle Screening Inventory manual.* Spencer, IN: Spencer Evening World.

Miller, G., & Kaplan, B. (1996). Testifying in court. *Psychotherapist in Private Practice, 15,* 15–32.

National Institute on Alcohol Abuse and Alcoholism (U.S. Department of Health and Human Services). (1995). *Assessing alcohol problems: A guide for clinicians and researchers* (NIH Publication No. 95-3745). Bethesda, MD: Author.

Sattler, J. M. (1992). *Assessment of children* (3rd ed.). San Diego: Author.

Selzer, M. L. (1971). The Michigan Alcohol Screening Test: The quest for a new diagnostic instrument. *American Journal of Psychiatry, 127,* 1653–1658.

Selzer, M. L. (1985). Michigan Alcoholism Screening Test. In D. J. Keyser & R. C. Sweetland (Eds.), *Test critiques: Volume III* (pp. 439–446). Kansas City, MO: Test Corporation of America.

Selzer, M. L., Vinokur, A., & vanRooijen, L. (1975). A self-administered Short Michigan Alcoholism Screening Tests (SMAST). *Journal of Studies on Alcohol, 36,* 117–126.

Senay, E. C. (1997). Diagnostic interview and mental status examination. In J. H. Lowinson, P. Ruiz, R. B. Millman, & J. G. Langrod (Eds.), *Substance abuse: A comprehensive textbook* (3rd ed.) (pp. 364–369). Baltimore: Williams & Wilkins.

Shaffer, H., & Kauffman, J. (1985). The clinical assessment and diagnosis of addiction. In T. E. Bratter & G. G. Forrest (Eds.), *Alcoholism and substance abuse: Strategies for intervention* (pp. 225–258). New York: Free Press.

Straussner, S. L. A. (1993). Assessment and treatment of clients with alcohol and other drug abuse problems: An overview. In S. L. A. Straussner (Ed.), *Clinical work with substance-abusing clients* (pp. 3–30). New York: Guilford.

Vereby, K. G., & Buchan, B. J. (1997). Diagnostic laboratory: Screening for drug abuse. In J. H. Lowinson, P. Ruiz, R. B. Millman, & J. G. Langrod (Eds.), *Substance abuse: A comprehensive textbook* (3rd ed.) (pp. 369–377). Baltimore: Williams & Wilkins.

Winters, K. (1991). *Personal experience screening questionnaire.* Los Angeles: Western Psychological Services.

CHAPTER

3

Assessment and Diagnosis of Dual Disorders

PRETEST

1. What are some definitions of *dual diagnosis?*
2. What are some of the historical struggles between the two fields of chemical dependency and mental health counseling?
3. What are general treatment guidelines for working with clients who have dual disorders?
4. What are common problems in diagnosing clients with dual disorders?
5. What are some effective approaches for counselors working with violent clients?
6. What are some of the different types of sexual addiction?
7. What are some common personality disorders among addicts and how can they be worked with in counseling?
8. What are some clues to the presence of a dual diagnosis?
9. How can clients with dual disorders be recognized in addiction treatment? In mental health treatment?
10. What treatment modifications may need to be made for clients with dual disorders in terms of time, medication, confrontation, psychiatric support, self-help groups, and use screening?

Principles of Diagnosis and Treatment

Clients with dual diagnoses are those who have both psychiatric and substance abuse problems (Zimberg, 1993). Although the term *dual diagnosis* means that the client can have either a substance abuse or dependence problem (Evans & Sullivan, 1990), this discussion will be limited to clients who are addicted and have a psychiatric problem. Sometimes additional terminology is used to describe this population. For example, the New York State Office of Mental Health has used the terms *MICAA (MICA)* and *CAMI* to describe dual diagnosis clients. Originally, the term *MICAA* (Mental Illness Chemical Abuse and Addictions) was used. This term was later changed to *MICA* (Mentally Ill Chemically Addicted), to diagnose clients with severe, persistent mental illness (Axis I disorder in *DSM*) with an accompanying abuse/addiction problem, whereas those who have an addiction problem accompanied by other mental illness (often Axis II personality disorders in *DSM*) were call *CAMI* (Chemically Addicted Mentally Ill) (Shollar, 1993). Because these terms created communication confusion as well as caused clients to feel stigmatized, the New York State Office of Mental Health is currently using the term *Persons in Dual Recovery—Co-occurring Psychiatric and Addictive Disorders,* and encouraging clinicians to make more precise diagnostic terminology under that larger umbrella.

Historical Struggles between the Fields

Dual diagnosis clients, due to the nature of their problems, require an exceptional amount of teamwork between professionals in both the mental health and addictions fields. A dually diagnosed client needs to have a psychiatrist, addictions counselor, and mental health counselor who can work collaboratively and flexibly together in order to assure that the client's needs are met. For example, at one point in the client's recovery, the psychiatric problem may be top priority, and at another point, the chemical dependency problem may need to be the top priority. Such flexibility by counselors requires a great amount of honest communication, trust, and cooperation.

One of the main problems in working with dual disorders is the separateness of mental health and addiction counselor training. Often, counselors who have been trained in mental health have little or no experience in diagnosing or working in the addictions field. Also, counselors who have been trained in addictions counseling often have little or no experience in diagnosing or working in the mental health field. Furthermore, there continues to be a suspiciousness between the two fields regarding the quality and integrity of the counselors in each field. Mental health counselors may believe that if the underlying problems were addressed, the addiction would diminish, whereas addiction counselors may not see the psychiatric problems as being severe and may not believe in the need for medication (Evans & Sullivan, 1990).

Another issue between the two fields is territorial. Because the dual-disordered client needs assistance from counselors in both fields, counselors need to share information openly with one another. Yet, counselors in each field may hesitate to share information about their perceptions of the client for fear that they may be ridiculed, ignored, or misunderstood. They also may be hesitant to share information out of concern that the other counselors may not be open to suggestions; therefore, they may have a sense of "Why bother?"

Part of the problem is historical. Initially, when mental health workers did not know how to assist addicted individuals and found them, as a whole, to be difficult clients (i.e., they would lie, relapse, struggle with those in authority), addicted clients mainly had to rely on themselves, whereby the self-help organizations, such as Alcoholics Anonymous (AA), developed. The addictions field, then, became much more of a grassroots movement with its early professional counselors eventually evolving out of that context. The mental health field had a more professional development separate from a grassroots movement.

These early developmental differences laid the groundwork for another difficulty between the areas, which is in the framework and language used by each field.

One example of this is Gold's (1995) outline of different viewpoints between the self-help focus and the psychiatric focus. In terms of the self-help focus, groups such as AA may be viewed as lifesavers for the addict, whereas psychiatry may view them as possibly missing psychiatric problems in the individuals who attend them. Another difference is in the area of medication. Here, the self-help focus may view taking medication as potentially harmful to the addict, while psychiatry may view it as helpful. Also, the self-help focus may see psychological problems as resulting from the alcohol/drug use (therefore, such problems will stop when the person sobers up), whereas psychiatry may be concerned that problems were present prior to the alcohol/drug use. The differences between these two areas indicate the potential struggles when addiction counselors and mental health counselors begin to work together.

Evans and Sullivan (1990) describe these differences between the two fields in terms of models. They describe the *recovery model* as one where the client is always recovering, needs to abstain from alcohol/drug use, needs to develop various coping skills, and typically needs to attend self-help meetings, obtain a sponsor, and work the steps of recovery. The *mental health model* for recovery looks more at physiological problems, developing systems that reinforce certain behaviors and developing coping skills in the client, which includes an awareness in the client of his or her thoughts, feelings, and behaviors. These differing perspectives can lead to difficulties in communication and trust between the counselors in the addictions and mental health fields. One way of avoiding or minimizing these conflicts is for professionals to work hard at communication and collaboration. Increased awareness of dual disorders may enhance communication and collaboration.

General Guidelines

To be aware of the presence of a dual disorder, the counselor needs to note behaviors outside those expected of the general addiction population. This would include differences in how the client interacts with others and how the client responds to treatment. Extremes in thoughts, feelings, and behaviors, or unusual aspects in these three areas, can alert a counselor to the possible presence of a dual diagnosis. Although this terminology is vague, seasoned counselors, in both the mental health and addiction fields, develop a sense of what are normal behaviors and problems for the populations with which they work. Neophyte counselors, then, need to rely on supervision to determine if a client's behavior is unusual.

It is also helpful to watch the client's addiction recovery process. If the client is unable to remain sober, there may be an accompanying mental health problem. The client may be self-medicating by relapsing. In addition, if, as part of the treatment process, a client routinely takes psychological tests, the counselor can use these tests to determine if psychological problems are diminishing as the client receives more treatment and has a longer period of time in recovery. The same is true for the mental health client. If the mental health client is not responding typically to treatment, the counselor may want to examine his or her substance use. Finally, if a client responds to psychiatric medication, then a dual diagnosis is present (Evans & Sullivan, 1990).

Problems with Diagnosing

Zimberg (1993) reports that alcohol and drug use can make a client appear to have psychological problems. Many of these apparent psychiatric symptoms disappear as the abstinence of the individual increases (Scott, 1995). Further complications are evident in that the two problems interface and make it harder to treat them (Evans & Sullivan, 1990). One suggestion made by Inaba (1995) for coping with clinical uncertainty is that counselors make flexible diagnoses when working with this population. *Flexible diagnosing* means the use of provisional diagnosis until the clinician has enough information to make an established diagnosis. Two other aspects that affect the diagnostic process, sobriety time and client history, are further explored here.

Sobriety Time
In order to determine if a client has a dual diagnosis, it is helpful to have him or her remain sober for a period of time. What may appear to be psychiatric symptoms may naturally disappear when the client is sober and thereby clarify the client's diagnosis. The recommended length of sober time varies according to experts in the field: three to six weeks (Zimberg, 1993), four weeks (Evans & Sullivan, 1990), or four to eight weeks (Scott, 1995). Unfortunately, the catch-22 with dual diagnosis clients is that they may have a more difficult time achieving and maintaining sobriety. In this latter case, the counselor needs to make the best diagnosis possible, keeping in mind Inaba's suggestion (1995) that it be flexible.

Client History
It is also important to determine if the psychiatric problem was present prior to the addiction, if it emerged alongside of the addiction, or if it emerged after the addiction began (Zimberg, 1993). As Evans and Sullivan (1990) state, it is easier to make a dual diagnosis if the psychiatric problems were present prior to the addiction problems. A thorough client history, then, is the best way to ascertain if and when a psychiatric problem began to coexist with the addiction problem. As discussed in Chapter 2, it is important for the counselor to obtain information from significant others as well as the addicted individual in order to be assured of obtaining accurate information. In addition to the client history of mental health problems, the counselor also should ask about a history of mental health problems in the family in order to help determine a possible genetic predisposition to mental health problems.

Types of Dual Diagnosis

Prevalence Rates of Types

Estimations of the prevalence of dual diagnosis vary. Nace (1992) reports that 44 percent of male alcoholics and 65 percent of female alcoholics may have an accompanying psychiatric diagnosis in their lives. Mirin and Weiss (1991) state that approximately 30 percent of psychiatric patients have a substance abuse problem. Evans and Sullivan

(1990) estimate that more than 50 percent of the young, chronically mentally ill population abuse mood-altering chemicals. Regier and colleagues (1990) found the co-occurrence of addictive and psychiatric disorders (lifetime prevalence) as follows: 47.0 percent schizophrenia, 14.7 percent anxiety disorder, 35.8 percent panic disorder, 32.8 percent obsessive-compulsive disorder, 32.0 percent affective disorder, and 60.7 percent bipolar disorder.

Homelessness

Since the early 1980s, research with the homeless has shown high rates of mental illness and substance abuse, both severe in nature and more common with this population than the general population (Koegel, Burnam, & Baumohl, 1996). Every homeless study reports pathology in both social and personal realms, but the estimates for drinking problems range from 29 to 55 percent and for other substance dependencies, estimates range from 10 to 30 percent; whereas 20 to 84 percent have emotional disturbances or are mentally ill (Wright & Lam, 1990).

Alcoholism is common among homeless people because they drink to cope and to socialize (Daly,1996). The subculture of homelessness allows for heavy drinking (Schutt & Garret,1992). Homeless men are three times more likely to be alcoholic than homeless women (Daly,1996), and the homeless have a four-time greater chance of having a problem with alcohol as well as higher morbidity rates when compared with other alcoholics (Schutt & Garret, 1992).

There is a relationship between homelessness and mental illness. Often, the chronically mentally ill have been deinstitutionalized, which may result in alcoholism (Daly, 1996). However, while homelessness may cause mental health and substance abuse problems, these problems may also cause homelessness (Koegel, Burnam, & Baumohl, 1996). For most homeless alcoholics, heavy drinking is present prior to the homelessness (Schutt & Garret, 1992). Their problems of homelessness, substance abuse, and mental health may all interact to make treatment for these problems difficult: Mental health and substance abuse issues may keep them from homeless programs and their homelessness may keep them from receiving help from mental health and substance abuse programs (Oakley & Dennis, 1996).

Violence

A tendency toward violence may accompany a diagnosis of addiction. Nuckols (1995) states that many addicted individuals may exhibit violence for different reasons. One reason may be organic. For example, lower serotonin levels may be related to poor impulse control. Also, some alcoholics have had closed head injuries that have resulted in violence due to head trauma. Another cause may be psychosis, which can be treated with antipsychotics. A third cause may be characterological problems related to personality (e.g., antisocial, borderline, or post-traumatic stress disorder survivors who may use the anger as a protective mechanism).

Nuckols (1995) reports that clients who hurt deeply may feel that retaliation toward others is a right. Nuckols's suggestions for counselors is that they work with the anger as grief work by establishing rapport, drawing out the emotional pain, and controlling countertransference with regard to violence. Verbal management of these clients includes the counselor being calm, appearing in control, speaking softly, listening to the client, and showing concern for his or her (counselor) own safety in the situation, and, if possible, both counselor and client should be sitting. Finally, the counselor should assess the level of violence and know his or her own personal reactions to anger, violence, and the client (Nuckols, 1995).

Sex

Sexual addiction, as defined by Goodman (1997), is when sexual behavior results in pleasure and a decrease in pain, where the client repeatedly cannot control the behavior and continues it in spite of harmful consequences. The majority of people who experience this addiction are men. The addiction seems to begin before age 18, and the behavior is at its height between ages 20 and 30 (Goodman, 1997). Treatment has included pharmacology and various therapies (cognitive-behavioral, group, couples, family, psychodynamic) (Goodman, 1997). Carnes (1995) presents 10 different types of sexual addiction that may co-occur with an alcohol/drug addiction:

1. Fantasy sex (masturbating compulsively, stalking others)
2. Seductive role sex (focusing on conquest and power)
3. Voyeuristic sex (accessing information through one primary sensory mode such as visual [e.g., "peeping toms"])
4. Exhibitionism (exposing oneself to others, which can take different forms)
5. Trading sex (replicating fearful childhood sexual experiences, only this time having the sense of being in control)
6. Paying for sex (paying another for sexual acts)
7. Intrusive sex (using violation to experience eroticism, which was paired with boundary violations as a child)
8. Anonymous sex (seeking instant gratification)
9. Pain exchange (experiencing arousal when hurt is repetition of earlier trauma and may include objects as part of the violence experienced)
10. Exploitive sex (seeking a vulnerable individual to exploit)

Carnes states that these individuals share a common core of pain with alcohol/drug addiction. He suggests that these sexual addicts are trying to appease their pain through alcohol/drugs and sex. Treatment for these dual-disordered clients needs to address the common source of pain they are responding to through their alcohol/drug addiction and their sexual addiction.

Post-Traumatic Stress Disorder (PTSD)

Nace (1992) recommends that individuals who have PTSD and an addiction problem be treated for the addiction first. Following that treatment and an attainment of sobriety, then the traumatic experiences(s) can be explored gradually so the experience is slowly integrated into the individual.

Evans and Sullivan (1995) state that often PTSD clients invite counselors to become involved in some part of the Karpman Triangle. In the Karpman Triangle, one person is the rescuer, another is the victim, and the third is the persecutor. They suggest that counselors work at staying off of the triangle by resisting choosing the role of rescuer, victim, or persecutor and instead work from a point of strength and balance. When a counselor experiences the anger of a PTSD survivor, it may be helpful to determine what the client is fearing. Peer groups tend to mean a lot to these individuals and can be used by counselors as a resource in their treatment of survivors (Evans & Sullivan, 1995).

Evans and Sullivan (1991c) also suggest working with PTSD clients to accept both diagnoses and work at being abstinent. They suggest that clients emphasize that they are survivors rather than victims, and that they are actively involved in their recovery from both of their diagnoses by obtaining support from other individuals, practicing self-care, working through their trauma, and possibly obtaining psychiatric medication.

Personality Disorders

Antisocial and borderline personality disorders will be examined in this section because addicted clients often show these symptoms (Solomon, 1993). When parents of both adopted and biological children have an Antisocial Personality Disorder, the children have a greater chance of developing an Antisocial Personality Disorder, a Substance-Related Disorder, and Somatization Disorder (*DSM-IV;* APA, 1994). In an adult who has a Substance-Related Disorder and shows signs of antisocial behavior, the diagnosis of Antisocial Personality Disorder is not given unless these antisocial behaviors were present from childhood into adulthood (APA, 1994). This caution with diagnosis of an Antisocial Personality Disorder is because addicted individuals may commit antisocial acts in conjunction with their addiction. Goodwin and Gabrielli (1997) state that the percentages of alcoholics who also meet the criteria of an antisocial personality vary too much to be quoted. Approximately 84 percent of individuals with antisocial personalities have alcohol problems (*Harvard Mental Health Letter,* 1996). When working with antisocial personality disorder clients, a therapeutic alliance may not be possible (Shollar, 1993). Confrontation regarding substance abuse may then be required. When referring these clients to self-help groups for support, the counselor needs to help the client examine his or her dysfunctional behavior at meetings in order to help the client change (Zaslav, 1993).

Nace, Saxon, and Shore (1983) estimate that 12 to 39 percent of alcoholics have a borderline personality disorder. These clientele tend to be younger, use more drugs and use them earlier in life, have more self-destructiveness (e.g., suicide attempts) and dissatisfaction with self and others, dysphoria, and alcohol cravings. Fayne (1993) indicates that these clients may react with intense anger to limits set with them or when they experience emotions and may be involved in community struggles. Zaslav (1993) suggests referring these clients to supportive self-help groups, which are very tolerant of individuals' idiosyncracies.

Cognitive Impairments

Individuals with cognitive impairments, which are chronic in nature, may appear that they are not interested in the treatment or may be viewed as defiant. In reality, they have difficulty in sustaining attention and concentration, controlling their emotions and being empathic to others, as well as being logical and engaging in a self-awareness process. Counselors working with these clients may need to watch for cues of problems with memory, empathy, logic, and self-awareness. Counselors may consider a referral for psychiatric assessment of their limitations, which could be incorporated into their treatment plans.

Depression

Approximately 30 to 50 percent of alcoholics have a major depression (Goodwin & Gabrielli, 1997). Solomon (1993) reports that depression is a common withdrawal symptom from alcohol, which begins several hours after the last drink and can continue for up to 48 hours. Therefore, it is helpful if the client has been sober for a period of time to determine if the depression is drug related. It is also important to note that because depression appears to be connected to alcohol/drug relapse (Loosen, Dew, & Prange, 1990), it is critical that it be addressed as a part of the client's recovery. First and Gladis (1993) indicate that one of the first things to consider for the client who is both depressed and addicted is psychotropic medications. They suggest antidepressants for the client whose depression is the primary diagnosis, but possibly a medication such as Antabuse for the client whose primary diagnosis is addiction.

Anxiety Disorders

Solomon (1993) reports that anxiety, like depression, is a common withdrawal symptom in the early stages (several hours up to 48 hours) of alcohol withdrawal, thereby requiring some sober time for the client to accurately diagnose an anxiety disorder. Anxiety disorders have various behavioral symptom profiles.

Approximately one-third of alcoholics have an anxiety disorder (Goodwin & Gabrielli, 1997). Nace (1992) reports that one of four people who have obsessive-compulsive disorder (OCD) is also alcoholic and that the alcohol is used to provide relief from the disorder. In addition, Nace (1992) states that social phobia and agoraphobia are highly related to alcohol abuse and addiction and again suggests that the alcohol is used to medicate the problems. Lurie (1995) reports that 19 percent of social phobics have alcohol abuse and 13 percent of them are drug abusers. Nace (1992) suggests that generalized anxiety disorders and panic disorders typically occur after the individual has established a pattern of alcohol abuse/addiction.

Screening

Chapter 2 discussed the importance of doing a thorough assessment in the different areas of the client's life (social, legal, family, medical, employment) to determine if there is a problem with substance abuse. Evans and Sullivan (1990) report five areas of similarities between the chemically dependent client and the dual-disordered client: loss of control, protecting one's alcohol/drug supply, denial of a alcohol/drug usage problem, negative consequences of alcohol/drug use, and problems with various systems in one's life. The authors also report four difficulties within this population: difficulty distinguishing between blackouts and memory loss, difficulty determining a change in tolerance due to sporadic use of alcohol/drugs, difficulty determining progression of the addiction due to memory problems and sporadic use, and the masking of withdrawal symptoms by psychiatric symptoms.

Scott (1995) suggests that there are historical clues to a possible dual diagnosis. These cues include a history of sexual abuse, persisting symptoms during abstinence, using alcohol/drugs to change how one feels, difficulty staying sober, later onset of substance abuse (over age 20), and use of four or more different substances.

Recognition of Problems in Different Settings

Some behavioral characteristics occur across different drug treatment settings that will alert a clinician to the possible presence of a dual disorder. One of those characteristics, which commonly occurs across settings, is that the client does not "calm down" during the treatment process. Rather, the clinician will find the client becomes more agitated the longer he or she is sober. Another common characteristic is that such clients will become more troublesome to the center—they simply are more difficult to work with than other clientele. A final clue is that they may become scapegoated by others in the setting because their behaviors are different and bothersome.

Addiction Treatment

Fayne (1993) describes some of the ways a counselor can detect a dual-disordered client during the detoxification process. These clients may be quite needy, but have a difficult time relating to others particularly in a group setting. The author cautions that depression in these clients may not be picked up by the staff because of their irritating behaviors.

In the inpatient rehabilitation process, Fayne (1993) indicates that, once again, the difficulty relating to others in a group may pose a problem. In addition, such clients may have trouble being close with others emotionally and experiencing confrontation. As a result of these problems, they may either withdraw or become more agitated in the setting. Fayne also reports that in the outpatient setting there may be problems in group counseling: Clients may either withdraw from others or be ostracized by them because they are different. There is also a tendency for these clients either to split off from emotions or become explosive. Finally, these clients may have difficulty staying sober.

Mental Health Treatment

On an inpatient psychiatric unit, Fayne (1993) makes specific suggestions as to behaviors to examine that may indicate a substance abuse problem. Physiological problems (e.g., neurological difficulties or withdrawal syndromes, medication-seeking behaviors), as well as comparatively better social skills with an alternating threatening manner, may be present in a substance-abusing client.

In an outpatient psychiatric clinic, Fayne (1993) suggests some possible behaviors that can alert the counselor that he or she is working with a dual-disordered patient. These behaviors include numerous treatment failures, medication noncompliance, absenteeism, inconsistent behavior, superficial sessions, consequences that could be the result of alcohol/drug use, and the therapist's clinical sense that something is not right about the treatment.

Treatment Modifications

General Guidelines of Treatment

Orlin and Davis (1993) indicate some similarities in addiction and psychiatric treatment that may facilitate the counselor's attempt to treat the client who has problems in both areas. Both treatment styles have in common that they are attempting to educate clients and provide supportive counseling, group and family counseling, case management, crisis intervention, and relapse prevention approaches. These treatment similarities can assure the counselor of a general approach to take with clients who have dual disorders, keeping in mind that some modifications need to occur.

Also, Zweben (1995) suggests that counselors can enhance the treatment process by joining dual-disordered clients in their pain, avoid punishment of their ambivalence about recovery, and encourage them to try a period of abstinence. One possible source of bibliotherapy for clients are the Dual Diagnosis Series of brochures published by Hazelden (Evans & Sullivan, 1991a, 1991b, 1991c; Fields &

Vandenbelt, 1992a, 1992b; N., 1992). These pamphlets discuss both diagnoses in layperson's terms, the overlap between the diagnoses, and recovery suggestions.

Time

Dual diagnosis clients may require a longer time frame to achieve abstinence (Orlin & Davis, 1993) and may relapse more often (Zimberg, 1993). Zimberg (1993) also recommends that treatment be more frequent for this type of client (i.e., two to three times weekly). Orlin and Davis (1993) suggest a brief psychiatric hospitalization, followed by rehabilitation treatment for 6 to 12 months, followed by a combination of outpatient psychiatric care and self-help groups. In addition, they suggest that although abstinence is a goal for treatment, a relapse should not be used as a reason for discharge from treatment.

Medication

Psychotropic medication will sometimes assist the recovery process of dual-diagnosed patients (Orlin & Davis, 1993). Evans and Sullivan (1990) suggest the use of nonmood-altering medications when possible. Inaba (1995) also suggests avoiding the use of reinforcing drugs for this population. For example, Evans and Sullivan (1991c) recommend that PTSD survivors use such medications as antidepressants, beta-blocker antihypertensives, and antipsychotics, when appropriate, while avoiding tranquilizers, sedative-hypnotics, and painkillers.

Changing Confrontation Style

Scott (1995) recommends that counselors working with this population be quite flexible in their work, especially in terms of confrontational style. This clientele may require a less confrontive style of counseling (Orlin & Davis, 1993) in order for treatment to be effective. Zimberg (1993) cautions counselors that dual-disordered clients may stir more transference and countertransference issues and that treatment be less rigid and confrontational in particular with regard to giving up the use of alcohol/drugs. The counselor walks a thin line when working with dual diagnosis clients about giving up alcohol/drugs. Although it is important for the counselor to be aware that these clients may have more difficulty initially achieving and maintaining sobriety, the counselor needs to be careful that he or she does not set up an enabling pattern with the client. It is also important for the counselor to believe in the client's capacity to become sober, regardless of the client's diagnosis. This hope and belief in the client can facilitate treatment for clients who live in difficult life circumstances. As Inaba (1995) states, counselors need to remember that dual diagnosis is treatable.

Psychiatric Service Support

Zimberg (1993) suggests that the symptoms for both diagnoses be stabilized and treated simultaneously in order to be effective with this clientele. Addiction counselors need to work closely with psychiatric services in order to facilitate the client's recovery (Orlin & Davis, 1993). Scott (1995) supports this approach by encouraging the counselor not to work alone with these clients. Zimberg (1993) suggests that one counselor be the primary counselor for the client, and, if there is more than one counselor involved in the client's treatment, they should talk frequently. Orlin and Davis (1993) view a team approach as critical for effective treatment with this population.

Self-Help Groups

Zimberg (1993) indicates that effective treatment for dual diagnosis clients cannot be limited to the attendance at self-help groups such as Alcoholics Anonymous, yet, these groups can be an important resource for them. As discussed in Chapter 7, self-help groups can be an important, cost-free resource for addicted clients. They can also pose some problems for those people with dual diagnoses. One place of difficulty for clients may be the 12 Steps of Alcoholics Anonymous (AA) (or other programs based on the 12 Steps). As Thiesse (1984) states, AA generally encourages its members to be free of chemicals. However, the dual diagnosis client may interpret this suggestion to mean he or she should not be on any psychotropic medication, which could be hazardous for recovery from both problems. The counselor needs to forewarn the client who attends self-help meeting that advocate total abstinence that this suggestion does not include psychotropic medication.

Other possible difficulties with 12-step programs may be the very steps of recovery (Thiesse, 1984). In the first step, there is an emphasis on acknowledging powerlessness; however, the dual-disordered client needs to have a sense of power with regard to addressing his or her mental health problems. In the second and third steps, a higher power is reportedly going to restore the client to sanity. The difficulty with these steps for the dual-disordered client is that this concept may fuel mental health delusions of the past. The fourth and fifth steps, which address taking a moral inventory of oneself, may be difficult for the dual-disordered client because of low ego strength and high vulnerability. Finally, the eighth and ninth steps involve amends to other individuals. Again, low ego strength and difficulty in personal relationships due to social skill deficiency may make these steps difficult for the dual-disordered client.

Double Trouble groups are for those individuals who have both mental health and addiction problems (Zaslav, 1993). Their steps are a revised version of the 12 Steps of Alcoholics Anonymous. The concerns expressed by Thiesse (1984) with regard to the first three steps (a sense of powerlessness and a higher power restoration to sanity) are not present for this program. The emphasis in the revised first three steps is on personal control. The fifth step changes the word of *wrongs* to *problems,* which may eliminate some of the sense of morality from this step. A counselor interested in referring clients to Double Trouble groups needs to find out if they exist in the area where the client lives by contacting via Internet: LISTPROC@CAIRN.ORG

In addition, there is Dual Recovery Anonymous (DRA), a national self-help program based on the 12 Steps of Alcoholics Anonymous. Dual Recovery Anonymous began in Kansas City in 1989. It focuses on illnesses in an attempt to avoid relapse to alcohol/drug use and a return of emotional/psychiatric symptoms. Information about this organization can be obtained by contacting Dual Recovery Anonymous (DRA), Central Service Office, P.O. Box 8107, Prairie Village, KS 66208, 888-869-9230, http://webs.linkport.com/~grimnir/dra

Whatever self-help group to which the counselor refers the dual-disordered client, spots of difficulty, such as those just stated, need to be anticipated through an acquaintance of the steps or guidelines for the program. For example, some excellent samples of modified 12-step work for schizophrenic/organic mental disordered, manic-depressive, borderline, and antisocial clients are provided by Evans and Sullivan (1990). In addition, the counselor needs to check with the dual-disordered individual to determine how he or she is being received at the meetings and what he or she is learning about the process of recovery, which may have a negative or positive impact on his or her mental health problems.

Screening for Use
The importance of relapse prevention will not be discussed here since it is discussed extensively in Chapter 6. However, one manner of assuring that dual diagnosis clients are being truthful about their abstinence is to use screening devices to validate their sobriety. Urine monitoring and breathalyzers may be necessary to facilitate recovery for the dual-disordered client to stay sober (Orlin & Davis, 1993). Such screening devices, however, need to be used in a respectful manner, which involves informed consent of the client. It is most beneficial if the screening approaches are discussed early in the treatment process, the client is aware that it is a standard procedure for someone who has a dual disorder, and it is introduced as a tool to assist in recovery rather than as a punishment for relapse.

Summary

Working with dual diagnosis clients requires the clinician to exhibit sensitivity in assessment, treatment, and aftercare in mental health issues as well as substance abuse issues. In addition, the chemical dependency counselor needs to work closely and collaboratively with other mental health professionals to ensure that the client obtains the best possible care. Providing treatment that effectively meets the needs of both problems is necessary for addiction recovery.

CASE STUDY: JANE

Jane is a 50-year-old woman who has had a 12-year history of severe alcoholism with four hospital detoxifications and four chemical dependency treatments, none of which had any significant impact on her drinking. She was court-ordered to treatment for her third DUI (driving under the influence). After two weeks in the treatment center, it was noted by the staff that Jane rarely was seen sleeping. At night, she would walk up and down the halls of the treatment center. She was also becoming more agitated in group therapy. She alternated in group therapy between very quiet yet agitated (unable to sit still) and very hostile when confronted or probed for information about herself by the counselor or other clients. She was the topic of most staff meetings, as counselors complained about how frustrating it was to work with her. There was discussion in the meetings of discharging her. The other clients increasingly refused to associate with her due to her highly critical manner and her tendency to be emotionally explosive.

1. What aspects of this situation indicate that Jane may be struggling with a dual disorder?
2. How would you initially intervene on the situation with Jane?
3. How would you approach the staff regarding the situation with Jane? The clients?
4. What form of therapy (individual or group) would you recommend for Jane?
5. How would you work with Jane in individual therapy? In group therapy?

CASE STUDY: WILLIAM

William is a 25-year-old male who has used drugs intravenously. He shared needles with his older brother, who died of AIDS about one year ago. William entered chemical dependency treatment because he was diagnosed one week earlier with being HIV positive (he had seen a doctor at a public clinic due to feeling ill). He had decided to come to treatment because he wanted to die with more peace than his brother when he died. After three weeks in treatment, he told his counselor in an individual session that he saw no point in trying to stay drug free. He said he was going to die no matter what and he wanted to die without any anxiety (e.g., being high on heroin). William shared that he had always felt down about life since his teenage years and he did not know "what possessed me a few weeks ago" to think that life could be any different.

1. What tentative dual diagnosis might you give William?
2. What would be your first intervention strategy with him?
3. What overall plan would you develop for dealing with his issues?
4. Are there any portions of his story that would make it difficult for you to work with him?

SUGGESTED READINGS

Daly, G. (1996). *Homeless: Policies, strategies, and lives on the street.* New York: Routledge.

Evans, K., & Sullivan, J. M. (1990). *Dual diagnosis: Counseling the mentally ill substance abuser.* New York: Guilford.

Fayne, M. (1993). Recognizing dual diagnosis patients in various clinical settings. In J. Solomon, S. Zimberg, & E. Shollar (Eds.), *Dual diagnosis: Evaluation, treatment, training, and program development* (pp. 39–53). New York: Plenum.

First, M. B., & Gladis, M. M. (1993). Diagnosis and differential diagnosis of psychiatric and substance use disorders. In J. Solomon, S. Zimberg, & E. Shollar (Eds.), *Dual diagnosis: Evaluation, treatment, training, and program development* (pp. 23–37). New York: Plenum.

Hamilton, T., & Samples, P. (1994). *The twelve steps and dual disorders.* Center City, MN: Hazelden.

Hazelden. (1993). *The dual disorders recovery book.* Center City, MN: Author.

Orlin, L., & Davis, J. (1993). Assessment and intervention with drug and alcohol abusers in psychiatric settings. In S. L. A. Strauss-

ner (Ed.), *Clinical work with substance-abusing clients* (pp. 50–68). New York: Guilford.

Shollar, E. (1993). The long-term treatment of the dually diagnosed. In J. Solomon, S. Zimberg, & E. Shollar (Eds.), *Dual diagnosis: Evaluation, treatment, training, and program development* (pp. 77–104). New York: Plenum.

Solomon, J. (1993). Management of acute problems in the dual diagnosis patient. In J. Solomon, S. Zimberg, & E. Shollar (Eds.), *Dual diagnosis: Evaluation, treatment, training, and program development* (pp. 57–76). New York: Plenum.

Zaslav, P. (1993). The role of self-help groups in the treatment of the dual diagnosis patient. In J. Solomon, S. Zimberg, & E. Shollar (Eds.), *Dual diagnosis: Evaluation, treatment, training, and program development* (pp. 106–126). New York: Plenum.

Zimberg, S. (1993). Introduction and general concepts of dual diagnosis. In J. Solomon, S. Zimberg, & E. Shollar (Eds.), *Dual diagnosis: Evaluation, treatment, training, and program development* (pp. 3–21). New York: Plenum.

REFERENCES

American Psychiatric Association. (1994). *Diagnostic and statistical manual of mental disorders* (4th ed.). Washington, DC: Author.

Carnes, P. (1995, October). *Sexual addiction.* Paper presented at the National Dual Disorder Conference, Las Vegas, NV.

Daly, G. (1996). *Homeless: Policies, strategies, and lives on the street.* New York: Routledge.

Evans, K., & Sullivan, J. M. (1990). *Dual diagnosis: Counseling the mentally ill substance abuser.* New York: Guilford.

Evans, K., & Sullivan, M. (1991a). *Understand-*

ing depression and addiction [Brochure]. Center City, MN: Hazelden.

Evans, K., & Sullivan, M. (1991b). *Understanding major anxiety disorders and addiction* [Brochure]. Center City, MN: Hazelden.

Evans, K., & Sullivan, M. (1991c). *Understanding post-traumatic stress disorder and addiction* [Brochure]. Center City, MN: Hazelden.

Evans, K., & Sullivan, M. (1995, October). *PTSD and the adolescent dual disorder patient.* Paper presented at the National Dual Disorder Conference, Las Vegas, NV.

Fayne, M. (1993). Recognizing dual diagnosis patients in various clinical settings. In J. Solomon, S. Zimberg, & E. Shollar (Eds.), *Dual diagnosis: Evaluation, treatment, training, and program development* (pp. 39–53). New York: Plenum.

Fields, R., & Vandenbelt, R. (1992a). *Understanding mood disorders and addiction* [Brochure]. Center City, MN: Hazelden.

Fields, R., & Vandenbelt, R. (1992b). *Understanding personality problems and addiction* [Brochure]. Center City, MN: Hazelden.

First, M. B., & Gladis, M. M. (1993). Diagnosis and differential diagnosis of psychiatric and substance use disorders. In J. Solomon, S. Zimberg, & E. Shollar (Eds.), *Dual diagnosis: Evaluation, treatment, training, and program development* (pp. 23–37). New York: Plenum.

Gold, M. (1995, February). *What can we learn from clinical research: Broadening the base of treatment options.* Paper presented at the North Carolina Governors' Institute, Greensboro, NC.

Goodman, A. (1997). Sexual addiction. In J. H. Lowinson, P. Ruiz, R. B. Millman, & J. G. Langrod (Eds.), *Substance abuse: A comprehensive textbook* (3rd ed.) (pp. 340–354). Baltimore: Williams & Wilkins.

Goodwin, D. W., & Gabrielli, W. F. (1997). Alcohol: Clinical aspects. In J. H. Lowinson, P. Ruiz, R. B. Millman, & J. G. Langrod (Eds.), *Substance abuse: A comprehensive textbook* (3rd ed.) (pp. 142–148). Baltimore: Williams & Wilkins.

Harvard Mental Health Letter. (1996). Treatment of alcoholism—Part II. *Harvard Mental Health Letter, 13,* 1–5.

Inaba, D. S. (1995, November). *Current advances in the medical management of dually diagnosed clients.* Paper presented at the National Dual Diagnosis Conference, Las Vegas, NV.

Koegel, P., Burnam, M. A., & Baumohl, J. (1996). The causes of homelessness. In J. Baumohl (Ed.), *Homelessness in America* (pp. 24–33). Phoenix, AZ: Oryx Press.

Loosen, P. T., Dew, B. W., & Prange, A. (1990). Long-term predictors of outcome in abstinent alcoholic men. *American Journal of Psychiatry, 147,* 1662–1666.

Lurie, S. (1995, November). Social phobia and chemical dependency. *The Amethyst Journal, 2,* 1–2.

Mirin, S. M., & Weiss, R. D. (1991). Substance abuse and mental illness. In R. J. Frances & S. I. Miller (Eds.), *Clinical textbook of addictive disorders* (pp. 271–298). New York: Guilford.

N., J. (1992). *Understanding bipolar disorder and addiction* [Brochure]. Center City, MN: Hazelden.

Nace, E. P. (1992). Emerging concepts in dual diagnosis. *The Counselor, 10,* 10–13.

Nace, E. P., Saxon, J. J., & Shore, N. (1983). A comparison of borderline and nonborderline alcoholics. *Archives of General Psychiatry, 40,* 54–56.

Nuckols, C. C. (1995, October). *Working with the angry/violent patient.* Paper presented at the National Dual Disorder Conference, Las Vegas, NV.

Oakley, D., & Dennis, D. L. (1996). Responding to the needs of the homeless people with alcohol, drug, and/or mental disorders. In J. Baumohl (Ed.), *Homelessness in America* (pp. 179–186). Phoenix, AZ: Oryx Press.

Orlin, L., & Davis, J. (1993). Assessment and intervention with drug and alcohol abusers in psychiatric settings. In S. L. A. Straussner (Ed.), *Clinical work with substance-abusing clients* (pp. 50–68). New York: Guilford.

Regier, D. A., Farmer, M. E., Rae, D. S., Locke, B. Z., Keith, S. J., Judd, L. L., & Goodwin, F. K. (1990). Co-morbidity of mental disorders with alcohol and other drug abuse. *Journal of the American Medical Association, 264,* 2511–2518.

Schutt, R. K., & Garret, G. R. (1992). *Responding to the homeless: Policy and practice.* New York: Plenum.

Scott, M. (1995, October). *Practical approach to dual diagnosis.* Paper presented at the National Dual Disorder Conference, Las Vegas, NV.

Shollar, E. (1993). The long-term treatment of the dually diagnosed. In J. Solomon, S. Zimberg, & E. Shollar (Eds.), *Dual diagnosis: Evaluation, treatment, training, and program development* (pp. 77–104). New York: Plenum.

Solomon, J. (1993). Management of acute problems in the dual diagnosis patient. In J. Solomon, S. Zimberg, & E. Shollar (Eds.), *Dual diagnosis: Evaluation, treatment, training, and program development* (pp. 57–76). New York: Plenum.

Thiesse, J. (1984). Working with dual disability clients. *The Grapevine,* 3–4.

Wright, J. D., & Lam, J. A. (1990). Lack of affordable housing causes homelessness. In D. L. Bender, B. Leone, & L. Orr (Eds.), *The homeless: Opposing viewpoints* (pp. 65–70). San Diego, CA: Greenhaven Press.

Zaslav, P. (1993). The role of self-help groups in the treatment of the dual diagnosis patient.

In J. Solomon, S. Zimberg, & E. Shollar (Eds.), *Dual diagnosis: Evaluation, treatment, training, and program development* (pp. 106–126). New York: Plenum.

Zimberg, S. (1993). Introduction and general concepts of dual diagnosis. In J. Solomon, S. Zimberg, & E. Shollar (Eds.), *Dual diagnosis: Evaluation, treatment, training, and program development* (pp. 3–21). New York: Plenum.

Zweben, J. (1995, October). *Engaging dual disorder patients into treatment.* Paper presented at the National Dual Disorder Conference, Las Vegas, NV.

4 The Treatment Process for Addictions

PRETEST

1. What are some important aspects of crisis counseling with addicted clients?
2. What are the five components of psychological first aid?
3. What are the four main goals of crisis resolution?
4. How are assessments of suicides and homicides similar and different?
5. How are interventions on suicides and homicides similar and different?
6. What are the stages of group development?
7. What are some issues common to addiction groups?
8. How can a leader care for himself or herself during the different stages?
9. What are common issues among addicted families?
10. What is the controversy regarding codependency? Adult children of alcoholics?

This chapter will examine four aspects of addiction counseling: crisis intervention, individual, group, and family. These areas will focus on counseling with an addictions emphasis. Each section will be followed by a case study reflecting that particular type of counseling framework. An overview of different treatment styles rather than specific interventions or approaches will be provided.

Crisis Intervention

Factors of a Crisis Situation

Slaikeu (1990) defines a *crisis* as a situation where known problem-solving techniques are not available to the client. For example, the client may be unable to recall a previous technique used at the time of the crisis, the client may not know a technique that would help in the crisis, or the client may be helpless in the circumstance and unable to use any coping techniques in order to survive the situation. The crisis, then, has the opportunity for the client to have a negative or positive outcome from the experience. The negative outcome would mean that the client does not come through the crisis with new knowledge and coping skills, whereas the positive outcome means that the client uses the opportunity to obtain new knowledge and coping skills.

The earlier the addicted person is in recovery, the more prone he or she may be to crisis situations. One of the problems for addicted individuals is learning what a crisis is. In some ways, particularly early in recovery (under two years of sobriety), everything for the addicted individual may feel like both a danger and an opportunity (a trigger). The individual is learning to live without alcohol/drugs and, as a result, may simply be more sensitive to the environment and the feelings he or she is experiencing. Thus, there may be many triggers to a crisis. The counselor plays an important role in assisting the individual in determining if the situation is or is not a crisis situation.

Also, the addicted individual needs to learn how to cope with a crisis—that is, how to deactivate the triggers of the crisis situation. The counselor is charged with helping the client find ways to calm himself or herself, reach out for support from others, and stay sober throughout the situation. These coping strategies can be and need to be taught to clients, regardless of whether the counselor believes the situation is actually a crisis.

The addicted individual also needs to learn what types of situations trigger crisis reactions in him or her. Once the crisis is passed, the counselor can help the client examine his or her thoughts and feelings that indicated that the situation was urgent. An awareness of these triggering events can cue the counselor as to coping skills that need to be learned by the client and respect for his or her own "soft spots" in the recovery process.

The counselor working with the addicted client needs to remain calm and supportive throughout the sessions. It is important to avoid judgment (e.g., "That is not a crisis") and simply to listen to the client's story. The client will also need assistance in sorting out and prioritizing issues to determine if the situation is a crisis and what needs to be done to address the circumstances. Finally, the counselor needs to help the client develop self-compassion both during and after the crisis. The client must learn that it is fine to reach out for assistance from others and that even if he or she overreacted to the situation, the important thing is that he or she made an effort to stay sober and learn from the experience.

There are some possible accompanying struggles that may occur for the addicted client, such as problems dealing with authority figures, difficulties trusting others, emotional reactivity, and poor impulse control. The counselor needs to be aware that the addicted client may view the counselor as an authority figure, who cannot be trusted, based on previous experiences the client has had with authority figures. Based on previous interpersonal experiences, the client may generally struggle with trusting others as well as be emotionally reactive and experience poor impulse control in interpersonal relationships. By remaining calm and supportive, the counselor can create an oasis for the client during the crisis. The counselor will need to keep these tendencies of addicts in mind in order to understand that it may take longer for an addicted individual to make a connection with a counselor in a crisis situation.

Short-Term Counseling

Slaikeu (1990) breaks crisis counseling into two components: first-order intervention (psychological first aid) and second-order intervention (crisis therapy). The main focus of psychological first aid is to help the client begin coping. Slaikeu (1990) reports that there are five components to this process:

1. *Psychological contact.* The counselor connects with the individual through the use of communication skills.
2. *Problem exploration.* The counselor looks at the crisis experience in terms of what led up to it, the strengths and weaknesses of the client, and what followed the crisis.
3. *Solution exploration.* The counselor helps the client prepare to address the crisis situation by looking at possible alternatives.
4. *Concrete action taken.* The client decides to take some action to address the crisis through the support and direction of the counselor.
5. *Follow-up.* The counselor and client have contact to see if the action taken helped the client's needs.

The themes of support and empowerment run throughout psychological first aid. The addictions counselor plays an important role of being present for the client throughout the crisis and helping the client see that he or she can survive this difficult situation sober.

During second-order intervention, crisis therapy, the counselor focuses on resolution of the crisis. Here, Slaikeu (1990) presents a BASIC personality profile to facilitate counselor assessment:

1. *Behavioral.* This area focuses on the client's behavior in terms of his or her strengths and weaknesses as well as behavioral antecedents and consequences.
2. *Affective.* The counselor assesses the client's feelings about these behaviors.
3. *Somatic.* The counselor assesses the client's physical health through sensations experienced.
4. *Interpersonal.* This area focuses on examining the number and quality of various relationships in the client's life.
5. *Cognitive.* The counselor assesses the thoughts and self-talk of the client.

The counselor using this framework with addicted clients is often using components of relapse prevention work. For addicted clients, a crisis situation is often paired with an urge to use. It is important that the counselor be aware that the addicted client in crisis may see only one way to cope with the situation: use alcohol/drugs. This myopic view of coping may be present for the client in spite of the length of his or her sobriety. As a result, the client will want to use the BASIC profile to examine the urge to use as well as to evaluate the crisis situation.

Slaikeu (1990) continues by encouraging the counselor to apply the BASIC profile to four specific crisis-resolution tasks: surviving the crisis physically, being able to express one's feelings with regard to the crisis, mastering the crisis cognitively, and learning to make adjustments behaviorally and interpersonally that will have an impact on the client's future. The BASIC profile information gathered by the counselor will guide the development of the crisis-resolution tasks. As stated under the BASIC profile, the counselor will want to verify that the client is also focused on tasks to stay sober as well as survive the crisis.

Common Addiction Recovery Crises

Often, addicted individuals have interpersonal problems such as marital problems, separation or divorce problems, domestic violence, parenting issues, and sexual orientation concerns. They may also have extensive trauma related to experiences such as rape, physical or sexual abuse, and war incidents. They may also be dual diagnosed or diagnosed with a life-threatening illness such as HIV/AIDS. Consequences such as financial or legal concerns resulting from their using may also be an issue. Finally, these individuals may be suicidal or homicidal. While the other areas may be effectively addressed through the crisis therapy previously discussed, there will be a special emphasis placed on suicidal and homicidal tendencies of the client.

It is critical for the counselor to assess suicidal tendencies and possible means of intervention. Many times, clients who are suicidal have ambivalent feelings about hurting themselves; the counselor must work to find that the part of the client that wants to remain alive. In order to connect with the part of the client that wants to live, the counselor must first watch for signals of possible suicidal tendencies.

One such means for assessment is the SAD PERSONS scale (Patterson, Dohn, Bird, & Patterson, 1983). This scale focuses on 10 factors that are correlated with suicide:

1. *Sex.* Males are more likely to complete suicide and choose more lethal means.
2. *Age.* Individuals under age 18 and over age 35 are higher-risk groups.
3. *Depression.* Clients who are depressed are more likely to commit suicide, especially if they begin to feel better and have more energy after being severely depressed.
4. *Previous attempts.* Clients who have attempted suicide before may find it easier to attempt again.
5. *Ethanol.* The presence of alcohol/drugs is connected with suicide.
6. *Rational thinking loss.* If a person has thought disorders, he or she may not be able to find ways to cope with the crisis.
7. *Social supports lacking.* If a client feels isolated and does not have enough relationships of meaning, there is an increased chance of suicide.
8. *Organized plan.* If a client has an organized plan, this means that the lethality level is high.

9. *No spouse*. Single individuals are more likely to commit suicide.
10. *Sickness*. If a client has a serious physical illness, he or she is more prone to commit suicide.

Another way to assess suicide potential is to memorize three questions to ask clients who seem to feel hopeless:

1. Are you thinking of hurting yourself?
2. How would you hurt yourself?
3. What stops you from hurting yourself?

Asking these questions in a calm, direct manner may assist the counselor in clarifying the lethality of the situation. For example, a client thinking of suicide who has a plan, access to means, and nothing of value to self that would inhibit an attempt is at high risk for suicide. Yet, while these questions may clarify the level of lethality, any suicidal indention should be taken seriously, and a counselor may need to consult with a supervisor or colleague to assist in lethality assessment (Zaro, Barach, Nedelman, & Dreiblatt, 1996).

Interventions on suicidal clients can be carried out a number of ways (Sunich & Juhnke, 1994). Generally, focusing on developing support and exploring alternatives is helpful; one option is increasing the frequency of the counseling sessions (Zaro et al., 1996). If a client's risk appears low or moderate, it may be appropriate to ask him or her to sign a contract agreeing not to attempt suicide for a specific period of time and agreeing to take some action (e.g., contact the counselor if he or she decides to hurt himself or herself). This contract may be written or verbal. For moderate- to high-risk clients, hospitalization and medication may be required. The counselor needs to remember that confidentiality is waived in a situation such as this and it may be helpful to notify close friends and family of the client's intent. Finally, Corey, Corey, and Callanan (1998) recommend counselors know their own limits in working with suicidal clients as well as carefully document their clinical work with these clients.

The process of assessment is similar for homicide. The counselor can use the same three questions to assess the lethality level:

1. Are you thinking of hurting someone?
2. How would you hurt this person?
3. What stops you from hurting this person?

Some of the factors positively correlated to homicidal behavior are similar to those of suicidal behavior: sex (males are more likely to commit homicide), history of violent behavior, excessive use of alcohol/drugs, and psychotic or paranoid disorders (Wicks, Fine, & Platt, 1978). In addition, these clients may exhibit reckless behavior or be accident-prone, have a sense of failure and low self-esteem, and have neurological problems, especially if there has been a head injury (Wicks, Fine, & Platt, 1978).

Intervention regarding a homicidal threat requires that the counselor not only examine the need for hospitalization and medication but also notify the individual who the client has threatened to harm. This crisis situation overrides the commitment to confidentiality, as evidenced in the case of *Tarasoff* v. *Regents of the University of California* (Bersoff, 1976).

CASE STUDY: JOHN

John is a 26-year-old, single man. He was divorced four years ago, and since that time has dated a number of women. He has been in private practice therapy (with the same counselor) since his divorce. He sobered up at the time of his divorce and has remained alcohol/drug free. He attends a weekly 12-step group (Narcotics Anonymous) and has a sponsor whom he contacts frequently. Two years ago, John tried to kill himself: He had a gun to his head and called his therapist for help. He was committed to a psychiatric hospital. This attempt followed the break-up of a relationship. He has little contact with his family and few friends. Today, John is calling his counselor because he does not want to live anymore. His most recent relationship ended earlier today because of his overcontrolling, demanding nature.

1. How well does John fit the SAD PERSONS scale?
2. What questions would you want to ask John to determine his level of lethality?
3. What are your intervention options with John?

Individual Therapy

Individual therapy can be very important for the recovering addict. It is here where the addict can learn to apply both general and specific recovery techniques to his or her own life situation. The counselor who is both willing and able to assist the client in this critical personalization process can provide the client with an anchor in his or her recovery.

Individual therapy with individuals who are addicted will probably flow out of the theoretical framework of the counselor. However, whatever the counselor's theoretical framework, awareness of some similarities among addicted individuals may enhance individual therapy by the use of specific approaches. These approaches include genuine counseling, collaborative relationships, and challenging interactions. Individual therapy also involves making sure that the client is in an appropriate treatment setting. Because of two recent streams of information regarding client treatment matching, the American Society of Addiction Medicine (ASAM) placement criteria and Project MATCH, these two areas will be discussed at the end of this section in terms of their impact on individual counseling.

Genuine Counseling

Being genuine with clients is an important element in counseling all clients, and is even more critical when working with addicted individuals. Because addicts often have difficulties in interpersonal relationships and especially in trusting others, the genuineness of the counselor can be useful in facilitating the therapeutic relationship.

A counselor working with addicted individuals needs to be very direct, honest, and genuine. For whatever reason, addicts are able to spot phoniness and insincerity relatively quickly. They will not tolerate someone who exhibits these behaviors. In order for a counselor to establish a therapeutic relationship where healing around addiction issues can occur, there needs to be a core of honesty to the relationship.

This core of honesty will involve the counselor being direct regarding what he or she feels and thinks with regard to the client. The counselor will need to determine how much self-disclosure fits his or her personal style of therapy, but regardless of the amount, the counselor needs to be quite congruent with the addicted client. If the client finds discrepancies within the counselor's thoughts, feelings, and behaviors, the client may simply write off the counselor as another individual who will not be helpful to him or her. A counselor who is genuine with the addicted client will find that this genuineness will pave a solid baseline for work. An addicted client who trusts his or her counselor will give that individual a lot of room when addressing and working with personal issues.

A second important core component is in the establishment of a collaborative relationship. Many addicted individuals are suspicious and distrustful of authority figures. This lack of trust may be based in family of origin or later life experiences that led to or evolved from their experiences with addiction. The counselor who tries to hide behind or use authority with addicted clients will have a difficult time helping the addicted individual trust him or her. However, if the counselor begins to work with clients in a more collaborative manner, the addicted clients are more likely to be honest in sessions and work closely and deeply with the counselor on the issues that fuel the addiction. Collaborative counseling means that the counselor may present ideas and options to the client, but always stresses the client's right to make a choice that fits him or her. Although it may be difficult for the counselor to allow a client to make mistakes in the treatment or recovery process of addiction, the empowerment experienced by the client communicates a deep respect for individual choice.

Addicted individuals have tendencies to push the limits on relationships with others as well as have excuses for their behavior in an attempt to avoid consequences. Counseling with addicted clients requires the counselor to be clear and firm about limitations and consequences. If a counselor does not provide this type of structure to the addicted client, the counseling will not help the addict with his or her addiction. The counselor needs to particularly examine personal views on relapse and any consequences in counseling given for this behavior.

One of the main difficulties in working with addicted individuals can be the challenging interactions that arise with them. As stated earlier, addicts may not be able to determine what a crisis is, so they may inadvertently "burn out" counselors and others in their lives with their most current crisis. There is also an adage some-times used by counselors of addicted individuals that they "want what they want when they want it." Therefore, if the addicted individual decides in that moment that he or she wants help, then that is often the expectation made. Often, there is a lack of willingness to delay gratification or trust the process that individuals are trying to help them even though a delay is involved. Combining this level of demanding with a general distrust of authority can make the addicted client very difficult to counsel.

A counselor working with this population in an individual setting needs to set firm, yet supportive, limits with the client. The counselor needs to stay calm, yet hon-est, and communicate clearly with the client regarding the difficulties of client behav-ior in their interaction. By remaining a calm, steady influence with clients, the counselor can teach them to slow down the reaction process and learn some helpful communication and social interaction skills.

Finally, it is important to discuss the aspect of matching of the client with the appropriate treatment. First, the American Society of Addiction Medicine Patient Placement Criteria-2 (ASAM PPC-2) (1996) suggests that clients be assessed in terms of six dimensions:

1. Intoxication and/or complications in terms of withdrawal
2. Conditions and complications in terms of biomedical aspects
3. Conditions and complications in terms of emotional and behavioral aspects
4. Acceptance and resistance levels in terms of treatment
5. Potential for relapse or continued use
6. Living environment with regard to recovery

The ASAM handbook is an excellent reference for counselors because it out-lines the specific criteria that need to be met for different aspects of treatment (admis-sion, ongoing stay, discharge, etc.) at all levels of treatment for both adolescents and adults (Perkinson, 1997). Because these criteria are being increasingly used in treat-ment programs throughout the United States (Shulman, 1997), counselors would be well advised to obtain a manual for reference in the assessment and treatment pro-cess.

In 1989, the National Institute on Alcohol Abuse and Alcoholism (NIAAA) began Project MATCH (Matching Alcoholism Treatment to Client Heterogeneity), involving 1,726 treatment centers throughout the United States, including women (25 percent) and minorities (15 percent) (NIAAA, 1997). The two main arms of the study were outpatient clients who came from the community and aftercare clients who had just completed treatment (inpatient or intensive day hospital) (NIAAA, 1997). Cli-ents were randomly assigned to three types of treatment: twelve-step facilitation (TSF), cognitive-behavioral therapy (CBT), and motivational enhancement therapy (MET) (NIAAA, 1997). No control group was used because the project was focused on comparing treatments and because of the ethical dilemma of refusing to treat cli-ents who need treatment (Mattson & Fuller, 1997). Results of the study were summarized by NIAAA (1997): (1) patient treatment matching is not needed for treatment effectiveness, except that clients with few or no psychiatric problems were able to stay sober longer with TSF than CBT; (2) drinking and negative consequences were reduced in all three treatments; and (3) clients with previous supervised abstinence (aftercare clients) were better able to maintain abstinence than outpatient clients. Counselors, then, may not need to be as concerned with the type of treatment the client receives for the addiction as much as the importance that it be delivered by competent addiction professionals and to be aware that psychiatric problems and supervised abstinence may play a role in the abstinence of clients.

CASE STUDY: JERRY

Jerry has been in individual counseling for his addiction because he has been unable to attend any group sessions due to his work schedule. Whenever he meets with his counselor, he appears angry and belligerent. He has told his counselor he feels miserable being sober and angry that he cannot drink. He said he cannot believe that his counselor is in this "racket" for anything other than the money. When Jerry gets upset in an individual session, he simply gets up and leaves the session.

1. If you were the counselor, how would you approach Jerry on his behavior?
2. What would make it difficult for you to work with someone like Jerry?
3. What limits would you set on Jerry's behavior and how would you set them?

Group Therapy

A common difficulty for addicted individuals is interpersonal problems (Capuzzi & Gross, 1992). For this reason, group therapy can be very healing for an addict's recovery process. As Yalom (1985) states, group therapy is a microcosm of the real world. Therefore, how an addict operates in the real world will show up in the group, allowing the addicted individual to work through those issues differently.

Types of Group

Group therapy is a common form of therapy used in chemical dependency treatment centers in the United States (Capuzzi & Gross, 1992). Therefore, it is critical that addiction counselors have a basic understanding of group counseling approaches and techniques.

Corey (1995) discusses different types of counseling groups: educational, vocational, social, and personal. Addiction groups may be a combination of educational, social, and personal types. Also, there are more structured groups that focus on a theme of recovery from addiction. The leader of an addictions group needs to determine the goal he or she has for the group and then look at how to set up norms to encourage the achievement of that goal.

It works best if these norms are clearly stated in a pregroup interview. If possible, it is a good idea to interview individuals who are going to join the group before they attend their first session. A 15- to 20-minute interview can allow the leader time to educate the client about the purpose and norms of the group as well as allow the client to obtain a sense of the leader and the group. A balance between safety and risk needs to be discussed with each member. Yet, members need to be encouraged to "do life differently." This encouragement may assist them in breaking out of lifelong interactional patterns.

Many times, however, addiction counselors do not have the luxury of a pregroup interview. In these cases, it is helpful for the leader to make some type of contact with the individual either prior to or in the group, even if it is as simple as shaking the person's hand and introducing himself or herself. If a new member joins a group without a pregroup interview, the other group members can educate that individual to the norms of the group.

If the counselor does not have the luxury of determining who is or is not in his or her groups, this issue must be discussed within the work environment. A counselor may face having someone in the group who he or she believes is very disruptive to the group process. This issue needs to be discussed with a supervisor in order to determine a policy of how this difficulty may need to be handled.

A leader must be careful in setting the tone for the group. One of the important bases of a group is the norms that are established. For instance, the leader needs to make sure that people attend the group, and if they cannot, they must know that it is their responsibility to call the leader. It is helpful to ask members to attend the group maybe five or six times to get a "feel" for the average group before deciding if they like or dislike the group. Group members must know that they cannot be sexual with one another in the group, because of how such a relationship would affect the dynamics of the group. They need to understand that if they do want to be involved with another group member, it is best to bring up the issue with the leader, who must then consider separating the individuals into different groups. Group members also need to be told the importance of confidentiality as well as the leader's limitations on enforcing such confidentiality.

If a member leaves the group, the leader needs to allow the group and member a chance to say good-bye. If a member needs to leave the group and there is not a chance for the group to say good-bye, the leader may ask the member if he or she wants a statement to be read to the group or, at the very least, allow the group a chance to acknowledge the absence of the member in the next session.

It is also important to make sure that there are enough chairs in the group for everyone, including members who are not present. Even though it may sound odd to have empty chairs in the group for individuals who are not there, it communicates an important message to the group that members are still part of the group, even if they cannot make it to one session.

Also, a leader needs to decide how to open and close sessions to see if these actions will reinforce targeted behaviors. The use of exercises in the group also needs to be examined. Although exercises can be helpful in providing clients with a framework for the group (thereby reducing their anxiety), they may also reinforce dependency on the leader.

Finally, if a counselor has a co-leader in the group, the dynamics of this relationship can have a powerful effect on the group. The communication between coleaders must be very honest and open with issues being addressed between them. If there are communication problems, these will be acted out in a group, just as marital problems in a family are acted out in the children's behavior.

Stages of Group Development

Different group theorists frame group development in various stages (Corey, 1995; Yalom, 1985). The framework used in this chapter will be Corey's (1995), which discusses four group stages: Initial Stage—Orientation and Exploration (Stage 1), Transition Stage—Dealing with Resistance (Stage 2), Working Stage—Cohesion and Productivity (Stage 3), and Final Stage—Consolidation and Termination (Stage 4). The counselor needs to remember that these group stages are not fixed or clear cut. Groups may show evidence of going back and forth between the stages, depending on membership changes in the group or issues that arise in the group.

The first stage of group development is what may be called the "cocktail party" stage, where members are nervous about attending the group. During this stage, members generally are involved in superficial chit-chat that does not reveal much about themselves. As Corey's (1995) title implies, members are trying to orient themselves to the group and explore how they are expected to function within the group. A central issue for members is the theme of trust (Corey, 1995). As members are determining group rules and norms, they are also trying to determine a sense of whether they belong in this group and whether they will be accepted by the other group members as well as by the group leader.

Addiction clients may show these initial group development behaviors in specific ways. For example, superficial chit-chat may be "junkie of the year" competition bragging. Here, a client may talk with other clients about how many different types of drugs he or she has done, how much of certain drugs have been taken, or how many consequences have been experienced (e.g., the number of DWIs). This information sharing may appear both deep and meaningful, but the client is truly sharing information that, to some degree, is already known by the counselor and other individuals in the client's life. This chit-chat may serve as a distraction from the painful issues in the client's life that led to or resulted from the addiction. At the same time, this information is important for the client to share to determine how similar or dissimilar he or she is to other group members and if these members will be judgmental. The group leader, then, aware of the need for such information to be shared by members, also needs to monitor if this information sharing is an avoidance technique being used by the clients.

Stage 2 of group development is often a difficult stage for both clients and the leader. In this stage of group development, the leadership of the group is challenged. Prior to this stage, the leader may have looked like an omnipotent parent to members (Yalom, 1985). During this time, members are questioning the leader's ability to direct the group. Actually, the members are really trying to find out how safe the group is for them. Knowledge of this level of safety emerges from struggles with power and control. Typically, this challenge is initially directed to the leader. In part, this is to determine what the leader acts like when stressed in situations. It is a parallel process to what one may do in an intimate relationship to find out how safe one is with an individual by fighting with him or her. Once the leader has been challenged, group members will repeat this process with other group members. These conflicts will show how the leader responds to conflict and what other members in the group are like when they are challenged.

At this stage of development, addicted clients may challenge the leader in a variety of ways. The leader, if not a recovering addict, may be asked what he or she knows about addiction and how he or she dares to work with addicts when he or she has never actually faced these issues. If the leader is a recovering addict, he or she may be challenged by being asked what types of drugs were done or how long he or or he used. The leader may also be challenged on gender or ethnicity differences, again questioning how well the leader can understand the struggles of the members. Whatever the form of the challenge, the leader is basically questioned regarding his or her competence. This questioning process reflects the underlying anxiety of the group members and the level of resistance or willingness they have to discuss concerns at a deeper level. Group leaders, while responding to questions directed to them, also need to redirect the focus from self by refocusing the group's attention to the underlying anxiety and resistance, and processing this anxiety and resistance with the group.

In the working stage of group development, Stage 3, group cohesion has developed and members trust each other and feel close to one another. At this stage, members share information about themselves on a deep and meaningful level. In the context of the group, they are now willing to look at issues with which they have struggled. Members are comfortable being direct and confrontational with one another. The leader is seen by group members in a more realistic light of having both strengths and weaknesses.

In working with addicts at this stage of group development, the leader may find members willing to discuss their personal issues in depth. Rather than simply discussing drugs they have used, they may be willing to discuss the shameful and embarrassing actions they took to obtain drugs. They may discuss how they felt as children growing up in alcoholic homes. Issues that emerge are discussed with expression of vulnerability and openness. At this stage, members are willing to be supportive and share their own places of pain with others in the group.

In the final stage of group development, members are facing issues of termination and attempting to integrate their experiences in the group into their daily lives. Strong feelings about termination may emerge for members as well as concerns regarding how well they may apply these group experiences to their lives. Themes regarding loss and grief may appear. The loss of loved ones through death or through the consequences of one's drug use may be present. Feelings of abandonment and betrayal may also emerge. The leader, for example, might be accused of not really caring for the addicted individuals because the group will end and they will not be able to see the leader again.

Group Leader Techniques

Group leaders can facilitate the transitions in the stages of group development by acknowledging the need for certain factors to be present and encouraging the presence of those factors in the group. Because 2 of Yalom's (1985) 11 therapeutic factors for group development, installation of hope and universality, seem especially related to the issues of addicted clients, they will be discussed here.

Installation of hope is a very powerful tool in working with addicted clients. These individuals may have previously tried to address their addiction and found themselves back in it in spite of their best efforts. If a leader can communicate hope to clients, this may assist them in making important changes in their lives. The leader's belief in the client's ability to change may assist with the client's motivation level as well as provide him or her with support to make changes around addictive behavior. For example, the therapist can simply encourage clients to "do it differently" in the context of group—that is, to try different behaviors in an attempt to achieve and maintain sobriety. This experience can lead to what Yalom (1985) calls the corrective emotional experience: The client heals from a previous trauma by reexperiencing the emotions in the group and having a chance to reflect on them. For example, a client may have let down many people in his or her attempts to be sober and, as a result, has been ostracized from significant others because of the addictive behavior. If a client relapses in a group and has the experience to process his or her own feelings and thoughts regarding the relapse within an honest, caring, supportive group that holds the client responsible for the relapse behavior, the client may experience hope about staying sober. In addition, he or she also has the corrective emotional experience of still being cared for and supported by the group to make another attempt at recovery.

Universality is the sense that one is not unique in one's problems or situations (Yalom, 1985). This sense can reduce a feeling of social isolation for the addicted individual. One way for this sense to be encouraged is for the therapist to work in the here and now. In other words, the therapist is aware of what is happening in the group at the present moment and watches for times of similarity between members. Commenting on such similarities can assist with the sense of universality, which can provide a strong basis for the group to explore specific issues related to addictions because of the experiences they have in common. Also, the experience of universality can be healing in and of itself because of the tendency for addicted individuals to be isolated from others as a result of their addiction and related behaviors. The universality can provide the addict with the sense of belonging to a community. For example, a client who has had extramarital affairs related to alcohol/drug use may have been isolated from his or her partner, children, church members, neighbors, and friends, who thought the affairs were a statement on what a bad person the addict is. Coming to a group and hearing how others made the mistake of having extramarital affairs may be healing for the addicted client and encouraging for him or her to discuss other issues related to dependency.

Leaders may find some other group techniques helpful when working with clients who are addicted. In general, group leaders need to listen actively, reflect meaningfully, facilitate goal achievement, and clarify, summarize, empathize, interpret, question, confront, support, diagnose, evaluate, and terminate appropriately within the group context. One technique helpful to group development is called *linking.* In this technique, the leader watches for ways to encourage interaction among the members by connecting the words and actions of one member to the concerns of another. This focus on common concerns among group members can facilitate the cohesion of the group (Corey & Corey, 1992).

Another technique is *blocking,* which is helpful in group development because the leader blocks member behaviors that work against group cohesion. At the same time, the leader does not attack the individual client demonstrating those behaviors in the group. Corey and Corey (1992) report some behaviors that need to be blocked: asking too many questions, gossiping, telling stories, invading privacy, and breaking confidences. For example, the therapist can block too many questions being asked by interrupting with a reframing comment such as, "It seems that the group members are wanting to know you better. What would you like us to know about you?"

Finally, group leaders need to use techniques that are a good match with the characteristics of the addicted clients with whom they work (Capuzzi & Gross, 1992). The leader needs to be directive by being focused and disciplined, which is important for addicted clients who may have low frustration tolerance and impulsiveness. They also need to confront both indirectly and directly to help clients break self-defeating patterns. The leader must also be tolerant toward emotionalism expressed by members and nondefensive especially with regard to anger and hostility. By being directive, respectfully confrontive, tolerant, and nondefensive, the leader can assist the group in becoming more cohesive as well as provide addicted clients with role modeling behaviors helpful to their recovery process.

Specific Issues

When working with addicted individuals in a group, the therapist needs to address relapse issues. For example, each leader needs to think about the conditions under which individuals who relapse will be allowed to remain in the group (Capuzzi & Gross, 1992). There is a thin line between compassion for how difficult it is to change a habit and encouraging the addicted individual to continue using. Relapse is understandable in the case where an individual has a commitment to sobriety and is willing to learn from the relapse by exploring it in the group therapy context, as well as possibly individually with the therapist (Miller, Kirkley, & Willis, 1995). It is important that group members accept consequences for their relapses. It is best that these consequences be clearly outlined in the group before a relapse occurs. An example of this type of situation would be when the counselor in the pregroup interview tells each recovering client that he or she is expected to remain sober, but if a relapse occurs, the client must let the counselor know of the relapse. This relapse would then be discussed openly in the group in order to determine what needs to be done differently to help the client stay sober. The client must understand that relapse does not automatically mean dismissal from the group, but that repeated relapses mean that the client's recovery is not working and so he or she may have to explore treatment alternatives with the counselor as well as the group.

Typically, addicts have problems with authority figures, trusting others, emotional reactivity, and poor impulse control. Problems with authority figures is discussed next (Therapist Self-Care); the other three themes need to be monitored throughout the group development stages.

Because trust of others may be a serious issue, the group leader needs to work hard at encouraging individuals to be both honest and respectful toward one another throughout the group care. An atmosphere of such honesty will assist members in trusting one another. At the same time, addicted members need to learn to work with their emotional reactivity and their poor impulse control. They must be encouraged to listen to their emotions and their impulses, but to delay acting on them until they have seriously anticipated the consequences of their behavior.

Two areas that may pose problems in a group with addicted individuals are denial and resistance (Capuzzi & Gross, 1992). Group members who have denial need to be confronted on the discrepancies of their behaviors, thoughts, and feelings. This does not have to be a highly emotional confrontation, but it needs to be anchored in behavior. If possible, it is highly effective to have members confront one another on the presence of denial or resistance. The counselor should note, however, that resistance in an addicted individual may be quite healthy in that the client may be aware that there is not enough support in his or her life to address such issues.

Therapist Self-Care

One of the main areas that will assist a group in developing is the ability of the therapist to work with the group's transference on his or her leadership role (charactersitics projected on to the leader). As Yalom (1985) states, the leader must remember that the transference is connected to the role. At the same time, the leader also needs to be aware that struggles with the leadership will be shaped by the traits/style of the leader.

During the first stage of group development, the leader is closely watched by group members. When the therapist enters the room, the room might become very quiet, and during discussions, members may turn often to the leader for feedback and suggestions. Group leaders will likely react differently to this focus of attention. For some, it may be uncomfortable to be under the magnifying glass of the group. These leaders may need to learn how to relax and be themselves when in the spotlight. For others who like to have the spotlight and be seen as having all the answers, they may need to proceed cautiously with feedback to members. In short, these leaders need to keep their egos in check for the sake of the group development.

The primary goal for the leader in the first stage of group development is to help the members feel comfortable in the group by making the group an inviting place for them to attend. The leader also wants to allow members to have superficial conversations while also inviting them to look at deeper issues. The therapist must closely monitor his or her behavior so the norms being set for the group are the ones he or she wants to have set.

During the second stage of group development, the leader encourages criticism from the group members. Here, the leader is monitoring for verbal and nonverbal signs of disagreement with the leadership. It is important for the leader to facilitate such challenges so that the group members learn how to confront one another in the group and so they learn that they are safe even if they challenge the authority structure of the group.

The counselor knows that it is impossible to please all members of the group at this stage. Whatever action he or she takes, the group members will find some fault with it. If the therapist is caring, the group may say it wants more authority. If the therapist is authoritative, the group may say that it wants more flexibility. The group attack on the leadership will never be unanimous (Yalom, 1985), but to some degree, it will be personal.

The leader must acknowledge his or her flaws and possibly apologize to the group. The group will be closely watching the leader to see how he or she deals with being confronted. By remembering that the members are transferring their projections from previous experiences with authority figures, the leader will be less likely to be overwhelmed by the experience. It may also help to remember that allowing the group the process of challenging the leadership is exactly what will help the group move into the working stage.

Thus, it is necessary for the counselor to learn how to take on the criticism of the group. He or she must model an openness to feedback and find a way to "ground" himself or herself during the challenge. This process of anchoring may vary among group leaders. Some may find it helpful to take a deep breath before responding to criticism. Others might place both feet on the floor and uncross their arms while doing a visualization that they are connected to the earth and that they will survive this confrontation. It is imperative that the therapist not strike back at the group member(s) who is doing the challenging. He or she must realize that the individual is simply the mouthpiece of the challenge for the group.

Because many addicted clients have had negative experiences with authority figures, stage 2 is critical in an addictions group. The leader needs to firmly guide the group through this stage of development by being honest, open, and willing to work through the challenge. Becoming resistive or defensive can stop the group at this stage of development.

During stage 3 of group development, the leader turns over different leadership functions, such as beginning and ending the group and establishing the focus of the group session. This may be difficult for leaders who have a high need for control, but it is important for the group members who have grown in their sense of autonomy.

During stage 4 of group development, the leader must be comfortable with issues of death and loss. He or she needs to help members process their own grief reactions to the group ending as well as allow himself or herself a chance to grieve the ending of the group.

An important part of self-care as a leader is allowing oneself some supports in being a therapist. The feedback of trusted colleagues, a supervisor, or a mentor will assist in this area.

CASE STUDY: TREATMENT GROUP

You have taken over an aftercare group from a female counselor. You have no control over the size of the group (the agency simply places people in the group by the night they can attend), and so there are 16 members. You sat in on the group once before taking over the facilitation of the group alone. You noticed that the former leader did not allow the group members to go into their feelings very deeply. You sensed a lot of frustration in the group toward the leader and other group members.

1. What group norms will you need to change in the group and how will you go about changing them?
2. What level of development is this group in?
3. What would you expect to happen in the group if you encourage members to express their emotions at a deeper level?

Family Therapy

Basic Concepts of Addiction Family Counseling

Family can play an important part in both the active addiction and recovery process for the addicted client. Stanton and Heath (1997) report that a family may affect abuse and overdose incidents, drug usage role modeling (parental), the need of drug abuse for homeostasis, and the enabling of the active addiction. McIntyre (1993) indicates that there are basically two functions for substance abuse in a family system. The first is that the abuse is primary and in itself causes problems within the family. The second is that the abuse is a symptom of lacking skills or needs that have not been satisfied. The counselor, then, needs to determine how the family uses alcohol/drugs in the system in order to determine how to most effectively intervene.

The counselor must examine the family boundaries in terms of how the family is divided both inside and outside the system (i.e., the types of rules that guide the family) (Kaufman, 1985). The counselor also needs to look for homeostasis: how the family stays in balance. It is also necessary to examine what conditions led to the alcohol/drug use, who the scapegoat (identified patient) is who acts out the family pain, and what triads exist in the family to keep symptom behavior alive (Kaufman, 1985). In addition, communication patterns and cross-generational coalitions need to be understood (McIntyre, 1993). This information can be beneficial in examining the alcohol/drug use impact on the family.

Family therapy is a way of looking at problems from the view of the overall system and intervening on interactions within the system (Stanton & Heath, 1997). The counselor looks for the strengths the family has developed through the process of addiction (McIntyre, 1993). Knowledge of the strengths can assist the counselor in finding cornerstones on which the family therapy can be built. The counselor also needs to carefully determine who will be involved in the family therapy. One of the items of concern may be how much to involve the children. Perhaps the children need to be involved in order to understand the impact on them, but not necessarily involved in any work that does not directly concern them (e.g., marital problems).

Individuals in the family will likely need help in understanding the role they play in the system (McIntyre, 1993). This awareness can help them understand themselves and the system better and thereby be freer to make choices about their behaviors rather than automatically responding according to the role they have been assigned or taken on. One way to facilitate awareness is to help them look at family of origin issues regarding alcohol and drugs (McIntyre, 1993). Without realizing it, parents may be bringing their unresolved issues regarding alcohol/drug use in their family of origin to their family of creation.

Buelow and Buelow (1998) frame treatment of families within their developmental stages: early abusive, middle dependent, and late deteriorative. In the early abusive stage, the family holds the value of sobriety even when members abuse drugs. Treatment prognosis for the family at this stage is good. In the middle dependent stage, the drugs have been integrated into the daily functioning of the family, and the counselor needs to realize that progress with the family at this stage may be slow. In the late deteriorative stage, the family dysfunction is severe, with family members split off from one another. Here, it is advocated that the counselor take on an educator or consultant role.

Often, treatment centers will have "family weeks" to help families both support and confront each other. Buelow and Buelow (1998) recommend that prior to these intensive weeks, the counselor should meet with the family to discuss confidentiality issues, set limits on focusing on those behaviors that will bring the family closer together, and provide ground rules for the group.

Types of Addictive Families

Kaufman (1985) describes four types of alcoholic families: functional, neurotic enmeshed, disintegrated, and absent. The *functional alcoholic family* has a stable system. In this type of family, drinking is usually in its early phase and is connected to conflicts that are social or personal in nature. The recommendation for counseling with this type of family is educational in nature (Kaufman, 1985).

The *neurotic enmeshed family* may be regarded as the stereotypic alcoholic family, where drinking is either a symptom of family problems and/or a means to cope with family problems. This type of marriage has sometimes been labeled the "alcoholic marriage" (Doweiko, 1990). Communication is indirect, fighting is frequent, marital partners compete with one another, and the nonalcoholic is in charge in the family (Kaufman, 1985). It is recommended that the family of this type be educated as well as have therapy that is behavioral, structural, and psychodynamic.

The *disintegrated family* is one where there is some temporary separation between the alcoholic and the other family members. This is generally the neurotic enmeshed family that has progressed to a later stage of development. Here, it is recommended that the focus be on the individual, with some exploration of potential family support.

The fourth type of family is called the *absent family,* where there is permanent separation between the alcoholic and his or her family. In this family system, there is basically no longer a family to whom the addict can turn. Here, the counselor can be most effective by helping the addicted individual develop new support systems.

Codependency

Codependency is a controversial topic in the addictions field. Zelvin (1993) reports that the term *codependency* started in Minnesota in the 1970s when the individuals close to alcoholics/addicts were seen as affected by the addiction and requiring assistance. Some theorists estimate that 96 percent of Americans are codependent (Zelvin, 1993).

Doweiko (1990) defines a *codependent* person as someone trying to connect with the addicted individual to obtain personal strength. In essence, the codependent individual focuses on the addict's need(s) to the point of not noticing his or her own needs. Zelvin (1993) describes codependency as the result of not developing completely as an individual and thereby focusing externally to obtain a sense of fulfillment. Both Doweiko and Zelvin recommend viewing codependency on a continuum. Doweiko's model (1990) views the ends of the continuum as being totally dependent on others for one's sense of self-worth (e.g., being a people pleaser) to totally disregarding the feedback of others. Zelvin (1993) states that there are three aspects to codependency: focusing too much on the opinions of others, not knowing what he or she likes or wants, and being drawn to relationships where others are needy.

The other view of codependency is that it does not exist, or at least not in the framework just described. Collins (1993) reports that no research empirically supports the construct. Kasl (1992) describes codependency as a lack of personal development, where the individual does not have an internal sense of power and security, does not believe he or she can exist on his or her own, has strong feelings of being alone and responsible, and is uncomfortable with being assertive. There is an argument that the definitions of codependency blame the victim (Kasl, 1992; Van-Wormer, 1989). Kasl (1992) states that stereotypic codependent behavior of submissiveness and passivity are reinforced in women (e.g., codependency is the oppression of women internalized).

It is important to remember that although some counselors and writers of self-help books use this term, the diagnosis is not listed in the *DSM-IV*. Myer, Peterson, and Stoffel-Rosales (1991) state that there is a lack of consensus about codependency because of the lack of specific criteria describing codependent behavior. In order to use the term clinically, then, it requires more precision and more clinical research to support the term (Mannion, 1991).

Counselors may walk this line between whether codependency is a diagnosis by working within the client's frame of reference. If a client uses this term to describe himself or herself, it would be wise for the counselor to ask what the client means by the term. It would also be wise for the counselor to be careful with regard to using this term so that clients do not think they are being diagnosed clinically. Until further research is obtained, it may be best to use descriptions of the symptoms (poor boundary setting, lack of assertiveness skills, overfocus on others, relationship problems around power and control, or extremes in complimentary role behaviors) rather than the term *codependency*. Even without the label of codependency, the counselor can help the individual become more aware, accepting, reflective, and responsible with regard to self (Whitfield, 1997).

Although counselors should be cautious with regard to labeling clients as codependent, the use of the concept of enabling in therapy may assist family members and significant others in examining their own behavior with regard to the addicted individual. *Enabling* is the process of encouraging the alcohol/drug use by unintentional behavior (Zelvin, 1993). It involves preventing the addicted individual from experiencing the consequences of his or her chemical usage by making excuses for behavior, lying to others for the benefit of the addict, attempting to control the addict's behavior, taking over the addict's roles, protecting the addict from consequences, and rescuing the addict from trouble (Perkinson, 1997; Zelvin, 1993). The process of enabling fuels the addicted person's denial about the presence of an addiction problem, the belief that the chemical usage is controllable, and the belief that responsibility for the problem lies within the control of the nonaddicted individuals (Perkinson, 1997; Zelvin,1993). The counselor can assist the family and significant others as well as the addicted client in the recovery process by encouraging all members to take responsibility for themselves and allow others to experience the consequences of their behaviors. If family members and significant others can recognize and cease their enabling behavior of the addiction, the vicious cycle of addiction can be broken or hampered because the outside supports for the addiction are gone.

Children of Alcoholics

There are similar struggles when looking at the characteristics of the children of alcoholics, sometimes called adult children of alcoholics (ACOAs). The self-help groups of ACOA began in the 1970s and are not affiliated with Alcoholics Anonymous or

Al-Alanon (Doweiko, 1996). Those theorists who believe that ACOA issues exist describe these individuals as not trusting themselves and struggling with boundaries, awareness of feelings, impulse control, trust, and guilt over parental alcohol use (Doweiko, 1990). The belief is that these individuals struggle in the present due to a dysfunctional alcoholic system in which they were raised.

The critics of the existence of ACOA issues state that this viewpoint is another victim-blaming perspective that keeps the focus of the issues away from the individual (Doweiko, 1990). Once again, there is a struggle with using this label with clients because there is not enough specific, behavioral criteria to substantiate the use of such a label (Doweiko, 1990).

Again, the counselor would be well advised to use the term *ACOA* with great caution, since it is not listed in the *DSM-IV* and there is no consistent pattern of behavior on which to base the diagnosis. Also, if a client is using this term, it is important to ask the client's definition of what this means to the client and then use his or her definition to help guide treatment planning.

Recovery Process

No matter what terms counselors use to describe the impact of being involved closely with an individual who is addicted, it is important to have a healing process for the person who cares about someone who is addicted. A core concept here is that of enabling, where the nonaddict encourages the addict's chemical use by buffering him or her from the consequences of the addiction (Zelvin, 1993). The counselor needs to help the individual examine how he or she is feeding the problem of addiction by his or her behaviors. Zelvin (1993) indicates that it is common for people not to see themselves as having any kind of problem connected with the addiction. If family members and significant others do not receive treatment, they may undermine the addict's treatment (Stanton & Heath, 1997).

Zelvin (1993) states two goals in treating the individual are (1) to stop the enabling behavior so that the addict can feel the full consequences of his or her usage and (2) to enhance the sense of self-responsibility. One way to help meet these goals is to support the individual in attending self-help groups (Al-Anon, Nar-Anon, Co-Anon, Families Anonymous, Codependents Anonymous [CoDA], and ACOA), which may be beneficial (McIntyre, 1993; Zelvin, 1993). (See Chapter 7 for suggestions on how to help clients find the best group for themselves. Also, at the end of Chapter 7 is a listing of some support groups that may be contacted for information regarding the groups and how to establish one.)

It is important to note here that Al-Anon developed out of conversations had by wives of alcoholics when their husbands were at AA meetings. These women met and talked about their own problems of living with alcoholic men. At some point in these conversations, they decided to apply the 12 Steps to their own lives. In 1948, the Al-Anon Family Group modified the 12 Steps and 12 Traditions to meet the needs of families of alcoholics. The only change to the 12 Steps was that the word *alcoholics* in the 12th step became *others*. In 1957, Al-Anon was modified for the concerns of teens. It used the same 12 Steps as Al-Anon and encouraged the view that the teenager had not caused the alcoholic to drink.

Codependents Anonymous and Adult Children of Alcoholics meetings may also be helpful to clients. Whether the diagnoses of codependency or ACOA exist or not, clients may find comfort in attending these meetings that offer them support and encouragement in their daily lives.

Markowitz (1993) adds some comments about working with children of addicted families. The author suggests that young children need to look at their denial about the impact of the alcohol/drug usage as well as allow themselves a chance to become angry and have their reactions to the usage supported. With adult children, the author recommends addressing the following issues in therapy: compulsivity, low self-esteem, shame, lack of self-awareness, and boundary problems.

CASE STUDY: THE JONES FAMILY

The Jones family has an alcoholic/prescription-addicted mother who has been brought to addiction treatment by her husband. She has been a successful treatment client in that she has examined her addiction and has been attending self-help groups during her short time of recovery. Shortly before discharge from the treatment program, her family has been brought in for a counseling session. Her husband and her two teenage daughters do not see why they needed to come in because now that Mrs. Jones is sober, they do not anticipate any more family problems.

1. How would you address the denial and resistance that the family is experiencing?
2. What options of treatment would you offer this family in terms of counseling? Self-help groups?
3. If the family refuses all treatment options, what areas would you address with your addicted client before she leaves treatment?

SUMMARY

In this chapter, specific areas common in the treatment of addiction were discussed: crisis intervention as well as individual, group, and family therapies. An overview of basic concepts was provided, with suggestions on how to apply these concepts to counseling.

SUGGESTED READINGS

Corey, G. (1995). *Theory and practice of group counseling* (4th ed.). Pacific Grove, CA: Brooks/Cole.

Kaufman, E. (1985). Family therapy in the treatment of alcoholism. In T. E. Bratter & G. G. Forrest (Eds.), *Alcoholism and substance abuse* (pp. 376–397). New York: Free Press.

Markowitz, R. (1993). Dynamics and treatment issues with children of drug and alcohol abusers. In S. L. A. Straussner (Ed.), *Clinical work with substance-abusing clients* (pp. 214–229). New York: Guilford.

McIntyre, J. R. (1993). Family treatment of substance abuse. In S. L. A. Straussner (Ed.), *Clinical work with substance-abusing clients* (pp. 171–195). New York: Guilford.

Slaikeu, K. A. (1990). *Crisis intervention: A*

handbook for practice and research (2nd ed.). Boston: Allyn and Bacon.

Zelvin, E. (1993). Treating the partners of substance abusers. In S. L. A. Straussner (Ed.), *Clinical work with substance-abusing clients* (pp. 196–213). New York: Guilford.

REFERENCES

American Society of Addiction Medicine. (1996). *Patient placement criteria for the treatment of substance-related disorders* (2nd ed.). Chevy Chase, MD: Author.

Bersoff, D. N. (1976). Therapists as protectors and policemen: New roles as a result of Tarasoff. *Professional Psychology, 7,* 267–273.

Buelow, G. D., & Buelow, S. A. (1998) *Psychotherapy in chemical dependence treatment.* Pacific Grove, CA: Brooks/Cole.

Capuzzi, D., & Gross, D. R. (1992). *Introduction to group counseling.* Denver, CO: Love.

Collins, G. (1993). Reconstructing codependency using self-in-relation theory: A feminist perspective. *Social Work, 38,* 470–476.

Corey, G. (1995). *Theory and practice of group counseling* (4th ed.). Pacific Grove, CA: Brooks/Cole.

Corey, G., & Corey, M. (1992). *Groups: Process and practice* (4th ed.). Pacific Grove, CA: Brooks/Cole.

Corey, G., Corey, M. S., & Callanan, P. (1998). *Issues and ethics in the helping professions.* Pacific Grove, CA: Brooks/Cole.

Doweiko, H. F. (1990). *Concepts of chemical dependency* (2nd ed.). Pacific Grove, CA: Brooks/Cole.

Doweiko, H. F. (1996). *Concepts of chemical dependency* (3rd ed.). Pacific Grove, CA: Brooks/Cole.

Johnson, V. E. (1973). *I'll quit tomorrow.* New York: Harper and Row.

Kasl, C. D. (1992). *Many roads, one journey: Moving beyond the 12 Steps.* New York: Harper Perennial.

Kaufman, E. (1985). Family therapy in the treatment of alcoholism. In T. E. Bratter & G. G. Forrest (Eds.), *Alcoholism and substance abuse* (pp. 376–397). New York: Free Press.

Mannion, L. (1991). Codependency: A case of inflation. *Employee Assistance Quarterly, 7,* 67–81.

Markowitz, R. (1993). Dynamics and treatment issues with children of drug and alcohol abusers. In S. L. A. Straussner (Ed.), *Clinical work with substance-abusing clients* (pp. 214–229). New York: Guilford.

Mattson, M. E., & Fuller, R. K. (1997, June). Reply from NIAAA. *Epikrisis, 8,* 2.

McIntyre, J. R. (1993). Family treatment of substance abuse. In S. L. A. Straussner (Ed.), *Clinical work with substance-abusing clients* (pp. 171–195). New York: Guilford.

Miller, G., Kirkley, D., & Willis, M. (1995, January). *Blending two worlds: Supporting group functions within an addictions' framework.* Paper presented at the meeting of the Third National Conference of the Association for Specialists in Group Work, Athens, GA.

Myer, R. A., Peterson, S. E., & Stoffel-Rosales, M. (1991). Co-dependency: An examination of underlying assumptions. *Journal of Mental Health Counseling, 13,* 449–458.

National Institute on Alcohol Abuse and Alcoholism. (1997, April). Patient-treatment matching. *Alcohol Alert, 36,* 1–4.

Patterson, W. M., Dohn, H. H., Bird, J., & Patterson, G. A. (1983). Evaluation of suicidal patients: The SAD PERSONS Scale. *Psychosomatics, 24,* 343–349.

Perkinson, R. P. (1997). *Chemical dependency counseling: A practical guide.* Thousand Oaks, CA: Sage.

Shulman, G. D. (1997, May). The ASAM patient placement criteria-2: Making it work. *Epikrisis, 8,* 2.

Slaikeu, K. A. (1990). *Crisis intervention: A handbook for practice and research* (2nd ed.). Boston: Allyn and Bacon.

Stanton, M. D., & Heath, A. W. (1997). Family and marital therapy. In J. H. Lowinson, P. Ruiz, R. B. Millman, & J. G. Langrod (Eds.), *Substance abuse: A comprehensive textbook* (3rd ed.) (pp. 448–454). Baltimore: Williams & Wilkins.

Sunich, M. F., & Juhnke, G. A. (1994, November). Substance abuse and suicide. *The Amethyst Journal, 1,* 1–2.

Van-Wormer, K. (1989). Co-dependency: Implications for women and therapy. *Women and Therapy, 8,* 51–63.

Whitfield, C. L. (1997). Co-dependence, addictions, and related disorders. In J. H. Lowinson, P. Ruiz, R. B. Millman, & J. G. Langrod (Eds.), *Substance abuse: A comprehensive textbook* (3rd ed.) (pp. 672–683). Baltimore: Williams & Wilkins.

Wicks, R. J., Fine, J. A., & Platt, J. J. (Eds.). (1978). *Crisis intervention: A practical clinical guide.* New York: Charles B. Slack.

Yalom, I. D. (1985). *The theory and practice of group psychotherapy* (3rd ed.). New York: Basic Books.

Zaro, J. S., Barach, R., Nedelman, D. J., & Dreiblatt, I. S. (1996). *A guide for beginning psychotherapists.* Cambridge: Cambridge University Press.

Zelvin, E. (1993). Treating the partners of substance abusers. In S. L. A. Straussner (Ed.), *Clinical work with substance-abusing clients* (pp. 196–213). New York: Guilford.

CHAPTER

5 Treatment-Related Issues

PRETEST

1. What are the effects of sexual abuse in men? In women?
2. What are the differences in counseling work with a perpetrator of sexual abuse and a survivor?
3. How can sexual orientation influence treatment and recovery?
4. What are the transmission processes of HIV/AIDS?
5. What are common issues for clients with HIV/AIDS?
6. What is the difference in counseling focus with a batterer and a survivor of domestic violence?
7. When is a couples treatment of domestic violence appropriate?
8. What multicultural concerns arise regarding domestic violence?
9. What are the different diagnostic categories of eating disorders?
10. What are three treatment stages in working with clients who have eating disorders?

This chapter will review three areas that are often related to addictions treatment: sexual issues (sexual abuse, sexual orientation, HIV/AIDS); domestic violence; and eating disorders. These three areas will be summarized in terms of general findings with specific recommendations made for addiction counseling. Each section will be followed by a case study to facilitate understanding of the material.

Reading this information may be overwhelming for a counselor because of the numerous issues that may interact with addiction. The following summary of these issues is meant to be an overview and hopefully serve as a reference in working with addicted clients. No counselor can remember to work with all of these issues all of the time, but an awareness of the possible presence of these issues, combined with careful listening to the client's story, can provide a holistic approach to addiction counseling.

Sexual Issues

Sexually related struggles may take different forms in the addiction treatment and recovery process. Four areas of possible concern are discussed in this section: rape, sexual abuse, sexual orientation, and HIV/AIDS. Although these areas are not inclusive of the sexual concerns of addicted individuals, they are common areas that emerge in the treatment of addictions. A general overview as well as counseling approaches specific to addictions will be provided.

Rape

Forcible rape is underreported in official statistics, especially when it involves someone known to the victim (e.g., date rapes, marital, group, and gang), because of personal reactions to threats of the rapist and feelings of shame and fear (of rejection from others, publicity, embarrassment, courtroom experiences, etc.) (MacDonald, 1995).

The relationship between alcohol consumption and acquaintance rape has been demonstrated particularly among college students (Parrot, 1991a, 1991b). The enormity of the problem with this population is supported by studies done by Koss and colleagues (1987, 1988) where the *MS.* Magazine Project on Campus Sexual Assault found 53 percent of the women of the 6,000 students studied said they had unwanted sexual contact; 15 percent of them reported completed rapes and 12 percent reported attempted rapes.

The *DSM-IV* notes that 3 to 58 percent of victims of criminal violence may experience posttraumatic stress disorder (PTSD). Although rape victims may be only a portion of those individuals, the statistics indicate the potentially strong trauma experienced by someone who has been raped. For example, in a study of PTSD with methadone patients, the most common stressor for women was rape (Villagomez, Meyer, & Lin, 1995).

Frazier, Harlow, Schauben, and Byrne (1993) report that women who blamed themselves and external forces for the rape experienced more distress in the recovery process. In contrast, women who had a sense of control over their futures and belief that they could avoid future assaults were more successful in the recovery process. Cognitive restructuring resulted in less distress, whereas higher distress was connected with the expression of emotion. Gilmartin (1994) suggests that although crisis counseling can be helpful in terms of assisting the victim to attach blame on the perpetrator(s) and access resources, the counselor needs to be careful not to minimize the woman's experience and her sense of the impact of that experience on her.

Gilmartin (1994) encourages society to look at the long-range effects of rape and to look at how symptoms such as drug and alcohol abuse/addiction may be metaphors for the struggles of victims recovering. The author suggests that these symptoms may indicate that the victim's view of self and the world has been altered or even shattered.

Counselors working with individuals who have been raped must be sensitive in processing the experience with the individual. They must connect sensitively with these victims by caring for them both during and after the relating of the story and by avoiding simplistic responses (Gilmartin, 1994). Rather, therapists need to hear and emphasize with the broad range of thoughts and emotions the victim may be experiencing.

CASE STUDY: TRUDY

Trudy is a 22-year-old female who has come in for outpatient chemical dependency treatment. She has been involved with the program for about two weeks and has just completed her first step on powerlessness over her addiction. She turns in her written first step to you. You notice that Trudy has an item written about the powerlessness she experienced at a fraternity party in college. Her comments seem vague and unclear. In your next individual session, you ask Trudy to clarify that section of her first step and she begins to cry. She tells you that she went to a fraternity party when she was a sophomore in college, had too much to drink, and passed out. She woke up in a bedroom in the fraternity house while someone was having sex with her. She said the experience terrified her, but she did not fight back, even though three more males raped her after she woke up. She said she did not press charges against them for three reasons: (1) she was drunk and felt like she was responsible for what happened, (2) she knew most of the males who raped her and described them as "basically good guys," and (3) one of the males she knew the best came in after the rape ended, cried, apologized, and begged her to not file charges against them. Trudy flunked out of college that semester because of her heavy drinking and her inability to concentrate on her studies after the rape. She never returned to college. She did not tell anyone about the rape until this conversation with you.

1. What would be your overall response to Trudy's story?
2. How would you address her rape as a part of her treatment plan?
3. What concerns would you have for Trudy in her recovery because of her being raped?

Sexual Abuse

With regard to sexual abuse, more females are studied than males, with prevalence rates in the United States and Canada ranging from 3 to 31 percent for males and 6 to 62 percent for females (Peters, Wyatt, & Finkelhor, 1986). Over one-third of female children in the United States have been sexually abused (Russell & Wilsnack, 1991) and 15 to 38 percent of women and 6 percent of men were sexually abused as children (Hiebert-Murphy, 1992). However, there are difficulties with the prevalence rates.

First, in terms of gender, females are studied more than males, boys may underreport (abuse does not fit stereotype, fears related to homosexuality, girls more easily seen as victims, etc.), and females may be abused in a less direct manner (Gonsiorek, Bera, & LeTourneau, 1994). Second, because of a lack of a clear definition of childhood sexual abuse, the statistics can be interpreted only within each study's definition of sexual abuse (Russell & Wilsnack, 1991). Third, research methodology problems (sensitivity of interviewers, number of subjects, randomness of subjects, etc.) affect the results (Russell & Wilsnack, 1991).

In spite of the variation of sexual abuse statistics, counselors working in the area of addiction need to remember that childhood sexual and physical abuse increases the chance of a substance abuse disorder (Brown & Anderson, 1991). The *DSM-IV* (1994) reports that substance abuse disorders may be related to posttraumatic stress disorder (resulting from childhood sexual abuse), but the pattern that precedes or follows the posttraumatic stress is unclear.

Effects
Finkelhor (1986) describes short- and long-term effects of sexual abuse for female survivors. Short-term effects include fear, anxiety, depression, anger, hostility, and inappropriate sexual behavior. Long-term effects are depression, self-destructive behavior, anxiety, sense of isolation and stigmatization, low self-esteem, a tendency toward revictimization, substance abuse, difficulty trusting others, and sexual maladjustment. Common to both are anxiety, depression, and sexual concerns. Gonsiorek, Bera, and LeTourneau (1994) describe the effects on males as committing aggressive acts, experiencing sexual identity confusion, having insecurity about masculinity, recapitulating the victimization, having more aggressive fantasies about others, and expressing more sexual interest in children.

Counseling Approaches with Survivors
Many addicted women are survivors of childhood sexual abuse (Hurley, 1991; Orrok, 1992) and may develop an addiction in response to sexual abuse (Blume, 1990). Similar relationships between addictions and compulsive behaviors and sexual abuse seem to be present for men (Bruckner & Johnson, 1987; Dimock, 1988; Krug, 1989; Olson, 1990; Urquiza, 1993).

When a counselor works with a client who is chemically dependent, it is important to ask if the individual has ever been sexually abused. A good approach to asking this question is to ask, "Has anyone ever touched you in a way that felt sexual and was uncomfortable for you?" This open question does not frame the answer in terms of sexual abuse, which is critical, since some clients may not realize that what was done to them was abusive. When a counselor asks this type of question and informs the client that this type of question is routine in an interview, the client may be more clear that the counselor is simply asking for information rather than suggesting that the client has been sexually abused (Knapp & VandeCreek, 1997).

In the late 1980s and early 1990s, claims of false memory syndrome became more frequent. The basis of this syndrome is that many cases of abuse are lies or distortions made by counselors (Gonsiorek, Bera, & LeTourneau, 1994). Lawsuits have increased against counselors in this area in recent years (Knapp & VandeCreek, 1997). Therefore, counselors who ask about sexual abuse in their clients need to be careful about how they ask about the abuse. There is no specific cluster of symptoms that automatically means a person was sexually abused. The counselor needs to find a balance between neglecting to address a significant childhood experience and assuming abuse happened without vivid memories or other evidence (Knapp & VandeCreek, 1997). A counselor using ethical standards, consultation, and supervision in conjunction with good clinical practices (firm boundaries, informed consent, careful diagnosing, clear diagnosis and treatment documentation, proven therapy techniques, and concern for future client-family connections) can find a balance between these extremes (Knapp & VandeCreek, 1997). In the area of assessment and diagnosis, a counselor is better off letting the client's story lead the counseling and let the client label whether or not he or she has been sexually abused. The counselor can always work with the client on the symptomatic problems and let go of the label of abuse. As Briere (1989) states, the counselor does not have to be the litmus test of truth.

For situations where abuse is suspected or self-reported, the counselor needs to establish an egalitarian relationship that is paced by the client (Briere, 1989). Rather than focusing on the label of sexual abuse, the counselor can focus on the presenting problems of the client. A safe environment needs to be established (Ratican, 1992), where trust is a core part of the therapeutic relationship (Hall, Kassees, & Hoffman, 1980). The counselor must be willing to completely accept the survivor and any feelings (Potter-Efron, 1989) as well as encourage the survivor to practice self-care (Armsworth, 1989). Two basic ingredients in effective counseling with a sexual abuse survivor are trust and self-care.

The survivor can learn to trust another by developing a relationship with a counselor (Miller, Sack, & Simmons, 1993). Also, the survivor needs to learn the symptoms of the abuse so he or she can practice self-care. For example, if a survivor tends to have outbursts of anger when something reminds her of the abuse, she needs to learn to recognize this as a symptom of the abuse having a current impact on her. In doing so, she will learn that such behavior does not control her, but rather guides her into self-care. The survivor also needs to learn how to calm himself or herself. This process of self-care is important for addicted survivors so that they do not turn to alcohol and drugs to self-medicate.

It seems most prudent to treat sobriety as a first priority because a sense of self-efficacy can be strengthened (Briere, 1989; Evans & Schaefer, 1987). Yet, when survivors stop using alcohol and drugs, they often have memories and flashbacks of the abuse (Bass & Davis, 1988; Briere, 1989) and may relapse in their addiction in order to cope with the memories of sexual abuse (Evans & Schaefer, 1987; Root, 1989). Therapy with the sexual abuse survivor, then, is a "dance" between the issues of addiction and sexual abuse: addressing the sexual abuse issues until signs of addiction relapse are present and then focusing on the addiction until the recovery process is stabilized and the sexual abuse issues can be examined once again (Miller, Sack, & Simmons, 1993).

The survivor and the counselor need to learn what the particular high-risk relapse situations are for the client in order to prevent relapse (Marlatt, 1985). These situations will be different for each survivor. For some, it may be a visit home; for others, it may be running into the perpetrator or someone who looks like the perpetrator. The counselor can help the survivor learn what the high-risk situations are for him or her by showing the survivor how to self-monitor (i.e., become aware of times of intense emotional reaction or an unexplainable reaction to circumstances). In this way, the survivor can then report the situation and reaction to the counselor and together they can determine what seemed to trigger the response.

The counselor and survivor can then work on approaches to cope with high-risk situations. Some examples of coping behaviors are encouraging self-talk, contacting a recovery sponsor or mentor, learning to detach from intense feelings (experiencing them without acting on them or repressing them), and developing missing coping skills such as assertiveness (Miller, Sack, & Simmons, 1993). The three recovery Ss (Miller, Sack, & Simmons, 1993) are *sobriety* becomes top priority, *strengthening* the addict's functioning, and *signs* of relapse are monitored. Throughout the counseling, the therapist needs to keep in mind the different effects that gender may have on the sexual abuse experience.

In the recovery process, a counselor will often refer a client to a self-help program or the client will already be involved in one. (Chapter 7 examines different self-help groups. In attempting to help an addicted survivor find a good match, the counselor needs to keep in mind the survivor's issues and, as outlined in Chapter 7, process the experience of the self-help groups with the survivor.)

An example of adapting a self-help program to benefit survivors is provided by Miller, Sack, and Simmons (1993), who suggest how counselors may translate the 12 Steps for addicted female survivors. In the first two steps, which discuss powerlessness—a feeling quite familiar to survivors—the counselor can assist the individual in understanding that acknowledging addiction powerlessness frees the survivor and helps him or her develop a sense of personal power (without drugs). In the third step, which uses the phrase "God as we understood Him," the survivor may need to find a group that uses the word *Her* rather than *Him,* or a group that translates this phrase in a broad, spiritual sense, or perhaps work on this issue alone. In the fourth and fifth steps, which encourage the person to admit his or her flaws, and in the sixth and seventh steps, which look at removing flaws in oneself, the survivor may need to be reminded that he or she did not cause the abuse and that the effects of the abuse need to be viewed with compassionate accountability: The survivor is responsible for his or her actions, but the survivor was doing the best he or she could to survive. In the eighth and ninth steps, where amends need to be made, a survivor needs to be reminded that he or she should be at the top of the amends list since he or she experienced the most pain of the addiction. Finally, with the last two steps, which are the recovery maintenance steps, the client needs to understand that he or she will make mistakes, to learn to communicate spiritually in a way comfortable for him or her, and to care for self and others.

This example of finding a way to translate a self-help recovery program can be done with any self-help group. The counselor simply needs to work with the client on his or her reactions to the recovery program and have the client translate concepts in a way that is helpful to the client staying sober.

Counseling Approaches with Perpetrators

When a counselor is treating a perpetrator of sexual abuse, it is very likely that the perpetrating client has previously worked with a sexual abuse offender expert; if not, the client needs to be referred to one to address the perpetration issues. Sexual abuse offender counseling is a specific area of specialization. Unless a counselor is specifically trained in this area, it is important to work closely with other counselors who have been. The counselor needs to remember that the client has a problem with both alcohol/drugs and sex offending, and treatment must focus on both areas or the problems may continue to feed into one another.

Finkelhor (1986) presents four preconditions that have to exist for the offender to sexually abuse; the first two must be present for the second two to occur. The first two are that the offender has to be motivated to abuse (be interested in sexually abusing another) and overcome any internal inhibitions with regard to abusing (e.g., the incest taboo). The second two are that the offender must overcome external obstacles against abusing (e.g., abusing in the presence of others) and has to overcome the child's resistance. Although alcohol or drugs can assist the offender in overcoming internal inhibitions against abuse, the motivation to abuse still must be present. The offender in treatment, then, cannot simply brush off the abuse to something that happened when he or she was drinking/using. Obviously, a second problem is present besides the problem with alcohol/drugs.

The *Juvenile and Family Court Journal* ("A Statement of Philosophy," 1988) provides a philosophy of managing and treating sex offenders. The first aspect of this philosophy is to make the community safe; therefore, there may be limits on confidentiality of sessions (e.g., the offender's plan to abuse someone). Second, treatment needs to complement the legal sentence given by the court, not reduce or void it. Next, treatment should fit the risk potential of abuse by the offender. Fourth, denial needs to be confronted and guilt must be admitted. Fifth, sex offenders need long-term treatment and follow-up. Last, a coordinated, multidisciplinary team is needed to address these issues.

The counselor working with a perpetrator needs to work as a part of a multidisciplinary team and in conjunction with the legal system so the perpetrator's behavior can be held accountable. Therapists will likely need to confront the "teflon defenses" (projection and denial) used by most perpetrators by pointing out inconsistencies and holding the perpetrators accountable for their behavior. The counselor working with the addiction aspects of the client's problems needs to stay focused on that aspect and not allow the client to use the addiction as an excuse for his or her behavior.

In terms of self-help recovery, the counselor must assist the client in finding groups that hold him or her accountable for personal behavior. The counselor may also need to translate program philosophy so the client does not use it to minimize his or her perpetration acts (e.g., "I was powerless over my behavior because I was drinking").

Sexual abuse counseling, whether it is with the perpetrator or the survivor, needs to be incorporated into addiction counseling in order to promote a complete recovery process. It is important that the addictions counselor is aware of these issues and their relationship with addictions through training, supervision, and/or consultation with colleagues.

CASE STUDY: SHARON

Sharon is a 40-year-old female who has had two previous addiction treatments. She has come to counseling because of work complaints: She has difficulty communicating with her supervisor. Sharon states that the stress is so high at her work that she often thinks about using alcohol/drugs. As she talks in counseling about her supervisor, she mentions that he looks a lot like her uncle who sexually abused her from ages 8 to 12. When encouraged to talk more about her concerns, she describes her problems with her supervisor with intense affect, but describes her childhood sexual abuse with a sharply contrasting flat affect. She states that she does not want to discuss her childhood experiences any more during the session. The day after her first counseling session, she calls you in the early morning, crying heavily. She reports sleeping only for brief periods during the night, wakened by nightmares of her uncle sexually abusing her. She states she is afraid that she will return to using alcohol and drugs.

1. What would be your first priority in working with Sharon?
2. In the short term, how would you balance her memories of the abuse and her addiction recovery?
3. What would be your long-range plan for working with the client?

Sexual Orientation

Cabaj (1997) describes sexual orientation as based on desire rather than sexual behavior that may or may not be connected to sexual orientation. *Homosexuality* means that the sexual interest in another person is toward the person of the same sex, whereas *bisexuality* is when that interest is toward people of both sexes. Although sexual orientation does not cause addiction, we live in a homophobic culture where individuals of homosexual or bisexual orientation experience discrimination. Heyward (1992) underscores the oppression and injustice experienced by gays and lesbians. Weinberg (1994) reports that in response to the oppression these individuals experience, friends may play important roles in their lives, thereby resulting in them drinking the way their friends drink. Cabaj (1997) states that high degrees of substance abuse with gay men and lesbians can be understood by their sexual orientation, "coming out" process, and homophobia, which is probably the most influential.

Some researchers state that approximately one-third of gays and lesbians in the United States abuse alcohol (Saghir, Robins, Walbran & Gentry, 1970; Weinberg & Williams, 1974). More recently, researchers (Stall & Wiley, 1988) found that only 19 percent of their sample of gay men were frequent, heavy drinkers, only some of whom were dependent. Cabaj (1997) states there is no firm agreement about the amount or incidence of drug use. Although there may be a range in the estimated number of alcoholics in this population, drinking is often a component in the socializing of gay men in terms of gay bars and parties, and this same process of role modeling/socializing may operate with the lesbian and bisexual populations (Weinberg, 1994). Heavy drinking may be more of a problem for older lesbians (over age 40) than younger lesbians (Eliason, 1996). In terms of drugs, gay and bisexual men tend to use more drugs than the general male population (Eliason, 1996). McKirnan and Peterson (1989) found no significant difference between frequency of use when comparing lesbian and bisexual women to the general population, although these women tended to use more marijuana and cocaine during their lives.

Gays, lesbians, and bisexual men and women report experiences with discrimination and harassment in chemical dependency treatment centers (Eliason, 1996). J. Hall (1994) states that there are three barriers in addiction treatment for lesbians: (1) distrust in terms of not feeling that sexuality issues are understood or that they are discriminated against, (2) incongruence between the client's and the provider's views of the problem and treatment, and (3) provider styles are not helpful (e.g., paternalistic and confrontational). When these individuals enter into recovery from addiction, their sexual orientation must be addressed, without prejudice, as a part of their recovery. One such organization, the Pride Institute, which focuses on mental health and addictions treatment for gay, lesbian, bisexual, transgender (GLBT) clients, began in 1986 (Amico & Neisen, 1997).

In 1973, the American Psychiatric Association stated that homosexuality, by itself, cannot be considered a psychiatric disorder (Finnegan & McNally, 1987). As a result, counselors do not have the professional support to view homosexuality or bisexuality as a psychiatric illness. Yet, due to heterosexism and homophobia, some counselors tend to operate in that manner with their homosexual and bisexual clients. *Heterosexism,* the belief that heterosexuality is better, results in *homophobia,* negative stereotypes and feelings toward gays/lesbians.

One of the main concerns for the heterosexual counselor, then, is his or her countertransference issues with a client's sexual orientation. Each counselor working with an addicted individual who is homosexual or bisexual needs to examine his or her own reactions and biases toward that person's sexual orientation. Negative biases can be addressed in counseling, with colleagues, and/or a supervisor.

Each client, regardless of sexual orientation, has a right to be treated with respect. If a counselor truly believes he or she cannot work with homosexual or bisexual addicted clients, the agency should be informed of the counselor's limitation so that such clients are assigned to less homophobic counselors. If the counselor works alone, this limitation should be made clear to others who refer clients to him or her.

For the heterosexual counselor who works with the homosexual or bisexual addicted client, sexual orientation issues need to be integrated into the treatment recovery plan. Rather than assuming what these issues are, the counselor needs to work with the client to determine these concerns. Initially, each client needs to be asked about his or her sexual orientation in a relaxed manner as part of the normal treatment procedure (Finnegan & McNally, 1987). For those clients who are homosexual or bisexual, some concerns may be considered typical. Cabaj (1997), for example, recommends that counselors consider the following aspects of each individual in development of a treatment plan: life stage, "coming out" process, support available, current and past relationships with significant others and family, comfort with sexuality, and issues related to career, finances, and health. The "coming out" process is a series of steps taken over time where the client acknowledges his or her difference, pulls that difference into self-view, possibly acts on feelings, and then decides who to inform about his or her sexual orientation (Cabaj, 1997). Without the gay or lesbian client's own acceptance of his or her sexual orientation, relapse may occur. Also, the counselor needs to be aware that increased alcohol/drug usage or relapse may be related to verbal and/or physical attacks by others because of the client's sexual orientation.

Some clients might use "gaydar" to determine if a counselor is open to working with gays and lesbians. *Gaydar* is a term some gays and lesbians use to describe their internal "radar" or sense if someone is open to gays and lesbians. The counselor can demonstrate an openness by being relaxed when discussing sexual orientation, answering questions regarding the counselor's sexual orientation (if appropriate and comfortable for the counselor), and speaking an inclusive language that does not assume sexual orientation. An example of inclusive language would be a counselor talking with a client about intimate relationships and using a word such as *partner* rather than *boyfriend* or *girlfriend*.

Another concern of clients is not being able to go to gay bars to socialize. Gay bars serve a purpose broader than that of heterosexual bars. They are one of the few places in society that a client can safely assume that the others in the bar are gay or lesbian and can comfortably make connections with others (Finnegan & McNally, 1987). Therefore, a common counselor recommendation of avoiding bars may not be possible for this population. However, Finnegan and McNally (1987) suggest that clients who go to bars do so with other recovering gays, lesbians, and bisexuals after attending a recovery meeting. In whatever way the client attends these bars, it needs to be done in a self-protective manner that does not encourage relapse. For example, the client may be encouraged to go to a bar only when he or she is not out of balance physically or emotionally or only at times when he or she feels less vulnerable to the influence of others. In addition, it may be helpful for the client to scrutinize his or her motives for going to the bar and determine if those needs can be met somewhere else.

Typically, treatment for addiction will involve a client's partner or family members. The counselor needs to determine from the client if his or her partner and/ or family wants to be involved in treatment. It is possible that they may want to be involved, but do not want the homosexuality or bisexuality addressed in a group of predominantly heterosexuals. The counselor can work with the client to determine if group treatment is appropriate or if individual or family counseling in combination with the provision of educational literature regarding addiction recovery and sexual orientation is more appropriate. This approach would be respectful of the reality of homophobia in which the client and his or her partner and family live.

Lesbians often have some different issues that need to be addressed in treatment. Typically, they have less income, are more likely to be older when they "come out," have children, have their substance abuse ignored because they are female, experience bisexuality in terms of feelings or behavior, and are more likely to be in long-term relationships (Cabaj, 1997). Therefore, treatment with lesbians needs to focus on relationship-oriented issues such as parenting and domestic violence.

When counselors refer homosexual or bisexual clients to self-help groups in the community, they need to be aware that homophobia exists in such groups as well as the general population. It may be helpful if the counselor has contacts in the gay and lesbian community and in recovery and/or self-help groups in that community. Recovering gays, lesbians, and bisexuals can help clients adjust to the recovery process at times when the counselor may be inaccessible or in ways the counselor cannot assist the client (e.g., attending a self-help group with the client). Remember, too, that some homosexual clients may be hesitant to go to Alcoholics Anonymous or Narcotics Anonymous because he or she may connect these groups to religion, and often these clients have been ostracized by religions for their homosexuality (Cabaj, 1997).

If there is a self-help group in the community for gays, lesbians, and bisexuals, the counselor needs to remember to ask the client about the meeting experience. As with heterosexual meetings, the health of the group can vary a great deal. As with any individual in recovery, the client may find someone he or she wants to date at a self-help meeting, but that is not the intent of the meeting. The client may need to be reminded that the reason for attending meetings is to work on sobriety.

If there are no self-help groups specifically for homosexuals or bisexuals, the counselor needs to discuss with the client the possibility of experiencing discriminatory reactions if the client discloses to the group that he or she is gay, lesbian, or bisexual. Some recovering clients never let group members know their sexual preference and can live with that comfortably; they are comfortable using terms such as *partner* and avoiding terms such as *he* or *she* when discussing intimate relationships. If the client is not comfortable with that approach and wants to tell the group of his or her sexual orientation, the client needs to be reminded that some self-help group members may be very homophobic and that he or she may be ostracized in the group after disclosure of sexual orientation.

Another caution of self-help groups is with regard to sponsorship or mentorship. Some groups, such as 12-step groups, encourage the individual to choose a sponsor or mentor who is of the same gender. This advice is generally thought to discourage "13 stepping" (someone sober for a while being sexual with someone who is new in recovery). However, for gay, lesbian, or bisexual clients, this advice does not necessarily work. A client may be better advised to choose a sponsor or mentor to whom they can relate without a lot of sexual energy between them. This may be someone of the same sex or someone of the opposite sex.

Not all addicted clients will not have issues regarding sexual orientation, but the therapist working with addicted clients needs to have an awareness that such issues will be present for homosexual or bisexual clients. The counselor needs to work with this clientele in a respectful, honest manner with an ongoing awareness of the homophobia in the culture.

CASE STUDY: SANDRA

Sandra has just entered addiction treatment for the first time. She is in an outpatient setting with a mixed group of male and female clients. When she talks with you about her significant other, she always uses the word *partner,* and when she talks about her struggles in the group setting, she emphasizes that everyone in the group is married and most have children. She says after her first few sessions that she does not know if she will be able to stay sober, because much of her social life is around her friends who understand her and support her, but they often socialize together in a bar setting or in a social context where alcohol and marijuana are readily available. You believe that Sandra may be lesbian.

1. How would you bring up her sexual orientation with Sandra?
2. If she is a lesbian, how would you approach her social life in terms of relapse prevention?
3. If she is lesbian, how would you help her cope in the group treatment setting and in individual counseling with you?

HIV/AIDS

History
There are different theories as to the origin of HIV (human immunodeficiency virus), but it is not known for sure how it began and how it became introduced to humans (Kalichman, 1995). HIV can lead to acquired immunodeficiency syndrome (AIDS). AIDS cases were first identified by the Center for Disease Control and Prevention (CDC) when five homosexual men residing in Los Angeles had pneumocystis carinii pneumonia, a rare upper-respiratory infection (CDC, 1981). The virus that has caused

most of the AIDS cases was called human immunodeficiency virus type-1 (HIV-1) in 1986; a second AIDS virus, HIV-2, was discovered in 1986, but it has not spread as rapidly as HIV-1 (Kalichman, 1995).

The HIV virus reproduces itself by taking over the protein-producing functions of the host cell. The protein receptors of the immune system cells are the CD4 receptors through which the HIV virus enters in order to reach the protein receptor. Naturally, the immune system uses white blood cells, T helper cells and T suppressor cells, to address invading organisms: The helper cells tell the immune system to be alerted, whereas the suppressor cells tell it to not be alerted. After the HIV virus enters the helper cells and kills or hurts them, the suppressor cells provide stronger signals, which make the immune system less able to respond to the organism invading the body. The person infected with HIV/AIDS, then, is more susceptible to infections that might otherwise not be life threatening (APA, 1996)

Classification

The development of HIV infection to AIDS can take from at least 1 to 15 years (Bartlett, 1993). In 1987, the CDC developed a system for describing the four stages of the HIV disease: asymptomatic periods (stage 1 and stage 2); chronic lymphadenopathy, swollen, firm lymph nodes (stage 3); and later stages (stage 4: [A] weight loss, fever, chronic diarrhea; [B] neuropathology; [C] opportunistic infections; [D] tumors; [E] other problems) (Kalichman, 1995). Kalichman (1995) outlines three of the stages and their accompanying symptoms. In stage 1, which is known as the acute infection time, a person may have short-term flu-like symptoms such as fever or nausea. In stage 2, the individual is basically asymptomatic. In stage 3, the individual was often diagnosed historically as having AIDS-related complex (ARC), which means the symptoms were not considered severe enough to be labeled AIDS. However, the term *ARC* has been dropped, since some symptoms do not always occur before the onset of AIDS. In stage 4, the individual is diagnosed as having AIDS (Strom, 1993). In 1993, the Center for Disease Control revised its definition of AIDS. The new definition does not focus on manifestations of the virus, but on the CD 4 cell count being below 200 (Kain, 1996).

The most commonly used HIV test looks for the antibodies, because direct contact with HIV is not required and the test is less expensive (Saag, 1992). There are two possible levels of testing. The first test is called ELISA (enzyme-linked immunosorbent assay), which looks for HIV antibodies. If results are positive, another test, western blot procedure, must be given because the ELISA does not look just for HIV antibodies. As Saag (1992) points out, these two tests reduce the chances of a misdiagnosis to a low probability. A person who is tested for HIV and is found negative needs to be tested again in about three months, since the HIV may be in an incubation period.

Transmission

There are six routes of HIV transmission and therefore six risk behaviors: anal intercourse, vaginal intercourse, oral-genital contact, perinatal transmission, injection drug use, and blood transfusion (Kalichman, 1995). Condom use, particularly the use of latex condoms, helps protect the individual against the HIV virus (Conant, Hardy, Sernatinger, Spicer, & Levy, 1986). Although latex condoms reduce the risk of contracting the virus, they do not eliminate it, because condoms break, slip off, or have undetectable tears. Also, only lubricants that are oil free and water based should be used with the condoms, because oil products will break down the latex (Voeller, Coulson, Bernstein, & Nakamura, 1989).

The HIV virus can be transmitted to babies by crossing the placenta, having contact with blood and vaginal fluids during delivery, and during breast feeding (CDC, 1989). Babies can be tested for HIV; however, only conclusive tests can be done when the infants' HIV antibodies replace the maternal antibodies (Kalichman, 1995).

The virus can also be transmitted when injection equipment such as needles and syringes are used by an infected person and shared with others. Because drug abuse is considered deviant (Mondragon, Kirkman-Liff, & Schneller, 1991), HIV-infected drug users often experience a double discrimination. In the United States, individuals who received blood transfusions between 1978 (onset of the epidemic) and 1984 (first HIV-antibody test became available) are at the highest risk for infection (Kalichman, 1995).

Ramifications

HIV/AIDS may be similar in its ramifications to other terminal illnesses, but Moynihan, Christ, and Silver (1988) point out that HIV/AIDS has an impact on younger people and has both a unique disease process and unique social context. Other authors indicate that social support is inhibited (Turnell, 1989) and it involves more litigation (Huber, 1993). Kegeles, Coates, Christopher, and Lazarus (1989) report that HIV/AIDS-infected individuals commonly experience discrimination from others. This prejudice is in conjunction with fear of contracting the virus, risk group characteristics, and culturally negative attitudes toward death (Kalichman, 1995).

Often, individuals who have HIV/AIDS experience social rejection when they have a strong need for social support (Herek & Glunt, 1988; King, 1989). HIV/AIDS-infected individuals are often excluded from society (Bickelhaupt, 1986; Durham & Hatcher, 1984; Newmark, 1984; Nichols, 1985) as well as have a tendency to isolate themselves (McDonell, 1993). They may also experience discrimination in their employment and in their treatment from medical and mental health professionals.

Viney, Henry, Walker, and Crooks (1989) find that HIV/AIDS-infected individuals often feel helpless. Biller and Rice (1990) report that grief is compounded by multiple losses and a lack of time between the losses. Kain (1996) indicates that some of the losses include physical attractiveness, job, mobility and physical functioning, friends and significant others (HIV positive), future, and self (not knowing who they are due to all of the changes experienced).

Triple Diagnosis

Sometimes the term *triple diagnosis* is used to describe individuals who are diagnosed as being addicted to alcohol/drugs, having a mental health problem, and being diagnosed as having HIV/AIDS. Handling this type of situation is discussed next.

Counseling Approaches
The approach to treatment of HIV/AIDS-infected individuals hinges on a number of factors: where the client is in the process of having the disease, discrimination experienced around the disease, and losses with the disease.

In terms of the process of having the disease, the counselor should be familiar with the medical terms and conditions associated with the HIV/AIDS disease. Texts such as *Understanding AIDS: A Guide for Mental Health Professionals* (Kalichman, 1995) and *Positive: HIV Affirmative Counseling* (Kain, 1996) may be helpful references. A counselor would also be well advised to work as closely as possible with the client's physician or another physician/medical professional who is familiar with the medical diagnosis and treatment associated with the disease. Such information may facilitate the counseling approaches used in therapy by providing the therapist with current information regarding the client's physical condition. Issues related to that condition can be processed in counseling.

As Burke and Miller (1996) indicate, counselors need to work at separating their own countertransference issues from the client's counseling concerns. For example, when a client who has HIV/AIDS comes in for counseling, the counselor may assume that the client has death and dying issues. This may not be the reality of the client, but rather what the counselor anticipates what he or she would struggle with if diagnosed with HIV/AIDS. Other authors indicate that counseling may be negatively affected by the issues of the counselor: fear and denial (Rinella & Dubin, 1988), coping ability (Amchin & Polan, 1986), and loss and grief (Cho & Cassidy, 1994). Some mental health professionals may have negative attitudes toward these clients, similar to those of laypeople due to homophobia, anxiety about death, and negative stereotypes about drug users (Kalichman, 1995). Counselors, then, need to examine, on their own, and possibly with the assistance of colleagues and supervisors, their reactions to homosexuality, death, and/or drug users in order to reduce the impact of these biases on counseling.

Although familiarity with common issues facing individuals who have HIV/AIDS is important, the counselor also needs to remember to take the individual story into account. A counselor can easily stereotype an HIV/AIDS client based on reading literature and research written on the topic rather than clarifying the issues as perceived by the client. For example, the therapist may read that individuals who have HIV/AIDS experience discrimination at the workplace, however, the client may work in an environment that is very supportive of him or her. Therefore, even though there may be common experiences among individuals who have HIV/AIDS, the counselor needs to remember these tendencies do not apply to all such clients.

Client issues that might need to be addressed in counseling include, but are not limited to, positive test results, disclosure of positive test results to others (and possibly related disclosure of sexual preference [gay, lesbian, bisexual] and drug use history), diagnosis of AIDS, and issues related to dating and sexuality, loss, physical problems, medical treatment, helplessness/dependency on others, rational suicide, plans for death, spirituality, substance abuse, and quality of life (Kain, 1996; Kalichman, 1995). Given this list of concerns, it would be easy for a counselor to become overwhelmed when working with an person who is diagnosed as HIV positive. That is why it may be best for the counselor to work within the context of the individual's story and find out early in the counseling process, as well as ongoing, what the client feels will be the best approach to take in counseling and how to prioritize the issues being faced. As Szasz (1994) indicates, counselors need to ask clients what they want and if it seems reasonable, help them attain that wish or some sort of compromise.

When the HIV/AIDS client is also addicted, there are additional "twists" to the counseling process. If the client is still using alcohol/drugs, the counselor will want to facilitate the client receiving addiction treatment for these concerns. Although the client may believe that the alcohol/drugs are helping him or her cope with the diagnosis (Greene & Faltz, 1991), the alcohol/drugs are actually preventing the client from addressing the issues being faced and may increase HIV-transmitting behaviors (Kalichman, 1995). However, addiction treatment that best fits the clients' needs must be chosen (discussed in Chapters 4 and 7). For example, Springer (1991) recommends the harm reduction model, which is based on preventing HIV/AIDS as a higher priority than preventing drug use and avoiding a narrow focus on drug abstinence. The basis of this approach is that a focus on reduction of harm rather than abstinence may enhance communication about drug use and decrease the spread of HIV/AIDS. It is not a model that encourages drug use, but one that focuses on reduction of harm in a manner most appealing to the client. For example, rather than making abstinence a requirement for help, the counselor may initially focus on helping the person use less dangerously (i.e., avoid drinking and driving, use clean needles, etc.).

For the client who has recently stopped using alcohol/drugs or who has been sober for some time, the HIV/AIDS diagnosis may bring up issues of remorse, guilt, resentment, self-pity, loss, and hopelessness. He or she may feel punished for past mistakes. Also, those who have been "clean" may now face having to take mood-altering addictive drugs to cope with their physical decline, which may seem strangely ironic. Finally, these clients may feel discrimination by helping professionals whose personal issues arise when dealing with someone who has the HIV/AIDS diagnosis. For example, helping professionals may assume that the individual at some level "deserves" the illness because of involvement in risky sexual behaviors in the past. While such an attitude may not be expressed verbally, the client may detect judgmentalism, thereby making it difficult to share the struggles experienced by having an HIV/AIDS diagnosis. This discrimination may also be present with those who have the triple diagnosis of addiction, mental health problems, and HIV/AIDS. The counselor working with the addicted individual who also has HIV/AIDS (and possibly a third mental health diagnosis) needs to look at the client in a multifaceted manner. The counselor also needs to address his or her own issues that surface around an HIV/AIDS case diagnosis, particularly those focusing on sexual orientation and death. As stated previously, the counselor can address these issues in his or her own therapy, in conversation with colleagues who have resolved such issues, and/or with a supervisor who has previously addressed such concerns.

The client's concerns can work as an anchoring point in developing a treatment plan. What struggles is the client currently facing? What issues does the client anticipate or fear facing in the future? The counselor also needs to look at the setting in which the client is receiving addiction treatment. Who is supportive to the client in that setting? Are there other individuals who are HIV positive and addicted with whom the client can connect? Are there individuals within the setting who need to be educated regarding an HIV positive diagnosis? What are agency policies on working with someone who has HIV/AIDS? Upon leaving treatment, what community resources are present for the client? The importance of maintaining hope—by religion, work or vocation, or support of family and friends—is necessary for the HIV/AIDS client (B. A. Hall, 1994).

Most important of all, the client who has tested positive needs to be treated as any client who enters therapy: with respect and compassion. Respect does not mean that the counselor will avoid confronting the client on possible treatment issues (e.g., viewing the diagnosis as a death sentence), thereby reducing the importance of addiction treatment and recovery from the client's perspective. Rather, respect means that the counselor works with the client on issues pertinent to the recovery process and keeps the welfare of the client at the forefront of treatment. The counselor who is not able to work through personal prejudices needs to make co-workers and supervisors aware of this limitation. The counselor who has been able to address such concerns and is able to work with the HIV positive client with compassion can bring much healing to this addicted individual's life, especially if the counselor works through his or her own grief issues that arise.

CASE STUDY: CHARLIE

Charlie is a 20-year-old single male. He has attempted to sober up for the last two years, but he cannot make it beyond six months. His drug of choice is pot and he says he loves everything about it, especially how it calms him when he is nervous. He has smoked pot for 10 years, since his cousin introduced him to it. Charlie has been sporadically involved in AA and NA for the last two years and has had the same sponsor for that entire time. Charlie is well liked in the groups when he goes to meetings, but he is not respected in terms of his recovery and he says newcomers to recovery are warned about his "slippery" recovery.

Charlie has been sexual with both men and women and has at times prostituted during his use. He says he likes sex a lot, but does not like to have sex with people he feels close to emotionally.

When Charlie was about 10 years old, he was sexually abused by a female babysitter. At age 15, he was raped by a coach who he respected a lot. Charlie says he still loves that man, but he left town for another job when Charlie was 17 years old.

Charlie supports himself by living with anyone who will let him stay for a while. He dropped out of high school and does not know exactly how many credits he had when he dropped out at age 16. He said he thinks there is a God but that he has made too many mistakes for God to love and forgive him. Charlie has no contact with his family. He says there never was much of a family there. Charlie has come in for counseling at the recommendation of his sponsor, who has agreed to pay for his counseling.

1. What are Charlie's issues that interfere with his recovery?
2. Which issue(s) would you address first in counseling and how?
3. Are there any aspects of Charlie's story that would make it difficult to work with him, given your values?

Domestic Violence

Domestic violence and chemical abuse/dependency appear to be two issues that overlap. Generally, over half of the battering men have alcohol/drug use problems (Hamilton & Collins, 1981; Pernanen, 1991). Alcohol/drug use may be high in battering situations, but there does not appear to be evidence that it *causes* battering (National Woman Abuse Prevention Project, 1989; Walker, 1984). In addition, some women who are battered have alcohol/drug use problems (Eberle, 1982): The National Woman Abuse Prevention Project (1989) found that 7 to 14 percent of battered women have alcohol abuse problems. Therefore, alcohol and drugs are frequently involved in domestic violence situations, whether it is the batterer or the victim or both using them. The counselor who works with individuals who are addicted needs to understand how the dynamics of domestic violence interact with addiction. The counselor also needs to work in a coordinated, teamwork approach with domestic violence specialists in the community in order to control the behavior of batterers and assist survivors in being safe.

The two fields, chemical dependency and domestic violence, have typically not worked closely with one another. The Minnesota Coalition for Battered Women (MCBW) (1992) states that there is a lack of services for women in domestic violence situations that adequately addresses both areas. There are also barriers between these programs (Harner, 1987–88; Levy & Brekke, 1990; Rogan, 1985–86; Wright & Popham, 1982) that are based on different points of view and a lack of experience (Bennett & Lawson, 1994). Bennett and Lawson (1994) found in their study that substance abuse programs are less likely to refer to domestic violence programs, and they further state that conflict around how self-control is interpreted is one of the largest problems: Domestic violence programs view the violence as intentional and hold the batterer totally responsible for the violence, whereas the addictions programs studied believed in the disease model of addiction, which indicates that the addict is not in control of his or her behavior.

Diagnosis/Assessment

Findings such as those just discussed underscore the importance of counselors becoming aware of the dynamics of domestic violence. If the violence is not assessed and addressed in addiction treatment and/or recovery, the addicted individual may be more prone to relapse. Also, if the violence is not adequately addressed, the family may believe that once the addict sobers up, the violence will stop. The indications are that an addicted individual with a propensity for violence has two problems: the addiction and the violence (Minnesota Coalition for Battered Women, 1992). Both need to be addressed in order for treatment to be effective.

Prior to working with individuals in domestic violence situations, the counselor would be well served to examine any personal beliefs about domestic violence. The Minnesota Coalition for Battered Women (1992) states three common myths regarding domestic violence: battering occurs because of low self-esteem in the batterer, battering occurs because the batterer loses control of emotions, and battering is a disease. The MCBW (1992) responds by pointing out that many individuals with low self-esteem do not batter, the batterer batters in order to maintain control, and violence is a learned behavior.

Although both men and women have the potential to be batterers, 95 percent of all domestic violence assaults are crimes committed by men toward women (National Coalition Against Domestic Violence, n.d.). As a result, the following discussion for assessment will focus on men as batterers and women as victims.

The counselor working with a domestic violence situation needs to be able to make an assessment both of the batterer and of the victim, since either individual could be the client. In the case of the batterer, the counselor can look for some specific indicators (Brekke, 1987): hostility, rigid view of sex roles, patriarchal attitude, history of family of origin abuse, sense of women victimizing him, lack of significant nonfamily relationships, jealously (extreme), difficulty recognizing emotions other than anger, and dependency on partner for emotional needs (extreme). In the woman, the counselor can look for different symptoms (Brekke, 1987): physical injuries, depression, being afraid to express emotions and/or sexual intimacy, depersonalization, tendency to be passive, history of family of origin violence, hostility toward family members, self-deprecation, concern for children's safety (extreme), and suicide attempts.

Brekke (1987) also advocates an approach called *funneling,* which means bringing up the topic of abuse gradually in order to obtain complete information. This technique can be applied both to batterers and victims. The counselor may also find it more beneficial to interview the couple separately in order to obtain information about the violence. Otherwise, the victim may say little in the session out of fear of being abused later.

Probably the best theoretical format for understanding the dynamics of domestic violence emerge from the Domestic Abuse Intervention Project (Pence & Paymar, 1993). Its power and control wheel has eight sections that describe the dynamics of domestic violence: isolation; minimizing, denial, and blame; children; using male privilege; economic abuse; coercion and threats; intimidation; and emotional abuse (see Figure 5.1). All eight areas are ways in which the man tries to control the woman. In the area of isolation, he requires knowing at all times where she is going, what she is doing, and with whom she is interacting. In the next area on the control wheel, the man may use techiniques of minimization, denial, and blame to eliminate any responsibility for his own behavior. In the area of using the children, he may use the children as pawns to control the woman's behavior. In using male privilege, the man will

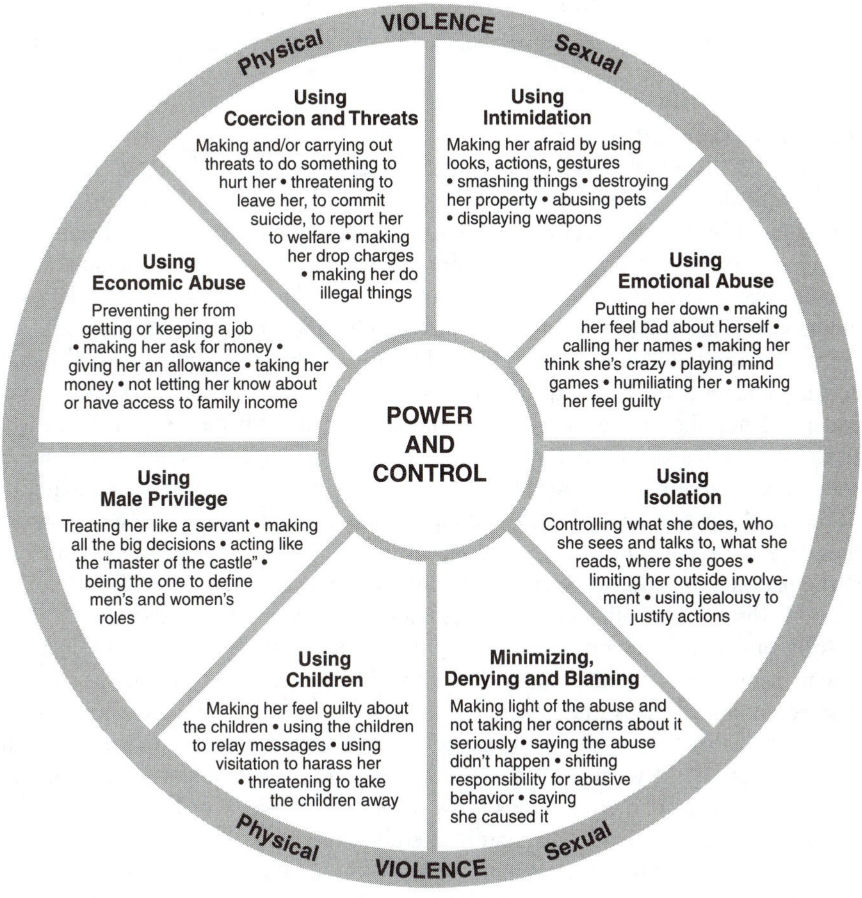

FIGURE 5.1 Power and Control Wheel: The Dynamics of Domestic Violence

Source: Domestic Abuse Intervention Project, 206 West Fourth Street, Duluth, Minnesota 55806, 218-722-4134. Reprinted by permission.

dominate the relationship and relegate the woman to a lesser status role. In economic abuse, he attempts to control the money situation, not allowing her to get or keep a job or requiring her to ask him for money. In the area of threats, he may make threats to try to hurt her emotionally. In intimidation, he may use a variety of subtle (looks) and not so subtle (destroying property) means to control her. In the area of emotional abuse, he may call her names or find other demeaning techniques of putting her down.

The cycle of violence has been described as having three phases (Walker, 1979). In phase 1, there is an increase in tension between the partners, as evidenced in increased fighting. In phase 2, the battering occurs in any of the eight forms listed in the power and control wheel. In phase 3, the relationship enters a calm phase where the male will be remorseful for his behavior. It is in the third stage that the batterer who uses alcohol/drugs may report that the abuse occurred because he had been high or drunk.

Treatment Approaches

Walker (1980) says that counselors often have inadequate training in addressing domestic violence. Some view the problem as a family problem (Minnesota Coalition for Battered Women, 1992) or one due to such addiction concepts as codependency (Frank & Golden, 1992): Neither concept holds the batterer wholly accountable for the violence. Viewing the problem as a family one and involving such techniques as mediation is based on an equal relationship, which is the opposite of the domestic violence situation (Golden & Frank, 1994). Therapists who work in that modality may actually endanger the battered woman (Jones & Schechter, 1992). In the labeling of codependence, the battered woman is a blamed victim again in that she may be viewed as sharing the responsibility for the violence, or as staying in the relationship due to something internally wrong with her. The label does not take into account the reality of the situation she faces with the batterer (Frank & Golden, 1992). The danger of these labels for the batterer is that he may view his violence as due to the woman's participation in the violent behavior (family problems, codependence issues, etc.).

As discussed in other chapters on addiction, the counselor needs to be aware of how his or her countertransference issues may emerge. Male counselors, for instance might dismiss the violence experienced by the woman as not as intense as she describes it due to a lack of empathy for the oppression of women or a lack of awareness of their own struggles with anger. Female counselors, for example, might become angry at the woman for not leaving, or might lack an understanding of how domestic violence can erode one's self-esteem and confidence. In male or female counselors, past experiences with family members or friends who left or did not leave abusive situations may influence their view of the struggle (e.g., wanting their clients to do the "work" that their loved ones were not able to do in their own lives).

Prior to discussing specific treatment approaches with survivors, the counselor needs to be aware of barriers in the survivor's escape or survival with regard to the violence. These barriers include abuser retaliation, inconsistent legal responses, lack of shelters, low income, loss of child custody, lack of housing, societal expectations, the myth of gender equality, and limited or negative assistance from family, clergy, and counselors (Minnesota Coalition for Battered Women, 1992).

The MCBW (1992) states six requisites for counselors working with survivors:

1. Safety of the woman should always be top priority.
2. The goal of counseling should be to empower the woman.
3. The therapy should be client based, with a focus on mutuality.
4. The therapy needs to take into account sociopolitical forces that are larger than the woman and her history and relationship.
5. Ethnicity and culture need to be considered in the counseling process.
6. The counselor should never take a stance of blaming the victim.

For the woman whose partner is in addiction treatment, she needs the therapist to think of her safety and advocate for her in clinical decisions. She also needs to be given the option of participation in the man's treatment and told that addiction and battering are separate issues (Minnesota Coalition for Battered Women, 1992). For the woman in addiction treatment, she needs to be educated about the different issues of battering and addiction, be provided with an advocate, and be given information about support for surviving the battering situation (Minnesota Coalition for Battered Women, 1992). Although a woman might drink or use drugs to cope with the battering, she needs to be reminded repeatedly that she cannot make the best decisions of survival for herself and her children if she is drunk or high.

It may be best for the counselor to assess all women, whether they or their partners are in addiction treatment or recovery, for domestic violence. If the woman does admit to domestic violence, she needs to be believed by the counselor and a safety or protection plan needs to be developed for her. Even if the woman insists that the violence will not occur again, the counselor needs to encourage her to prepare for the worst and give her a chance to rehearse what she will do if the violence does occur. A safety plan needs to include (Hodges, 1993) hiding extra money, car keys, and important papers in a safe place she can access quickly; keeping a packed suitcase hidden somewhere (inside or outside the house, at a friend's or relative's, etc.); having phone numbers of the local shelter and support network individuals available; giving a signal to children or neighbors that the police should be called; and knowing where to go in case of an emergency. It may underscore the seriousness of her situation and help her clarify these thoughts if the counselor draws up a simple checklist form that addresses each of these areas.

Women may address the issues of battering either individually and/or in groups. Emphasis should be on encouraging safety, giving gifts to oneself, moving out of the situation at the individual's own pace, working with the fear of failure, stressing positive aspects of the woman and her life, enjoying laughter, and sharing and being supportive to others (Goodman & Fallon, 1995). It is also critical to emphasize that the woman assert her rights, process her difficulties leaving, set boundaries with others, make decisions, and work through her feelings (Goodman & Fallon, 1995). Maybe most critically, the counselor needs to work at providing the battered woman with information regarding the domestic violence situation and then work at letting her make her own decisions. It is very important for the counselor not to convey information in a critical, judgmental attitude, which may only cause her to blame herself further and to isolate from others.

With regard to the batterer, the counselor needs to take a different focus. Many times, batterers will underestimate the violence and/or shift the blame to the survivor and/or other life circumstances (Adams & McCormick, 1982). The counselor needs to avoid being seduced by the defense mechanisms of projection and denial and hold the batterer accountable for his behavior. Also, as mentioned earlier, batterers who are also addicted need to be educated that the violence is a separate problem that needs to be addressed and that battering is a crime (Minnesota Coalition for Battered Women, 1992). If possible, the counselor can refer the client to a program that works specifically with batterers.

The violence by the batterer is an intentional act to gain power, and the goal in therapy is to stop the violent behavior (Edelson & Tolman, 1992). It is important to assess how the man has been abusive—how severely and how often. The batterer may experience intimate relationships with women as being dangerous and uncontrollable; this view, in combination with a high power need and a low verbal ability to assert oneself, results in violence (Edelson & Tolman, 1992). Batterers also seem to have high levels of depression and suicide (Ganley & Harris, 1978), are angrier than nonviolent men (Barnett & Planeaux, 1989), and have negative, sexist attitudes toward women (Edelson & Tolman, 1992).

Group intervention with batterers may be helpful in that they are receiving support from other men to be nonviolent: This holds them accountable for the violence and helps them learn ways to be nonviolent (Edelson & Tolman, 1992). The batterer's attitudes have to change to being responsible for all abusive behavior, having empathy for their partners, accepting confrontation from others, being aware of their socialization process (Edelson & Tolman, 1992), and being more aware of violence cycle cues (e.g., situational, cognitive, emotional, and physical). They need to sign an agreement to be nonviolent, become aware of their emotions (particularly those underlying the anger), learn to manage their arousal, take time-outs when upset, restructure their thoughts, and learn assertiveness and conflict resolution skills (Edelson & Tolman, 1992).

Couples treatment should occur only when (1) the man has made a commitment to be nonviolent, demonstrated this commitment by participating in treatment for the battering, and shown a commitment to nonviolence over time; (2) the woman feels safe; and (3) the couple wants to stay together (Edelson & Tolman, 1992). This treatment requires time, energy, and commitment on the part of the couple. A counselor would probably be most effective by requiring an evaluation of the couple, before beginning work with them, by an expert in the area of domestic violence.

Related Issues

Other issues such as family, religious, legal, and multicultural aspects enter into the reality of addressing domestic violence issues. Each of these will be briefly examined here in order to heighten the counselor's sensitivity to these concerns.

A battered woman can experience a wide range of family reactions to the domestic violence. Family members may offer support (emotional, physical, and financial), advice, transportation, and care of children. However, some family members of the battered woman may take a cold, detached stance with regard to assisting. Due to the batterer's control over the survivor, contact with the family may be limited, which may make bringing up the topic of abuse awkward and result in the family blaming the survivor for the abuse (Minnesota Coalition for Battered Women, 1992).

The counselor needs to assess the client's relationship with his or her family, regardless of whether the client is the batterer or the survivor. The closeness of the client to his or her family and how strongly the family views the situation will affect the client's views and decision-making process.

Battered women who are involved with religion may bring religious issues into the counseling setting (Whipple, 1987). Walker (1979) and Straus, Gelles, and Steinmetz (1980) report that domestic violence occurs across different religions. Concepts such as faith, forgiveness, submission, and a lack of acceptance of divorce may encourage a battered woman to remain in the relationship regardless of the level of damage to her and/or her family (Whipple, 1987). Depending on the woman's religion, other idiosyncratic aspects of her religion may be a place of struggle for her. The counselor is advised to do the following:

1. Have the woman educate the counselor about her religion in general. (If appropriate, the counselor might do some research on the religion.)
2. Have the woman educate the counselor about the specific religious creeds that seem to inhibit her taking an active response to domestic violence.
3. Work with the woman to find disagreement in religious creeds or in the lives of other parishioners that question any directives to remain in the domestic violence situation.
4. Work with the woman to find positive directives about relationships and views of women in religous creeds as well as in lives of other parishioners.
5. If possible, offer to connect the woman with a religious figure who is of her faith and has an understanding of domestic violence issues in order to facilitate a processing of the spiritual concerns.

For the counselor working with a batterer, a similar process can be followed. Even though the steps are similar, the counselor can work to help the batterer see that he does not have a right to perpetuate the violence.

All counselors must be aware of legal issues surrounding domestic violence concerns. Some state bar associations (e.g., North Carolina Bar Association, 1995) publish legal guides for survivors of domestic violence. The counselor needs to determine how the law defines domestic violence, provides protection against domestic violence, and allows for criminal and/or civil charges to be filed. If the counselor does not have the time to obtain all of this information, he or she may be able to contact the state bar association, a local attorney, or a local domestic violence shelter for a summary of use of the legal system to hold batterers accountable for their behavior and/or to support survivors of the abuse. Another option is to contact the National Coalition Against Domestic Violence or the state coalitions in which the counselor works. If the counselor works at an agency, it may be beneficial to have someone at the agency become specialized in domestic violence situations, given the frequency of the crossover between substance abuse and domestic violence.

Knowledge of the legal issues is critical in assisting individuals in domestic violence situations. Many states have temporary orders of protection or temporary restraining orders that protect women from future abuse (Ferraro, 1993). Some batterers respond to social controls and public humiliation; legal charges may reach them in ways that other information does not. However, it is important to keep in mind that a restraining order is just a piece of paper and that some batterers have no respect for or fear of the law. Survivors need to know what their rights are and the limits of legal protection so that they can make decisions that are best for them. In addition, it is helpful to know of local attorneys, magistrates, and judges who have an understanding of domestic violence.

Minorities are not immune to battering. Individuals from these sexual or ethnic orientation minorities typically experience discrimination and may be concerned about the increase in discrimination they may face if they discuss the domestic violence situation.

If gays and lesbians discuss the battering in their relationship, they will also be "coming out" to the counselor about their sexual preference at the same time. This reality may inhibit their disclosure of the battering in the counseling relationship. Also, Leeder (1988) reports that many of the dynamics of violence are similar to heterosexual couples, but the counselor needs to be especially aware of countertransference issues related to sexual preference, whatever the counselor's sexual preference. Finally, Benowitz (1986) states that lesbian batterers may have difficulty admitting to the battering because of fears of community reactions. Police may ignore the reality of gay/lesbian battering due to homophobia and may be less likely to intervene on the violence because of a tendency to see this group as deviant and thereby experiencing violence as a way of life (Ferraro, 1993).

In regard to racial minorities, White (1994) reports that even though African American women can be sensitive to the oppression and racism that African American men experience, this does not mean that the woman needs to tolerate abuse. When an ethnic minority woman does consider reporting the abuse, she may also be aware that, historically, police have oppressed people of color and have higher arrest rates higher for racial minority groups (Ferraro, 1993). Furthermore, these oppressed groups may also be viewed by police as deviants who experience violence as a way of life, thereby inhibiting police intervention on the violence (Ferraro, 1993).

Depending on the individual's ethnic minority, there may be other barriers to reporting violence. The individual may experience cultural and/or language barriers, be afraid of deportation, and experience poverty limitations (North Carolina Coalition Against Domestic Violence, 1995). The counselor needs to be aware of how each of these areas may inhibit the individual from addressing the battering situation. The counselor needs to approach the ethnic minority client with these different factors in mind.

Due to the frequent crossover between the areas of domestic violence and substance abuse, the counselor working with the addicted individual needs to keep this crossover in mind. Focus on domestic violence issues needs to occur at all levels of addiction counseling: assessment and diagnosis, treatment, and recovery.

CASE STUDY: JUNE

June is a 41-year-old female who has entered addiction treatment for the third time. She has been sent to treatment each time by her husband of 23 years. He threatens to leave her if she does not stop the pills and the alcohol, so she comes to treatment. After two weeks of treatment, she has confidentially admitted to you that she has trouble staying sober because her husband beats her frequently. She reveals that she never told any of her previous counselors about this situation because she did not want to admit that she had an affair during the early years of her marriage. June says that her husband began beating her when she told him about the affair shortly after it happened. She stated that he agreed not to bring it up in her treatment if she did not bring up his abuse. He tells her he would never have beaten her if she had not had an affair.

June is afraid to call a domestic violence shelter or take out a restraining order on her husband because of his threats of violence ("I'll kill you if you leave me"). She says he is a church-going man who is very kind to her in public, but very critical of her in private. According to June, the pills and the alcohol help her forget the pain and cope with her life. She drinks with her husband and says that he does not mind her alcohol use, but he does not like her taking Valium and Xanax because she becomes "listless." They have one son, age 22, who, according to June, was never hit by his father and never witnessed his father's violence toward his mother.

1. What aspects of June's story are typical for a survivor of domestic violence?
2. What would be your first priority in counseling her?
3. How would you help June address the domestic violence situation?
4. What internal and external barriers inhibit June from addressing the domestic violence situation in a different way?

Eating Disorders

Comparison to Addictive Behaviors

Eating disorders, framed as addictive in nature by some theorists, have similarities with other addictions (Scott, 1983; Zweben, 1987). Buchanan and Buchanan (1992) outline some of the similarities and the differences between eating disorders and other addictions. One of these similarities is the compulsive behavior that is combined with a sense of powerlessness and a preoccupation with food. Another similarity is avoidance of feeling and attaining a sense of relief by abusing food. A main difference, however, is that food, unlike alcohol and drugs, cannot be given up totally, so the client with an eating disorder needs to learn to manage the food differently.

Diagnosis

The *Diagnostic and Statistical Manual of Mental Disorders, Fourth Edition* (*DSM-IV*, 1994) has three categorizations of eating disorders: Anorexia Nervosa, Bulimia Nervosa, and Eating Disorder NOS. The Eating Disorder NOS (Not Otherwise Specified) is used for eating disorders that do not meet the criteria for the other two categories. The other two categories of eating disorders, Anorexia Nervosa and Bulimia Nervosa, will be discussed here.

Anorexia Nervosa

Anorexia nervosa is when a client does not maintain a normal body weight, is afraid of gaining weight, and has a distorted perception of his or her body. Anorexia comes from the Greek language meaning lack of appetite and food loathing and avoidance (Blinder & Chao, 1994). The *DSM-IV* (1994) reports four criteria for diagnosis:

1. Body weight is less than 85 percent of what is determined as normal for that person's age and height. Often, weight reduction is achieved through reducing food intake (eating very few foods), purging (vomiting, using laxatives/diuretics), and/or excessive exercise.
2. The person experiences intense fear of weight gain and being fat. Weight gain is a concern even when the person is losing weight.
3. The person has a distored view of the importance of his or her shape and weight as well as denies the impact low weight has on him or her physically.
4. Amenorrhea (having no menstrual cycles for at least three consecutive times) is present in postmenarcheal females. This condition is typically a result of weight loss.

The two types of anorexia nervosa are restricting (no binge eating or purging behavior during a recent episode) and binge-eating/purging (during the recent episode, binge-eating or purging behavior occurred). Those diagnosed as binge-eating/purging are more likely to be abusive in their use of alcohol/drugs. Anorexia nervosa occurs in .05 to 1 percent of the female population (late adolescence/early adulthood). The *DSM-IV* Manual (1994) states that there is limited information on the disorder in males and that it has increased in general in the last few decades. There is evidence that first-degree family members of these individuals may struggle more with anorexia nervosa and mood disorders, the latter diagnosis being more common with the binge-eating/purging clients.

Because these clients rarely are concerned about their weight loss and often experience denial with regard to its seriousness, the counselor will often need to contact parents or others who would have information so that an accurate diagnosis can be made (*DSM-IV,* 1994). It is also helpful for the counselor to have an awareness of predisposing causes for anorexia, since these causes can become relapse triggers for the client in the recovery process. Marx (1994) reports some of these causes to be:

1. Sociocultural factors (valuing women's excessive thinness)
2. Genetic (relatives may have anorexia nervosa, affective disorders, alcohol/substance abuse, etc.)
3. Personality (insecure, dependent, compliant, lack of spontaneity, etc.)
4. Family interaction (more disturbed, but research lacks to support it as the cause of the disorder)

The counselor can explore each of these factors with the client to determine which areas may be particular relapse triggers with regard to substance abuse and the eating disorder.

The *DSM-IV* (1994) lists a number of physical symptoms connected to anorexia nervosa: emaciated appearance, amenorrhea, skin-related changes (dryness, presence of fine downy hair, yellowing of skin, hand scars or callouses due to self-induced vomiting), dental problems, hypothermia, and hypotension. The clients can develop anemia, kidney, cardiovascular, dental, and osteoporosis problems. They may also complain about constipation, pain in the abdomen, feeling cold, feeling drowsy, and having too much energy. If the client is diabetic, blood sugar levels must be closely monitored (Goldner & Birmingham, 1994).

Goldner and Birmingham (1994) list some of the signs indicating the need for a medical assessment: quick weight loss, episodes of fainting/loss of consciousness, organic brain syndrome, heart rate of less than 50 beats per minute, frequent chest pain after exercising, irregular heartbeats, kidney problems or less than 400 cc of urine excreted daily, volume depletion (not retaining enough liquids in the body), tetany (spasmodic contractions of the arm and leg muscles), and decreasing exercise tolerance (rapid in nature).

Once the client has been medically stabilized, the counselor needs to develop a strong therapeutic alliance, assist the client in restoring weight, and promote healthy attitudes and behaviors around eating (Goldner & Birmingham, 1994). When working with adolescent or young adult females, counselors need to decrease treatment resistance by encouraging parents to help their daughter come to the session willingly. With adolescents, the counselor needs to align with both the adolescent and the parents as much as possible, and with young adult females, the counselor needs to help the client resume more self-responsibility (Pike & Wilfley, 1996). Although young adult as well as middle to late adulthood females are more likely to come in to counseling on their own because of a decrease in denial, the disorder has also had an impact on their lives for a longer period of time (Pike & Wilfley, 1996).

When doing outpatient work with this population, the counselor needs to set limits regarding the maintainance of a minimal weight and a lack of related physical problems. The counselor also needs to work with a treatment team, which includes a pediatrician, a nutritionist, and a school personnel representative (Pike & Wilfley, 1996). Finally, family therapy has been shown to be helpful with adolescents (Russell, Szmukler, Dare, & Eisler, 1987), whereas individual counseling with a cognitive-behavioral focus appears most helpful for young adults (Pike, 1994). Also with young adults, intermittent family therapy and group therapy may be additional counseling options (Pike & Wilfley, 1996). Treatment for females in middle to late adulthood is similar to that for young adults; however, older clients may need to work through feelings of guilt and failure as well as set realistic self-goals. Specific issues to be addressed in counseling adolescents are (1) developing a sense of self, (2) forming attachments in relationships, and (3) exploring their reactions to their physical and sexual development (Pike & Wilfley, 1996). Some of these same counseling themes emerge for young adults and people in middle to late adulthood: developing a sense of self without the self-definition of an active eating disorder, forming improved social relationships, and better individuation from parents (Pike & Wilfley, 1996).

Bulimia Nervosa

Prior to the 1960s and 1970s, bulimia was viewed as a form of anorexia nervosa, and in the 1980s, the *DSM-III* described it as a separate diagnostic category (Alexander-Mott & Lumsden, 1994). The *DSM-IV* (1994) describes the associated behaviors and types of bulimia nervosa. This category of eating disorder consists of binges (eating more food, usually high-calorie sweets eaten in secrecy, than one typically eats in a certain period of time) often followed by purging (forced vomiting) and/or the use of laxatives, diuretics, enemas, or fasting. The *DSM-IV* describes the three criteria necessary for the diagnosis of bulimia nervosa:

1. Having recurrent binge-eating episodes (more food eaten than most people would eat within a specific time frame and situation as well as a lack of a feeling of control over one's eating behavior)
2. Participating in behaviors that compensate for weight gain (vomiting; using laxatives, diuretics, and enemas; fasting; and exercising to excess).
3. Engaging in both of the preceding behaviors at least twice a week in a three-month period

There are two types of bulimia nervosa according to the *DSM-IV* (1994): purging (vomiting or abusing laxatives, diuretics, or enemas) and nonpurging (fasting, exercising excessively, but not purging behaviors).

The *DSM-IV* (1994) reports that bulimia nervosa appears in 1 to 3 percent of the population of females (late adolescence/early adulthood) and 1/10 of that frequency in males (10 to 15 percent of bulimics are male) (Gold, Johnson, & Stennie, 1997). Usually, individuals with this diagnosis are within their normal weight range, but there is some evidence that they are more likely to be overweight before they become bulimic. About one-third of individuals who have this disorder also have substance abuse or dependence problems, especially with alcohol and stimulants, with stimulants initially being used to control appetite and weight. Individuals with bulimia nervosa often have first-degree relatives who struggle with bulimia nervosa, mood disorders, substance abuse and dependence, and possibly obesity.

Binge eating is described in *DSM-IV* (1994) as secretive, planned or unplanned, and involving rapid eating of the food until the individual is simply too full to continue. Although the binge is often preceded by negative feelings, usually depression, it is often followed by negative self-criticism and a sense of loss of (or impairment in) control.

In terms of the causal factors for bulimia, most theorists look at how both psychological and social factors interact and some look at biological aspects, as well (Weiss, Katzman, & Wolchik, 1994). Weiss, Katzman, and Wolchik (1994) discuss four main models explaining bulimia: feminist, family, biological, and stress-coping. *Feminist models* address cultural bias toward thinness and against fat, perfectionistic tendencies regarding being feminine, tendencies to please others, and a desire simply to take up less space, symbolizing a lack of power. *Family models* examine factors such as disturbed relationships with parents throughout development, family patterns around food, and sexual and physical abuse. *Biological models* emphasize the presence of hypothalamic disturbances or major affective disorders biologically based. *Stress-coping models* focus on daily stresses, irrational beliefs, decreased sense of control, and personality deficits (e.g., low self-esteem may contribute to bulimia). The counselor working with a bulimic, then, can examine the client's view of cultural pressures regarding thinness, disturbed family relations, presence of major affective disorders, and/or stress-coping mechanisms. The information obtained from the client regarding these aspects can facilitate the client's recovery from the eating disorder as well as substance abuse by determining possible relapse triggers.

In the assessment process, the counselor may notice symptoms indicative of bulimia nervosa: teeth abnormalities (loss of teeth enamel, ragged appearing teeth, more cavities than normal), calluses or scars on the hand from vomiting, menstrual problems (irregularity, amenorrhea), laxative dependence, and fluid and electrolyte imbalances (*DSM-IV,* 1994). Additional medical problems can include enlargement of salivary glands, inflammation of the esophagus and pharynx, aspiration, tears in the upper digestive tract or the esophagus, heart and neurological dysfunction (caused by use of syrup of ipecac), metabolic problems, digestive system problems, dehydration, overstimulation and related effects, and musculoskeletal problems (Sansone & Sansone, 1994).

In terms of treatment for bulimia nervosa, cognitive-behavioral therapy and interpersonal psychotherapy, both of which are short term and focused in nature, appear to be quite effective (Pike & Wilfley, 1994). The cognitive-behavioral therapy focuses on cognitions and behaviors as they relate to weight and shape and eating practices, whereas the interpersonal psychotherapy looks at problems in interpersonal relationships (Pike & Wilfley, 1994). Counselors working with addicted clients who also have an eating disorder can emphasize cognitions and behaviors and/or interpersonal factors in their work with these clients.

Usually, these clients seek treatment on their own; however, they often try to keep their bulimia nervosa a secret. In fact, their counselor may be the first to hear of their disorder (Pike & Wilfley, 1994). An overvalue on appearance and unreasonable weight loss goals may make treatment difficult (Pike & Wilfley, 1994).

Once again, a treatment team may consist of an individual counselor, a family counselor, a medical professional, and a nutritionist (Pike & Wilfley, 1994). Although family therapy is not necessarily beneficial to this clientele, an emphasis on family issues may be an important part of therapy (Pike & Wilfley, 1994). In counseling, these individuals need to develop a sense of self-worth, improve social functioning (group therapy may help with this aspect), process reactions to physical and sexual development (adolescence), process major life decisions regarding relationships (middle to later adulthood), and discuss pregnancy-related concerns (middle to later adulthood).

Relationship with Sexual Abuse

In addition to crossovers between substance abuse and eating disorders, there may be a crossover between eating disorders and sexual abuse (MacDonald, Lambie, & Simmonds, 1995). There is disagreement as to whether child sexual abuse predisposes women to developing eating disorders (Rorty & Yager, 1996). It does appear that bulimics report more trauma than anorexics (Vanderlinden & Vandereycken, 1996). Nonetheless, a direct causal relationship cannot be drawn at this time between sexual abuse and eating disorders; however, Schwartz and Cohn (1996) argue that counselors who work with trauma need to have a familiarity with eating disorders.

It appears necessary, then, for addiction counselors who frequently work with traumatized clients to be prepared to assess for eating disorders in both their male and female clientele. An avoidance of examining such concerns could facilitate a relapse in either the eating disorder or the substance abuse/dependency, which could facilitate a relapse in the other. For example, the recovering addict who has an eating disorder relapse may drink in response to the guilt and shame experienced from the eating disorder relapse.

Assessment

This section discusses the assessment of addicted clients for eating disorders, but it is also important to remember that counselors of clients with eating disorders should also assess for substance abuse and dependency problems. Careful assessment for an eating disorder requires that the counselor ask questions, both of male and female clients, regarding eating behaviors in an accepting, supportive manner. For example, asking questions regarding the highest and lowest weights (the years of the weights) and how tall the client is can provide a baseline framework of information. Also, a few questions regarding eating behavior ("What is your relationship with food like?" "Did you ever 'fix' major problems in your life by eating or not eating?" "What types of weight loss measures have you taken?" [Bellofatto, 1993]) could enhance the overall assessment of the client's struggles and enhance the treatment of and/or the referral process to an eating disorders specialist.

From here, the counselor can ask about dieting behaviors, body image, exercise behaviors, dental problems, and the use of laxatives, diuretics, and enemas, watching for extremes in each of these areas. The counselor may also notice the client wearing a lot of layered clothes (to hide weight loss), complaining of coldness when others are not cold, spending time in the bathroom after meals or when in the bathroom, leaving the water running when in the bathroom, and, for female clients, having missed menstrual cycles. These behaviors indicate the need for the client to have a thorough physical and dental examination.

To determine the accuracy of the self-report, the counselor may involve significant others who can also provide information regarding eating behaviors. The therapist also needs to examine the dynamics in relationships with family and significant others to determine if there are problems that exacerbate the eating disorder (APA, 1993).

Another option to enhance the assessment process is to include an eating disorder inventory assessment. An example of such an assessment instrument is the Eating Disorder Inventory, 2 (EDI-2) (Garner, 1991). The EDI-2 has three subscales: body dissatisfaction, drive for thinness, and interoceptive awareness. Body dissatisfaction looks at shape and size of body areas of concern to clients, drive for thinness examines dieting and preoccupation with weight and weight gain, and interoceptive awareness measures the client's awareness of emotional and physical aspects of themselves (e.g., hunger/fullness) (Costin, 1996). The use of such a scale in the assessment process will assist the counselor in developing a more effective recovery treatment program for the client that takes into account both the chemical dependency and the eating disorder, thereby reducing the possibility of relapse in one or both areas.

Treatment

Buchanan and Buchanan (1992) recommend a three-stage treatment model: developing a relationship and educating the client about the eating disorder (stage 1); reducing symptoms by using cognitive-behavioral approaches, such as confronting irrational beliefs and learning positive self-talk (stage 2); and experiencing interpersonal therapy that is dynamic (i.e., using the therapeutic relationship to understand interpersonal dynamics and assisting the client in developing a support system) (stage 3). Cognitive-behavioral approaches appear effective in working with anorexics to change eating patterns. Other approaches that are cognitive, interpersonal, or dynamic in nature can be used to increase the client's coping behavior and insight into the eating disorder (APA, 1993). Once stabilized with regard to initial symptoms, clients respond to cognitive, interpersonal, and dynamic approaches (APA, 1993).

The counselor working with a client who has an eating disorder is wise to work closely with medical personnel until the eating disorder symptoms are stabilized. Sometimes tricyclic antidepressants and serotonin reuptake inhibitors (SSRIs) have been prescribed for depressed as well as not depressed eating disordered clients (Zerbe, 1996). Once the individual is somewhat stable medically, counseling to enhance coping skills and insights in the client is appropriate. Focusing on a need to control, self-care, and having a balanced life-style can be very effective with these clients. As with any compulsive behavior, an awareness of the compulsion, along with specific coping skills, can assist a client in breaking free of the eating disorder. A 12-step program, such as Overeaters Anonymous, may be helpful to the client, but, as with any self-help group, the group must be monitored for its health and its helpfulness to the client. The counselor needs to be aware of his or her limitations, however. If a counselor has never worked with an eating disordered, addicted client, it would be prudent to obtain supervision from someone who is skilled in both eating disorders and substance abuse addiction in order to learn the nuances of treating both. Also, it might be helpful for the counselor to obtain training in this area.

CASE STUDY: MARYANNE

Maryanne is a 28-year-old female who has come for counseling for the first time. She is the oldest of three children and reports that her parents are still married. She was referred to treatment by a physician who was concerned about her weight fluctuations and her admission to him of amphetamine use. She entered a combination inpatient/outpatient treatment and completed it about three weeks ago. She has not attended any self-help groups in her community, even though she was given referrals, because she did not want to bring further shame to her family. In her intake session, Maryanne reports a pattern of immersing herself in different addictive behaviors during her life. For example, for a time, she was involved with alcohol, then sex, then religion, then drugs, each in an addictive manner that appeared serial in nature. During the session, Maryanne brings food in with her: chips, cookies, candy, sugared soda, and the like. She eats these rapidly during the session and then midway through the session she says she needs to use the bathroom. When she returns, she appears slightly pale.

1. What do you say to Maryanne when she returns from using the bathroom regarding her behavior?
2. How do you need to work with other professionals in order to be helpful to this client?

3. What type of treatment plan would you develop for Maryanne?

Summary

This chapter has given an overview of three areas often related to substance abuse and dependence: sexual issues (rape, sexual abuse, sexual orientation, and HIV/AIDS), domestic violence, and eating disorders. No counselor can be an expert in all of these areas, but it is necessary for counselors to have some broad awareness of each area in order to better serve clients. Effective treatment and aftercare, including relapse prevention, relies heavily on the thoroughness of the assessment of the counselor. Struggles with related issues such as these can result in a relapse in substances, which can cause the client to feel like a failure. Although accurate assessment does not guarantee a client's sobriety, the counselor can be assured that addressing the issues as part of the treatment plan has fulfilled his or her responsibility as a counselor.

SUGGESTED READINGS

Cabaj, R. J. (1997). Gays, lesbians, & bisexuals. In J. H. Lowinson, P. Ruiz, R. B. Millman, & J. G. Langrod (Eds.), *Substance abuse: A comprehensive textbook* (3rd ed.) (pp. 725–733). Baltimore: Williams & Wilkins.

Edelson, J. L., & Tolman, R. M. (1992). *Intervention for men who batter: An ecological approach.* Newbury Park, CA: Sage.

Finkelhor, D. (1986). *A sourcebook on child sexual abuse.* Beverly Hills, CA: Sage.

Finnegan, D. G., & McNally, E. B. (1987). *Dual identities: Counseling chemically dependent gay men and lesbians.* Center City, MN: Hazelden.

Gonsiorek, J. C., Bera, W. H., & LeTourneau, D. (1994). *Male sexual abuse.* Thousand Oaks, CA: Sage.

Goodman, M. S., & Fallon, B. C. (1995). *Pattern changing for abused women.* Thousand Oaks, CA: Sage.

Kain, C. D. (1996). *Positive: HIV affirmative counseling.* Alexandria, VA: American Counseling Association.

Kalichman, S. C. (1995). *Understanding AIDS: A guide for mental health professionals.*

Washington, DC: American Psychological Association.

Knapp, S. J., & VandeCreek, L. (1997). *Treating patients with memories of abuse: Legal risk management.* Washington, DC: American Psychological Association.

L'Abate, L., Farrar, J. E., & Serritella, D. A. (Eds.). (1991). *Handbook of differential treatments for addictions.* Boston: Allyn and Bacon.

Minnesota Coalition for Battered Women. (1992). *Safety first: A guide for battered women.* St. Paul, MN: Author.

Minnesota Coalition for Battered Women. (1992). *Safety first: A guide for counselors and advocates.* St. Paul, MN: Author.

National Research Council. (1998). *Violence in families: Assessing prevention and treatment programs.* Washington, DC: National Academy Press.

Schwartz, M. F., & Cohn, L. (Eds.). (1996). *Sexual abuse and eating disorders.* New York: Brunner/Mazel.

Weinstein, D. L. (Ed.). (1992). *Lesbians and gay men: Chemical dependency treatment issues.* New York: Haworth.

REFERENCES

Adams, D. C., & McCormick, A. J. (1982). Men unlearning violence: A group approach based on the collective model. In M. Roy (Ed.), *The abusive partner* (pp. 170–197). New York: Van Nostrand Reinhold.

Alexander-Mott, L., & Lumsden, D. B. (1994). Bulimia nervosa. In L. Alexander-Mott & D. B. Lumsden (Eds.), *Understanding eating disorders* (pp. 159–160). Washington, DC: Taylor & Francis.

Amchin, J., & Polan, H. J. (1986). A longitudinal account of staff adaptation to AIDS patients on a psychiatric unit. *Hospital & Community Psychiatry, 37,* 1235–1238.

American Psychiatric Association. (1993). Practice guideline for eating disorder. *American Journal of Psychiatry, 150,* 207–228.

American Psychiatric Association. (1994). *Diagnostic and statistical manual of mental disorders* (4th ed.). Washington, DC: Author.

American Psychological Association. (1996). *Hope training manual.* Washington, DC: Author.

Amico, J. M., & Neisen, J. (1997, May/June). Sharing the secret: The need for gay-specific treatment. *The Counselor.*

Armsworth, M. W. (1989). Therapy of incest survivors: Abuse or support. *Child Abuse and Neglect, 13,* 549–562.

Barnett, O. W., & Planeaux, P. S. (1989, January). *A hostility-guilt assessment of counseled and uncounseled batterers.* Paper presented at the Responses to Family Violence Research Conference, Purdue University, Lafayette, IN.

Bartlett, J. G. (1993). *The Johns Hopkins Hospital guide to medical care of patients with HIV infection* (3rd ed.). Baltimore, MD: Williams & Wilkins.

Bass, E., & Davis, L. (1988). *The courage to heal: A guide for women survivors of child sexual abuse.* New York: Harper and Row.

Bellofatto, M. H. (1993, September/October). Look beyond the chemical dependency or eating disorder. *Addiction & Recovery, 13,* 1–2.

Bennett, L., & Lawson, M. (1994, May). Barriers to cooperation between domestic-violence and substance-abuse programs. *Families in Society: The Journal of Contemporary Human Services,* 277–286.

Benowitz, M. (1986). How homophobia affects lesbians' response to violence in lesbian relationships. In K. Lobel (Ed.), *Naming the violence: Speaking out about lesbian battering.* Seattle: Seal Press.

Bickelhaupt, E. (1986). Psychosocial aspects of AIDS. *Kansas Medicine, 87,* 66–83.

Biller, R., & Rice, S. (1990). Experiencing multiple loss of persons with AIDS: Grief and bereavement issues. *Health & Social Work, 15,* 283–290.

Blinder, B. J., & Chao, K. H. (1994). Eating disorders: A historical perspective. In L. Alexander-Mott & D. B. Lumsden (Eds.), *Understanding eating disorders* (pp. 3–35). Washington, DC: Taylor & Francis.

Blume, E. S. (1990). *Secret survivors: Uncovering incest and its aftereffects in women.* New York: Wiley & Sons.

Brekke, J. S. (1987, June). Detecting wife and child abuse in clinical settings. *Social Casework: The Journal of Contemporary Social Work,* 332–338.

Briere, J. (1989). *Therapy for adults molested as children: Beyond survival.* Mexico: Springer.

Brown, G. R., & Anderson, B. (1991). Psychiatric morbiditiy in adult inpatients with childhood histories of sexual and physical abuse. *American Journal of Psychiatry, 148,* 55–61.

Bruckner, D. F., & Johnson, P. E. (1987). Treatment for adult male victims of childhood sexual abuse. *Social Casework: The Journal of Contemporary Social Work, 68,* 81–87.

Buchanan, L. P., & Buchanan, W. L. (1992). Eating disorders: Bulimia and anorexia. In L. L'Abate, J. E. Farrar, & D. A. Serritella's (Eds.), *Handbook of differential treatments for addictions* (pp. 165–188). Boston: Allyn and Bacon.

Burke, M. T., & Miller, G. A. (1996). Using the spiritual perspective in counseling persons with HIV/AIDS: An integrative approach. *Counseling & Values, 40,* 185–195.

Cabaj, R. J. (1997). Gays, lesbians, & bisexuals. In J. H. Lowinson, P. Ruiz, R. B. Millman, & J. G. Langrod (Eds.), *Substance abuse: A comprehensive textbook* (3rd ed.) (pp. 725–733). Baltimore: Williams & Wilkins.

CDC. (1981). Pneumocystis pneumonia—Los Angeles. *Morbidity and Mortality Weekly Report, 30,* 250–252.

CDC. (1989). *AIDS surveillance/epidemiology.* Slide presentation.

Cho, C., & Cassidy, D. F. (1994). Parallel processes for workers and their clients in chronic bereavement resulting from HIV. *Death Studies, 18,* 273–292.

Conant, M., Hardy, D., Sernatinger, J., Spicer, D., & Levy, J. A. (1986). Condoms prevent transmission of AIDS-associated retrovirus. *Journal of the American Medical Association, 255,* 1706.

Costin, C. (1996). Body image disturbance in eating disorders and sexual abuse. In M. F. Schwartz & L. Cohn (Eds.), *Sexual abuse and eating disorders* (pp. 109–127). New York: Brunner/Mazel.

Dimock, P. T. (1988). Adult males sexually abused as children. *Journal of Interpersonal Violence, 3,* 203–221.

Domestic Abuse Intervention Project. Duluth, MN.

Durham, J., & Hatcher, B. (1984). Reducing psychological complications for the critically ill AIDS patient. *Dimensions of Critical Care Nursing, 3,* 300–306.

Eberle, P. (1982). Alcohol abusers and non-users: A discriminant analysis of differences between two subgroups of batterers. *Journal of Health and Social Behavior, 23,* 260–271.

Edelson, J. L., & Tolman, R. M. (1992). *Intervention for men who batter: An ecological approach.* Newbury Park, CA: Sage.

Eliason, M. J. (1996). *Who cares?: Institutional barriers to health care for lesbian, gay, and bisexual persons.* New York: National League for Nursing.

Evans, S., & Schaefer, S. (1987). Incest and chemically dependent women: Treatment implications. *Journal of Chemical Dependency Treatment, 1,* 141–173.

Ferraro, K. J. (1993). Cops, courts, and woman battering. In P. B. Bart & E. G. Moran (Eds.), *Violence against women: The bloody footprints* (pp. 165–176). London: Sage.

Finkelhor, D. (1986). *A sourcebook on child sexual abuse.* Beverly Hills, CA: Sage.

Finnegan, D. G., & McNally, E. B. (1987). *Dual identities: Counseling chemically dependent gay men and lesbians.* Center City, MN: Hazelden.

Frank, P. B., & Golden, G. K. (1992). Blaming by naming: Battered women and the epidemic of codependence. *Social Work, 37,* 5–6.

Frazier, P., Harlow, T., Schauben, L., & Byrne, C. (1993, August). *Predictors of postrape trauma.* Paper presented at the 101st Annual Meeting of the American Psychological Association, Toronto, Ontario.

Ganley, A. L., & Harris, L. (1978). *Domestic violence on trial* (pp. 155–173). New York: Springer.

Garner, D. (1991). *Eating disorder inventory-2.* Odessa, FL: Psychological Assessment Resources.

Gilmartin, P. (1994). *Rape, incest, and child sexual abuse: Consequences and recovery.* New York: Garland.

Gold, M. S., Johnson, C. R., & Stennie, K. (1997). Eating disorders. In J. H. Lowinson, P. Ruiz, R. B. Millman, & J. G. Langrod (Eds.), *Substance abuse: A comprehensive textbook* (3rd ed.) (pp. 319–330). Baltimore: Williams & Wilkins.

Golden, G. K., & Frank, P. B. (1994). When 50-50 isn't fair: The case against couple counseling in domestic abuse. *Social Work, 39,* 636–637.

Goldner, E. M., & Birmingham, C. L. (1994). Anorexia nervosa: Methods of treatment. In L. Alexander-Mott & D. B. Lumsden (Eds.), *Understanding eating disorders* (pp. 135–157). Washington, DC: Taylor & Francis.

Gonsiorek, J. C., Bera, W. H., & LeTourneau, D. (1994). *Male sexual abuse.* Thousand Oaks, CA: Sage.

Goodman, M. S., & Fallon, B. C. (1995). *Pattern changing for abused women.* Thousand Oaks, CA: Sage.

Greene, D., & Faltz, B. (1991). Chemical dependency and relapse in gay men with HIV infection: Issues and treatment. *Journal of*

Chemical Dependency Treatment, 4, 79–90.

Hall, B. A. (1994). Ways of maintaining hope in HIV disease. *Research in Nursing and Health, 17,* 283–293.

Hall, J. (1994). Lesbians recovering from alcohol problems: An ethnographic study of health care experiences. *Nursing Research, 43,* 238–244.

Hall, R. P., Kassees, J. M., & Hoffman, C. (1980). Treatment for survivors of incest. *Journal for Specialists in Group Work, 11,* 85–92.

Hamilton, C. J., & Collins, J. J. (1981). The role of alcohol in wife beating and child abuse: A review of the literature. In J. J. Collins (Ed.), *Drinking and crime: Perspectives on the relationship between alcohol consumption and criminal behavior* (pp. 253–287). New York: Guilford.

Harner, I. C. (1987–88). The alcoholism treatment client and domestic violence. *Alcohol Health and Research World, 12,* 150–152, 160.

Herek, G. M., & Glunt, E. K. (1988). An epidemic of stigma: Public reactions to AIDS. *American Psychologist, 43,* 886–891.

Heyward, C. (1992). Healing addiction and homophobia: Reflections on empowerment and liberation. In D. L. Weinstein (Ed.), *Lesbians and gay men: Chemical dependency treatment issues* (pp. 5–18). Binghamton, NY: Haworth.

Hiebert-Murphy, D. (1992). Group treatment for sexually abused girls: Evaluating outcome. *Families in Society, 73,* 205–213.

Hodges, K. (1993). Domestic violence: A health crisis. *Health Watch, 54,* 213–216.

Huber, J. T. (1993). Death and AIDS: A review of the medico-legal literature. *Death Studies, 17,* 225–232.

Hurley, D. L. (1991). Women, alcohol and incest: An analytical review. *Journal of Studies on Alcohol, 52,* 253–268.

Jones, A., & Schechter, S. (1992). *When love goes wrong.* New York: HarperCollins.

Kain, C. D. (1996). *Positive: HIV affirmative counseling.* Alexandria, VA: American Counseling Association.

Kalichman, S. C. (1995). *Understanding AIDS: A guide for mental health professionals.* Washington, DC: American Psychological Association.

Kegeles, S. M., Coates, T. J., Christopher, T. A., & Lazarus, J. L. (1989). Perceptions of AIDS: The continuing saga of AIDS-related stigma. *AIDS, 3,* 253–258.

King, M. B. (1989). Prejudice and AIDS: The views and experiences of people with HIV infection. *AIDS Care, 1,* 137–143.

Knapp, S. J., & VandeCreek, L. (1997). *Treating patients with memories of abuse: Legal risk management.* Washington, DC: American Psychological Association.

Koss, M. P., Dinero, T. E., & Seibel, C. A. (1988). Stranger and acquaintance rape: Are there differences in the victim's experience? *Psychology of Women Quarterly, 12,* 1–24.

Koss, M. P., Gidyca, C. A., & Wisiewski, N. (1987). The scope of rape: Incidence and prevalence of sexual aggression and victimization in a national sample of higher education students. *Journal of Consulting and Clinical Psychology, 55,* 162–170.

Krug, R. S. (1989). Adult male report of childhood sexual abuse by mothers: Case descriptions, motivations and long-term consequences. *Child Abuse & Neglect, 13,* 111–119.

Leeder, E. (1988). Enmeshed in pain: Counseling the lesbian battering couple. *Women & Therapy, 7,* 81–99.

Levy, A. J., & Brekke, J. S. (1990). Spouse battering and chemical dependency: Dynamics, treatment, and service delivery. In R. T. Potter-Efron & P. S. Potter-Efron (Eds.), *Aggression, family violence and chemical dependency* (pp. 81–97). New York: Haworth.

MacDonald, J. M. (1995). *Rape: Controversial issues.* Springfield, IL: Charles C. Thomas.

MacDonald, K., Lambie, I., & Simmonds, L. (1995). *Counseling for sexual abuse: A therapist's guide to working with adults, children, and families.* Melbourne: Oxford University.

Marlatt, G. A. (1985). Cognitive factors in the relapse process. In G. A. Marlatt & J. R. Gordon (Eds.), *Relapse prevention* (pp. 128–200). New York: Guilford.

Marx, R. D. (1994). Anorexia nervosa: Theories of etiology. In L. Alexander-Mott & D. B. Lumsden (Eds.), *Understanding eating disorders* (pp. 123–134). Washington, DC: Taylor & Francis.

McDonell, J. R. (1993). Judgments of personal responsibility for HIV infection: An attributional analysis. *Social Work, 38,* 403–410.

McKirnan, D. J., & Peterson, P. L. (1989). Alcohol and drug use among homosexual men and women: Epidemiology and population characteristics. *Addictive Behaviors, 14,* 545–553.

Miller, G. A., Sack, T., & Simmons, K. (1993). *Sexual abuse and alcohol: Women survivors [Summary].* Proceedings of the Fourth International Counseling Conference. Vancouver, British Columbia.

Minnesota Coalition for Battered Women. (1992). *Safety first: A guide for counselors and advocates.* St. Paul, MN: MCBW.

Mondragon, D., Kirkman-Liff, B., & Schneller, E. S. (1991). Hostility to people with AIDS: Risk perception and demographic factors. *Society of Science and Medicine, 32,* 1137–1142.

Moynihan, R., Christ, G., & Silver, L. G. (1988). AIDS and terminal illness. *Social Casework, 69,* 380–387.

National Coalition Against Domestic Violence. (n.d.). Fact sheet. Washington, DC: Author.

National Woman Abuse Prevention Project (NWAPP). (1989). *Understanding domestic violence.* Washington, DC: Author.

Newmark, D. (1984). Review of a support group for patients with AIDS. *Topics in Clinical Nursing, 6,* 38–44.

Nichols, S. (1985). Psychosocial reactions of persons with the Acquired Immunodeficiency Syndrome. *Annals of Internal Medicine, 103,* 765–767.

North Carolina Bar Association. (1995). *Domestic violence and the law: A practical guide for survivors.* Raleigh, NC: Author.

North Carolina Coalition Against Domestic Violence. (1995). *Project Esperanza: A guide to working with battered latinas.* Raleigh, NC: Author.

Olson, P. E. (1990). The sexual abuse of boys: A study of the long-term psychological effects. In M. Hunter (Ed.), *The sexually abused male: Volume 1. Prevalence,*

impact and treatment (pp. 137–152). Lexington, MA: Lexington.

Orrok, B. (1992). Diverse presentations of substance abuse and post-traumatic stress disorder in incest survivors. In S. Shapiro & G. Dominiak, (Eds.), *Sexual trauma and psychopathology* (pp. 113–142). New York: Lexington Books.

Parrot, A. (1991a). Institutional response: How can acquaintance rape be prevented? In A. Parrot & L. Bechhofer (Eds.), *Acquaintance rape: The hidden crime* (pp. 355–367). New York: Wiley and Sons.

Parrot, A. (1991b). Recommendations for college policies and procedures to deal with acquaintance rape. In A. Parrot & L. Bechhofer (Eds.), *Acquaintance rape: The hidden crime* (pp. 368–380). New York: Wiley and Sons.

Pence, E., & Paymar, M. (1993). *Education groups for men who batter: The Duluth model.* New York: Springer.

Pernanen, K. (1991). *Alcohol in human violence.* New York: Guilford.

Peters, S. D., Wyatt, G. E., & Finkelhor, D. (1986). Prevalence. In D. Finkelhor & Associates (Eds.), *A sourcebook on child sexual abuse* (pp. 15–59). Newbury Park, CA: Sage.

Pike, K. M. (1994, April). *Cognitive behavioral treatment in the relapse prevention of anorexia nervosa: A pilot study.* Paper presented at the Sixth Annual International Conference on Eating Disorders, New York.

Pike, K. M., & Wilfley, D. E. (1996). The changing context of treatment. In L. Smolak, M. P. Levine, & R. Striegel-Moore (Eds.), *The developmental psychopathology of eating disorders* (pp. 365–397). Mahwah, NJ: Lawrence Erlbaum.

Potter-Efron, R. T. (1989). *Shame, guilt and alcoholism: Treatment issues in clinical practice.* New York: Haworth.

Ratican, K. L. (1992). Sexual abuse survivors: Identifying symptoms and special treatment considerations. *Journal of Counseling and Development, 71,* 33–38.

Rinella, V. J., & Dubin, W. R. (1988). The hidden victims of AIDS: Health care workers and families. *Psychiatric Hospital, 19,* 115–120.

Rogan, A. (1985–86, Winter). Domestic violence and alcohol: Barriers to cooperation. *Alcohol Health and Research World, 9,* 22–27.

Root, M. P. (1989). Treatment failures: The role of sexual victimization in women's addictive behavior. *American Journal of Orthopsychiatry, 59,* 542–549.

Rorty, M., & Yager, J. (1996). Speculations on the role of childhood abuse in the development of eating disorders among women. In M. F. Schwartz & L. Cohn (Eds.), *Sexual abuse and eating disorders* (pp. 23–35). New York: Brunner/Mazel.

Russell, G., Szmukler, G. I., Dare, C., & Eisler, I. (1987). An evaluation of family therapy in anorexia nervosa and bulimia nervosa. *Archives of General Psychiatry, 44,* 1047–1056.

Russell, S. A., & Wilsnack, S. (1991). Adult survivors of childhood sexual abuse: Substance abuse and other consequences. In P. Roth (Ed.), *Alcohol and drugs are women's issues (Volume 1): A review of the issues* (pp. 61–70). Metuchen, NJ: Women's Action Alliance.

Saag, M. S. (1992). AIDS testing: Now and in the future. In M. A. Sande & P. A. Volberding (Eds.), *The medical management of AIDS* (4th ed.) (pp. 65–88). Philadelphia: Saunders.

Saghir, M. T., Robins, E., Walbran, B., & Gentry, K. E. (1970). Homosexuality: III. Psychiatric disorders and disability in the male homosexual. *American Journal of Psychiatry, 126,* 1079–1086.

Sansone, R. A., & Sansone, L. A. (1994). Bulimia nervosa: Medical complications. In L. Alexander-Mott & D. B. Lumsden (Eds.), *Understanding eating disorders* (pp. 181–201). Washington, DC: Taylor & Francis.

Schwartz, M. F., & Cohn, L. (1996). Introduction: Eating disorders and sexual trauma. In M. F. Schwartz & L. Cohn (Eds.), *Sexual abuse and eating disorders* (pp. ix–xii). New York: Brunner/Mazel.

Scott, D. (1983). Alcohol and food abuse: Some comparisons. *British Medical Journal, 3,* 301.

Springer, E. (1991). Effective AIDS prevention with active drug users: The harm reduction model. *Journal of Chemical Dependency Treatment, 4,* 141–157.

Stall, R., & Wiley, J. (1988). A comparison of alcohol and drug use patterns of homosexual and heterosexual men: The San Francisco Men's Health Study. *Drug and Alcohol Dependence, 22,* 63–73.

A statement of philosophy for management and treatment of sex offenders. *Juvenile & Family Court Journal, 39,* No. 2 (Preliminary Report from the National Task Force on Juvenile Sexual Offending 1988).

Straus, M. A., Gelles, R. J., & Steinmetz, S. K. (1980). *Behind closed doors: Violence in the American family.* New York: Anchor.

Strom, D. P. (1993). AIDS and intravenous drug users: Issues and treatment implications. In S. L. A. Straussner (Ed.), *Clinical work with substance-abusing clients* (pp. 330–350). New York: Guilford.

Szasz, T. (1994). *Cruel compassion: Psychiatric control of society's unwanted.* New York: Wiley.

Turnell, G. (1989). *Complications in working with AIDS patients in group psychotherapy.* Paper presented at the 97th Annual Meeting of the American Psychological Association, New Orleans, LA.

Urquiza, A. J. (1993, August). *Adult male survivors of child sexual abuse: Issues in intimacy.* Paper presented at the 101st Annual Convention of the American Psychological Association, Toronto, Ontario.

Vanderlinden, J., & Vandereycken, W. (1996). Is sexual abuse a risk for developing an eating disorder? In M. F. Schwartz & L. Cohn (Eds.), *Sexual abuse and eating disorders* (pp. 17–22). New York: Brunner/Mazel.

Villagomez, R. E., Meyer, T. J., & Lin, M. M. (1995). Post-traumatic stress disorder among inner city methadone maintenance patients. *Journal of Substance Abuse Treatment, 12,* 253–257.

Viney, L. L., Henry, R., Walker, B. M., & Crooks, L. (1989). The emotional reactions of HIV antibody positive men. *British Journal of Medical Psychology, 62,* 153–161.

Voeller, B., Coulson, A. H., Bernstein, G. S., & Nakamura, R. M. (1989). Mineral oil lubricants cause rapid deterioration of latex condoms. *Contraception, 39,* 95–102.

Walker, L. (1979). *The battered woman.* New York: Harper and Row.

Walker, L. (1980). *The battered woman* (2nd ed.). New York: Harper and Row.

Walker, L. (1984). *The battered woman syndrome.* New York: Springer.

Weinberg, M. S., & Williams, C. J. (1974). *Male homosexuals: Their problems and adaptations.* New York: Oxford University.

Weinberg, T. S. (1994). *Gay men, drinking and alcoholism.* Carbondale, IL: Southern Illinois University Press.

Weiss, L., Katzman, M., & Wolchik, S. (1994). Bulimia nervosa: Definition, diagnostic criteria, and associated psychological problems. In L. Alexander-Mott & D. B. Lumsden (Eds.), *Understanding eating disorders* (pp. 161–180). Washington, DC: Taylor & Francis.

Whipple, V. (1987). Counseling battered women from fundamentalist churches. *Journal of Marital & Family Therapy, 13,* 251–258.

White, E. (1994). *Chain, chain, change: For black women in abusive relationships.* Seattle: Seal Press.

Wright, J., & Popham, J. (1982). Alcohol and battering: The double bind. *Aegis, 36,* 53–59.

Zerbe, K. J. (1996). The emerging sexual self of the patient with an eating disorder: Implications for treatment. In M. F. Schwartz & L. Cohn (Eds.), *Sexual abuse and eating disorders* (pp. 134–154). New York: Brunner/Mazel.

Zweben, J. E. (1987). Eating disorders and substance abuse. *Journal of Psychoactive Drugs, 19,* 181–192.

6 Relapse Prevention

PRETEST

1. What is the balance a counselor needs to find in working with relapse prevention issues?
2. What are the five stages of addictive behaviors?
3. What is the main goal of the Marlatt Relapse Prevention (RP) model?
4. What are the two main parts of a specific habit-change goal according to RP?
5. The RP model is based on which four social learning theory assumptions?
6. According to the RP model, what are the three stages of changing a habit?
7. What is the distinction between a lapse and a relapse?
8. What do the terms *self-efficacy* and *AVE* mean, and what roles do they play in the RP model?
9. What are seven things counselors need to do to help their clients change specific target behaviors?
10. What four counseling techniques can be used in relapse prevention?

A lapse is different from a relapse. A *lapse* means the addict breaks the commitment to abstinence, but does not return to previous levels of use. *Relapse* involves an activation of the addictive process where the addict resumes drug use at previous levels. This usage occurs after a series of maladaptive responses on the part of the addict (National Institute on Drug Abuse, 1994b). Because of the lack of clear definition between a lapse and a relapse, viewing relapse as a continuum may be most helpful in the treatment process (National Institute on Drug Abuse, 1994b).

Sometimes self-help groups and addiction professionals will use the term *slip* to discuss resumed drug usage. There are two difficulties with the use of this term. First, a slip may not distinguish clearly between a lapse and relapse. Second, the term itself may encourage the client to view drug-taking behavior as accidental and outside of his or her control. Whatever terminology is used by the counselor *(slip, lapse, relapse),* it is important to help the client look at the experience and learn from it to decrease the chances of it occurring again.

Counselor Approaches

Relapse appears to be relatively common among addicted individuals: 20 to 80 percent of addicts relapse within a year of addiction treatment (Marlatt, 1985). Although relapse is common when clients try to break out of a habitual pattern of behavior (Prochaska, DiClemente, & Norcross, 1992), the counselor working on relapse issues with a client walks a fine line. He or she wants open communication with the client, building trust so that the client will bring up relapse situations in counseling sessions. However, the counselor does not want to encourage relapse or enable the client to use by reinforcing excuses for using behavior. The counselor, then, needs to create an atmosphere of trust so that the client feels comfortable discussing actual or potential relapses, as well as create an environment of accountability where the client looks at how his or her choices resulted in relapsing behavior.

Creation of a Trustworthy Atmosphere

The creation of a trustworthy atmosphere requires a nonjudgmental approach by the counselor. The component of relapse can make the work with recovering addicts very frustrating. It is hard to work with clients on their recovery, mutually enjoy the success of their changes, and then face their relapses with them in a nonjudgmental fashion. There are opportunities for countertransference issues to emerge in this aspect of recovery. Rather than examine the components of the relapse situation, the counselor may simply begin to assume that the client is not motivated or is "not ready" to recover from his or her addiction. There are also opportunities for transference where the client may blame the counselor for not doing enough to help him or her stay sober. Although the disappointment may be shared by both counselor and client, the counselor needs to maintain a nonjudgmental stance in order to work through countertransference and transference issues and thereby guide the individual into a discussion regarding the relapse situation.

Probably the best source of nonjudgmentalism for the counselor is awareness of any personal habit (overeating, smoking, gambling, drinking coffee, watching television, etc.) she or he has tried to change. Struggling with one's own habitual tendencies may help the counselor have compassion for the ongoing struggle it takes to change one's behavior. The client, struggling to change an addictive behavior, may sense this compassion in the counselor or at least feel comfortable talking with such a counselor.

In addition, many times, addicted clients may legitimately ask counselors how they can understand the recovery process. If a counselor has examined his or her own habitual tendencies, the counselor may choose to let the client know that there is an understanding for how hard it is to change a habit.

View of Relapse

In terms of accountability, the actual or potential relapse for the addicted client can be viewed as a signal that something has gone wrong with the client's recovery. Some clients may avoid looking at the relapse by stating that they just "slipped" or that they do, after all, have a "disease" and then want to move off the topic. Certainly, the therapist wants to avoid being judgmental of the relapse, but the client needs to be held accountable for the behavior. Thus, the client must learn to take responsibility for recovery choices and be aware of individual recovery "soft spots" or relapse triggers. Triggers that seem to be associated with relapse are stress, negative emotions, positive emotions, interpersonal conflict, social pressure, other substance use, and drug-related cues that stimulate cravings (National Institute on Drug Abuse, 1994b).

The relapse does not need to be viewed as a treatment failure (Marlatt & George, 1984) but, rather, as an experience from which one can learn and a chance to intervene on the relapse process (Mackay & Marlatt, 1990–91). Although it is understandably hard to discuss relapse, the counselor is not facilitating the recovery process by letting a phrase such as *I just slipped* or *I have a disease* suffice as an explanation of the relapse. In order to intervene on the addictive process, the counselor needs to help the client find the words to describe the relapse experience so it can be thoroughly examined in counseling, thereby allowing for an appropriate intervention.

Facilitation of Discussion

It may be best to start a discussion of the relapse or relapse potential by discussing a model of behavior change such as Prochaska, DiClemente, and Norcross's (1992) five stages of addictive behaviors: precontemplation, contemplation, preparation, action, and maintenance. Discussion of this model may provide a framework through which the relapse can be viewed as well as a common language for the counselor and client to discuss the relapse.

The *precontemplation* stage is apparent by the lack of intention to change the behavior. At this point, the person is unaware or underestimates the level of the problem and is resistant to changing it. During the *contemplation* stage, the individual is aware of the problem, is thinking about changing, but has not made a commitment to take any action to address the problem. In this stage, the individual is weighing how much it will "cost" to address the problem and if the price is worth the change. In the *preparation* stage, the individual is planning to take some action to make the behavior change, and has tried to change the behavior (without success) in the last year. During the *action* stage, the individual is making overt changes to address the addictive behavior by committing time and energy to the changes. In the authors' definition of this stage, the individual's addictive behavior has been changed anywhere from a day to six months. Finally, in the *maintenance* stage, the individual is preventing relapse of the addictive behavior by continuing the change process through stabilized behavior.

DiClemente, Prochaska, Fairhurst, Velicer, Velasquez, and Rossi (1991) point out that in this spiral cycle of change, the addicted individual can learn from mistakes made in the recovery process and make changes in his or her recovery plan based on what he or she has learned about changing the behavior. In addition, because the client's readiness to change is related to the outcome of treatment (Prochaska et al., 1992), the counselor needs to evaluate how ready the client is to make a change (Shaffer, 1997). Prochaska and colleagues (1992) recommend that therapists determine the change level their clients currently are at and then use that to determine the type of treatment intervention that can have an impact on relapse prevention. For example, a client at the contemplation stage may benefit more from therapy sessions that focus on the benefits and losses of making a behavior change than on action that needs to be taken to change the addiction. Further examples of application of this theory can be found in Prochaska and colleagues (1992).

Enabling Behavior

During relapse prevention work with a client, a counselor also needs to check himself or herself for enabling behavior that encourages relapse. In order to prevent enabling behavior for relapses, a counselor can ask himself or herself the following questions:

1. Am I telling the client that relapse is expected for all addicts?
2. Am I avoiding giving the client consequences for the choice to use?
3. Do I think that I would drink/use if I were in the same situation?
4. Am I keeping information about the relapse from others (e.g., intimate partners, bosses, parole officers, etc.) who I have agreed to update on the client's recovery process?
5. Do I find myself avoiding examination of the relapse situation with my client?
6. Do I avoid telling colleagues about the relapse because of how I, the client, the quality of our therapy work, or the impact on treatment may be viewed?

If the answer to any of these questions is yes, the therapist needs to examine the possibilities of enabling the client's usage. Three guidelines may assist a counselor in avoiding enabling behavior:

1. Question yourself and your motive in counseling around relapse situations.
2. Examine your history of care taking of addicts.
3. Use supervision and critical colleagues to question your reactions to relapse.

These guidelines are not a guarantee against enabling, but they can assist the counselor in keeping a balance between being judgmental and enabling during relapse prevention work.

Clients, then, need assistance in becoming aware of, making decisions regarding, and preparing to change their addictive problem. Therapists need to understand that clients may need to cycle through the stages of change a number of times before the behavior change is maintained. An awareness of this reality of changing addictive behaviors may assist both therapists and clients in being realistic about the difficulties that accompany changing an addictive behavior.

Relapse Prevention Models

Rawson, Obert, McCann, and Marinelli-Casey (1993) provide an excellent overview of nine relapse prevention models:

1. Marlatt and Gordon's Relapse Prevention Model
2. Gorski's CENAPS Model (Gorski, 1989a, 1989b, 1990; Gorski & Miller, 1986; Miller, Gorski, & Miller, 1982)
3. Wallace's Relapse Prevention Materials for Crack Cocaine Users (Wallace, 1989, 1990, 1991)
4. Annis's Relapse Prevention Approach for Alcoholism (Annis, 1986, 1990; Annis & Davis, 1988, 1989)
5. Roffman and colleagues' Relapse Prevention Treatment for Marijuana Dependence (Roffman & Barnhart, 1987; Roffman, Stephens, Simpson, & Whitaker, 1990)
6. Caroll and colleagues' Relapse Prevention for Cocaine Abuse (Carroll, Rounsaville, & Gawin, 1991; Carroll, Rounsaville, & Keller, 1991)
7. McAuliffe and colleagues' Recovery Training and Self-Help (RTSH) Model (McAuliffe, 1990; McAuliffe & Ch'ien, 1986; Zackon, McAuliffe, & Ch'ien, 1985)
8. Washton's Intensive Outpatient Model (Washton, 1989, 1990a, 1990b; Washton & Gold, 1987; Washton & Stone-Washton, 1990, 1991)
9. Rawson and colleagues' Matrix Neurobehavioral Model (Rawson, 1990; Rawson, Obert, McCann, & Ling, 1991; Rawson, Obert, McCann, & Mann, 1986; Rawson, Obert, McCann, Smith, & Ling, 1990; Rawson, Obert, McCann, Smith, & Scheffey, 1989)

A general overview of the nine models can be found in Rawson and associates (1993), or more detail about the models can be obtained from the specific references for each of the models. Gorski's CENAPS model will be briefly reviewed here because of the frequency of its use in chemical dependency treatment centers. However, the model that will be focused on will be the Marlatt and Gordon model, because it is a foundational model for the field of addictions upon which many of the other relapse prevention models are based.

Gorski's CENAPS Model

CENAPS stands for the Center for Applied Sciences. Gorski's model (Gorski, 1989a, 1989b, 1990; Gorski & Miller, 1986; Miller, Gorski, & Miller, 1982) has been used extensively in the private chemical dependency treatment centers (Rawson et al., 1993). Although Gorski's work provides a lot of clinical recommendations within a cognitive-behavioral view (Gorski, 1992), it lacks a specific methodology that can be examined in research (Rawson et al., 1993). Gorski's work has focused on alcohol and cocaine addiction. The model addresses client responsibility in terms of awareness of relapse triggers, the process of relapse, and coping behaviors other than the use of alcohol/drugs.

Marlatt and Gordon Relapse Prevention Model

The Relapse Prevention model (RP) (Marlatt & Gordon, 1985) is described as a self-management program that tries to increase the chances of a habit change being maintained. The goal is to teach clients how to anticipate and cope with actual and potential relapse. The model can be applied as maintaining a specific change or as a global life-style change. With regard to a specific habit, the goal is broken into two parts: (1) anticipation and prevention of a relapse after changing an addictive behavior and (2) recovery from a lapse prior to a full relapse. The proponents of the model (Marlatt & Gordon, 1985) believe it can be used on any addictive behaviors that consist of a compulsive habit pattern where the individual attempts to obtain immediate gratification.

This social learning theory model is based on four assumptions:

1. Addiction is an overlearned, maladaptive habit pattern.
2. Behavioral determinants and consequences have an impact on behavior.
3. People are not responsible for developing a habit or for not simply being able to stop it.
4. Escape from the addiction cycle hinges on changing habits through participation and responsibility.

The process of changing a habit involves three stages: (1) commitment and motivation, (2) implementation of the specific behavioral change, and (3) long-term maintenance of the behavioral change. The individual's view of the maintenance stage contributes significantly to the recovery process.

Relapse is viewed as a two-step process. Step 1 is a lapse, where the person violates the behavioral goal he or she has set. In step 2, the relapse, returning to the target behavior existing at the pretreatment level, depends on the individual's perception of the cause of the initial lapse. For example, the client may view himself or herself as a hopeless failure at staying sober after having one joint of marijuana (leading to a relapse of previous higher levels of marijuana use), or the client may view himself or herself as having made a mistake and needing to learn what preceded the marijuana use in order to prevent a relapse. The focus of RP is to assist people in viewing relapses as mistakes they can learn from rather than a behavior for which one is to be judged or punished.

CHAPTER 6

Relapse is a decision-making process: What occurs before and after the initial lapse is critical, and there are many opportunities that may increase or decrease the risk of relapse. A successful recovery from an addictive behavior is based on a high motivation to change and a high degree of self-efficacy. Self-efficacy consists of the self-judgments made about one's competency to adequately perform in a particular task situation. Self-efficacy affects behavior, thought patterns, and emotional arousal. Motivation is important because it underlines the commitment made to achieve a goal. Self-efficacy complements motivation by outlining how individuals can reach that goal and the degree to which they believe they can obtain the goal. For example, a client may be highly motivated to quit using alcohol and drugs due to family and legal problems. If the client can picture himself or herself as able to cope in different high-risk situations (high self-efficacy), there is a good chance of the client staying sober.

Most addictive behaviors involve a motivational conflict: Immediate gratification is desired but conflicts with the desire to avoid delayed negative effects. An addiction assists people in coping with natural emotional reactions that are unpleasant or aversive by decreasing the awareness of them. It is not the quitting of addictive behavior that is difficult, but the "staying quit" that is hard to maintain. Relapse frequently occurs when the person enters a high-risk situation (with regard to the addictive behavior). Often, seemingly irrelevant decisions are a part of the addicted person's decision chain, where choices result in exposure to the drugs and a risk of relapse (National Institute on Drug Abuse, 1994b). When the person enters a high-risk situation, does not know how to cope in the situation, and experiences diminished self-efficacy and positive outcome expectancies of the addictive behavior, a relapse is highly likely (see Figure 6.1).

To continue with the example of the client who wants to stay sober due to legal and family problems, the individual has a fight with his wife in the morning and then goes to court for the DUI and receives a severe sentence. This may be a high-risk situation because he feels like he is trying to change and yet his changes are not seeming to make a difference in his life situations. He may not know how to cope with these stressors other than using alcohol and smoking marijuana. His lack of coping responses affects his self-efficacy level: He does not view himself as able to stay sober with all of these stressors. He also begins to have positive outcome expectancies of drinking alcohol and smoking marijuana (e.g., "If I just drank and smoked a joint, I could relax and figure out how to handle this situation"). He uses alcohol (two beers) and marijuana (one joint) as a natural outcome of being in a high-risk situation, not knowing how to cope without the use of alcohol/marijuana, experiencing low self-efficacy (cannot see himself as being able to persist at staying sober), and expecting positive outcomes from using alcohol/marijuana (being able to relax and think clearly).

After the initial use, the individual experiences an abstinence violation effect (AVE), the psychological effect of violating the abstinent rule. AVE hinges on cognitive dissonance and the self-attribution effect. Cognitive dissonance is the discrep-

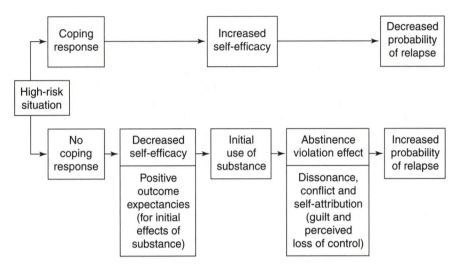

FIGURE 6.1   A Cognitive-Behavioral Model of the Relapse Process

Source: Relapse Prevention (p. 38) by G. Alan Marlatt and Judith R. Gordon (Eds.), 1985, New York: Guilford Press. Copyright 1985 by Guilford Press. Reprinted by permission.

ancy between what people believe about themselves and how they behave. This discrepancy requires individuals to change either their thoughts or behaviors in order to reduce the dissonance and have a consistent view of themselves.

For example, a person who wants to stop drinking alcohol enters an addiction treatment program and makes a commitment to herself that she will never drink again. Upon leaving treatment, there is a lapse: She has a beer. The behavior of drinking alcohol is inconsistent with the self-view of being a recovering alcoholic, so the person must either change her thoughts (stop believing that she is alcoholic) or change her behavior (stop drinking alcohol) to create a consistent self-view.

The self-attribution effect involves how a person explains the lapse (causal attribution). Was it due to a personal weakness or failure, or was it due to a unique response to a difficult situation? When considered as due to a personal weakness or failure, greater guilt, conflict, and AVE are experienced: An internal (self), stable (constant), global (general) attribution (uncontrollable) increases the likelihood of a strong AVE. A person, for instance, may use drugs after a period of abstinence and then believe that he or she may be a failure at staying sober because of lacking discipline (internal), will always lack discipline (stable), and will never be able to learn how to be more disciplined (general, uncontrollable).

On the other hand, if a person can explain the lapse as a unique response to a difficult situation, he or she will experience weaker guilt, conflict, and AVE: An external (environment), unstable (changeable), and specific causal attribution (controllable) decreases the likelihood of an intense AVE. Because a stronger AVE will increase the chances of relapse, the AVE in response to the lapse is a critical intervention point.

Returning to our same client who lapsed by drinking two beers and smoking a joint, his behavior is considered a lapse, because prior to treatment, he drank half a case of beer and smoked half an ounce of marijuana daily. If he returns to his pretreatment level of use, it is considered a relapse. At this point, however, he has only had a lapse into his addictive behavior. What determines if he returns to his pretreatment level of use is the AVE he experiences. If he experiences a strong AVE, he may make an attribution (an explanation) of his behavior that would underscore a sense of uncontrollability about changing the addictive behavior: "I used because I am a failure as a human being (internal) and I will always be a failure at staying sober (stable) no matter who tries to help me or what situation I am in (global)." This strong AVE combined with perceived effects of use (the alcohol/marijuana did relax him as he expected) will increase the chances of a full-blown relapse.

However, if he experienced a weaker AVE in response to his lapse, he may make an attribution (explanation) of his behavior that would underscore more of a sense of controllability with regard to changing his addictive behavior: "I used because of extreme stresses (external) that do not happen every day (unstable) and that were connected to my marriage and my legal status that are important to me (specific)." Although this may sound like enabling, it is not. This client may have an easier time tracking down the coping responses he lacked in the high-risk situation if he does not get caught in an intense, seemingly endless AVE, which will only encourage further relapse and a sense of hopelessness and uncontrollability with regard to making a change about the addictive behavior.

The RP model attempts to take a realistic, practical approach to recovery from an addiction. Viewing relapse as a normal part of recovery allows counselors to step out of a parental, authoritarian role with clients. Focusing on the likelihood of relapse provides counselors and clients the opportunity to develop prevention plans so relapse does not occur.

Counseling Techniques

The main emphasis in relapse prevention is for the counselor to assist the client in becoming more self-aware. The relapse prevention activities need to be personal. The client needs to take the abstract theory of relapse prevention and, with the help of the counselor, apply it to his or her own life. This personalization will result in an increased self-awareness. The self-awareness can generally be encouraged by the counselor by asking the client to watch himself or herself through such techniques as timing the length of the urge to use or logging his or her recovery experiences. Also, experiential activities such as role-plays (acting out relapse-triggering scenarios), guided imagery (focusing on positive thoughts and images while simultaneously imagining the difficult situation [Cormier & Cormier, 1998]), and empty chair (carrying on a dialogue with opposing parts of self by being the opposite self in each chair [Corey, 1995]) can help a client personalize the relapse prevention process through increased self-awareness. An increased self-awareness can assist the client in recognizing danger signs of relapse and developing a personal continuum of difficult recovery situations.

Marlatt and Gordon's Relapse Prevention Model

Marlatt and Gordon (1985) outline an intervention procedure for preventing relapse. With regard to specific target behaviors, counselors are encouraged to help clients learn the following:

1. Situations that are high risk for them
2. Skills to cope in high-risk situations
3. Relaxation and stress management skills
4. Examination of positive outcome expectancies: realistic outcomes of addictive behavior (sometimes described in self-help groups as "follow the drink through [to its inevitable outcome]")
5. Immediate and delayed effects of the addictive activity
6. Action to take if a relapse occurs
7. Control over behavior through programmed relapse

Martlatt and Gordon (1985) also recommend global recovery strategies, including examination of the client's life-style, development of positive addictions or substitutions for the addictive behavior, creation of an "observatory role" where clients learn from their urges to use rather than act on them, and development of the client's "relapse warning system" so early warning signals of relapse can be heard. For example, during the process of treating a middle-aged woman who is addicted to prescription medication and alcohol, the therapist will want to examine situations where she may have difficulty avoiding the use of prescription medication and/or alcohol to cope. The therapist will want to determine coping skills the client might lack, her view of the effects and consequences of her pill and alcohol use, and the action and control she needs to take to prevent a relapse. Also, the therapist will want to help this woman examine her overall life-style in terms of balance, positive addictions, capacity to self-monitor, and presence of a relapse warning system. Two techniques that may assist in this process are the decision matrix and mapping.

The *decision matrix* (Marlatt, 1985) is a chart that compares the consequences of quitting with continuing the addictive behavior. Figure 6.2, for example, shows what a decision matrix would look like for someone who wanted to quit smoking. The matrix has eight cells that are divided into two sections. The first section, which has four parts, looks at the positive and negative consequences for stopping (or remaining stopped) the addictive behavior. Both immediate and delayed consequences of stopping are addressed. Staying with the example of the middle-aged

	Immediate Consequences		Delayed Consequences	
	Positive	*Negative*	*Positive*	*Negative*
To stop smoking or remain abstinent	Increased self-efficacy Social approval Improved physical state Financial gain	Denial of gratification Withdrawal discomfort Frustration and anger Weight gain	Enhanced self-control Improved health (absence of disease) Financial gain Absence of social disapproval	Denial of gratification (becomes less intense)
To continue or resume smoking	Immediate gratification Removal of withdrawal discomfort Consistent with past self-image Weight loss	Guilt and attribution of no control Social censure Negative physical effects Financial loss	Continued gratification	Decreased self-control Health risks Financial loss Continued social disapproval

FIGURE 6.2   Decision Matrix for Smoking Cessation

Source: Relapse Prevention (p. 38) by G. Alan Marlatt and Judith R. Gordon (Eds.), 1985, New York: Guilford Press. Reprinted by permission.

woman, the therapist could use the matrix to understand the client's view of the consequences and effects of her addiction (see comments in parentheses):

1. Immediate positive consequences to stopping or remaining stopped in terms of the addictive behavior. (She likes feeling "clear-headed and energetic.")
2. Immediate negative consequences to stopping or remaining stopped in terms of the addictive behavior. (She does not like the feelings of anxiety she experiences when she is without pills or alcohol and in a stressful situation.)
3. Delayed positive consequences to stopping or remaining stopped in terms of the addictive behavior. (She hopes to earn the respect back from her children by being sober.)
4. Delayed negative consequences to stopping or remaining stopped in terms of the addictive behavior. (She is afraid she will not be able to cope with the anxiety every day of her life she is sober.)

The second section, which has four parts, looks at the positive and negative consequences for continuing (or resuming) the addictive behavior. Again, both immediate and delayed consequences are addressed:

5. Immediate positive consequences to continuing or resuming the addictive behavior. (She enjoys the feeling of relaxation she experiences when she takes pills and alcohol.)
6. Immediate negative consequences to continuing or resuming the addictive behavior. (Her children will not let her visit with her grandchildren if she resumes her chemical usage.)

7. Delayed positive consequences to continuing or resuming the addictive behavior. (She will feel capable to cope with her anxiety in stressful situations.)
8. Delayed negative consequences to continuing or resuming the addictive behavior. (Her children will lose respect for her again and possibly forever.)

In this example, high-risk situations would be those that the woman finds stressful and those that she uses pills and alcohol to cope with the stress. She lacks the stress management skills that could help her cope with the anxiety. If she can learn some stress management skills, which will help her stay sober, she may be able to choose actions in stressful situations that will allow her to control her behavior (stay sober) and work at regaining the respect of her children and the contact with her grandchildren, which are so important to her. By developing such a relapse warning system for high-stress situations and by learning to observe herself for signs of tension, the client can work at developing a more balanced life-style that incorporates some positive addictions to stress management activities.

The counselor and client need to work together on completing this matrix early in the treatment process to determine the client's motivation level and goals. Also, the matrix will help the counselor learn the values of the client that may not have been articulated. These values may enhance the client's motivation to change the addictive behavior.

Another relapse prevention technique is called *mapping* (Marlatt, 1985). The client and therapist draw out a relapse prevention map for the client. This map shows where the individual is and where he or she wants to go. The process leading to the final goal of abstinence from the addiction can be drawn out so the client gets an overall view of his or her recovery process. Different forks in the road can be drawn around high-risk situations, which can help increase the client's awareness of the antecedents and consequences to both using and nonusing behavior. The map can also assist the therapist in learning the aspects of relapse prevention that the client may be neglecting in his or her recovery.

In the previous example, the counselor and the client determine that a final destination for the client is to regain the respect of her children and contact with her grandchildren. Keeping these goals in mind, the client and counselor can anticipate high-stress situations for her based on her past use history and current life situation. Discussions can focus on what could lead the client to wanting to use pills and alcohol and what would happen to her if she does. Although the outcome may be similar to using the decision matrix, some clients may feel more comfortable with this exercise than one that lists short- and long-term effects, or the same information obtained in two different exercises may facilitate the client's awareness of relapse prevention.

In summary, Daley and Marlatt (1997) encourage counselors to help their clients see relapse as both an event and a process, identify high-risk factors and coping strategies, be aware of cues that can set off cravings, find different ways to cope with negative emotions, learn to cope with cognitive distortions, be aware of social pressure to use, develop a social network supportive of their behavior change, help those in residential treatment make the transition to outpatient/aftercare, consider pharmacological treatment, develop a balanced life-style, and develop a lapse/relapse plan.

Ten Most Common Dangers

An excellent overall counseling technique (National Institute on Drug Abuse, 1994a) to use with addicted individuals is an awareness of common dangers that addicts face in general when they are:

1. Around familiar drugs, drug users, or drug-related settings
2. Experiencing negative feelings
3. Celebrate positive feelings
4. Experiencing boredom
5. Getting high on any mood-altering substance
6. Experiencing physical pain
7. Focusing on getting high
8. Having a lot of money all of a sudden
9. Taking prescription medication that causes a high
10. Believing that occasional drug use (without problems) is possible

These are general relapse areas for the addicted individuals, in general; it is important to find out which of them are specifically a danger for the client with whom you are working. For example, a particular client may not struggle with experiencing positive feelings or negative feelings in general, but he or she may have an especially difficult time handling the feeling of loneliness.

TIPS for Coping with Stressful Situations

The National Institute of Drug Abuse (1994a) developed the acronym *TIPS* to remind addicts of how to cope with difficult situations: truth, information, priorities, and support. *Truth* means that the addict needs to let others know honestly about the struggle he or she is currently experiencing. *Information* encourages the addict to obtain facts about the situation at hand rather than react on assumptions or emotions. *Priorities* means that the addict sees as his or her number one priority to stay sober and focus on what is really important to the addicted person. *Support* reminds the addict to turn to others for support when in a difficult situation.

HALT

Another acronym used in some self-help groups is HALT (National Institute on Alcohol Abuse and Alcoholism, 1995). This acronym warns the addict about potential relapse by reminding him or her to not get too hungry, angry, lonely, or tired. When using this acronym with a client, discuss with him or her how to recognize how the client behaviorally acts out these feelings: What is he or she like when hungry, angry, lonely, or tired? This simple acronym may assist addicted clients when they find themselves in an upsetting situation that they do not know how to handle; it may remind them of simple self-care steps they can take to prevent relapse.

Relapse prevention is critical to the recovery process. In order to assist clients in maintaining their sobriety, therapists need to help them anticipate and prepare for difficult recovery situations. The following case studies are provided to facilitate awareness of coping with these issues.

CASE STUDY: FRANK

Frank is a 45-year-old male who is married for the third time. He completed one year of college, and has worked the night shift at a local factory for 20 years. All of Frank's friends are from his workplace, and their main recreational activity is focused on drinking. His first two wives left him because of his drinking and his third wife is currently threatening to leave him for the same reason. Frank has four children (two from each of his previous marriages), but none of his children have contact with him because of his aggressive personality when he is drinking. Frank's third wife has been Al-Anon for three of the five years they have been married. She arranges an intervention for him with regard to his drinking and he enters inpatient treatment primarily because "I love my wife and I will do anything to keep her."

During Frank's last few days in treatment, his wife admits during the family session that she has been having an affair with one of his best friends from the plant and that she arranged for Frank to go to treatment so she could leave the marriage without a guilty conscience. Frank is devastated by the news, and that afternoon one of his drinking buddies calls him at the treatment center and invites him to a retirement party for one of their friends at the plant. The party is scheduled for the day after Frank leaves treatment.

Frank decides to not tell anyone about the retirement party. He and his counselor make arrangements for him to live with another male new to recovery. When Frank leaves treatment, he goes to his house to collect the items he needs for his new apartment. His wife is there, but she refuses to talk with Frank. Frank has difficulty sleeping that night and has a lot of angry fantasies about seeking revenge on his wife and friend. When he gets to the retirement party, he sees his old friend who is involved with his wife. He decides to drink a beer ("to get some courage"). He then walks over to his friend and hits him as he is calling him names. His friends separate the two men and a number of them go with Frank to a local bar. Frank feels very ashamed that he drank, cannot imagine that he can live through the humiliation he feels about his wife's infidelity, and believes the alcohol has made him feel stronger and more confident about handling the situation.

After a couple months of drinking at his old rate, Frank contacts you for help.

1. How would you help Frank talk about his relapse?

2. How do you recognize the different aspects of the relapse prevention model (high-risk situations, lack of coping responses, decreased self-efficacy, positive outcome expectancies, lapse, AVE, perceived effects of use, increased relapse probability)?
3. What coping behaviors would you work on with this client?
4. How would you help Frank use techniques such as 10 common dangers, TIPS for coping, decision matrix, and mapping?
5. What changes does Frank need to make in his life-style?
6. What would you want to help Frank do with regard to positive addictions and/or substitutes?
7. How might the "observer role" help Frank?
8. How will learning early warning relapse signals help Frank?

Case Studies of Special Populations

Often addiction does not stand alone. It is frequently accompanied by additional issues such as domestic violence, sexual abuse, and eating disorders. Although these concerns are discussed at length in Chapter 5, some case studies of these special populations are presented here in order to facilitate the understanding of relapse prevention with regard to accompanying issues.

CASE STUDY: JEANETTE

Jeanette is a 22-year-old amphetamine addict who came to treatment at her doctor's recommendation. She had been obtaining amphetamines over the last five years by seeing different doctors for prescriptions ("doctor shopping") and by going to different pharmacies. One of the pharmacists notified one of her physicians of her amphetamine use and she was confronted by that doctor about her addiction during her next visit. Her doctor also asked her at that time about the bruises on her body and she admitted that her husband of two years beats her. She begged her doctor and her treatment counselor not to confront her husband because she is afraid a confrontation of the issue will accelerate the violence. She has done well in inpatient treatment, has attended both AA (Alcoholics Anonymous) and WFS (Women for Sobriety) self-help groups, has a sponsor/mentor in each of the self-help groups, and will be returning home in a couple days. While she is aware that she used drugs in part to cope with the violence (she used amphetamines to get more things done at home and at work so he would not be angry with her), she refuses to discuss the domestic violence in her home and her husband refuses to attend family sessions at the treatment center.

As her aftercare counselor, please answer the following questions:

1. What high-risk situations might Jeanette face when she returns home?
2. What coping responses might she lack?

3. What evidence is there of decreased self-efficacy and positive outcome expectancies?
4. What would be a main concern to address with Jeanette immediately in her aftercare plans?
5. Which counseling techniques (10 common dangers, TIPS for coping, decision matrix, mapping) would you see as appropriate to use with her at this time?
6. Do you see Jeanette as needing to make a life-style change in order to remain sober? If so, what changes do you see her needing to make and how would you recommend that she make them?

CASE STUDY: SUZI

Suzi is a 30-year-old female who has had one previous addiction treatment five years ago. She was able to stay sober for one year. Her treatment was court-ordered because of a DUI. She has come to you for counseling because she recently started drinking heavily again after a visit home over the holidays (during the previous four years, she says her drinking was limited to the weekends, but now she is back to daily drinking). She wants to quit drinking and using drugs again, but she wants to do it through private counseling with you rather than a formal treatment center, which she believes is a financial rip-off. She warns you that she is a "loser" when it comes to sobering up, because treatment did not work for her, nor did Alcoholics Anonymous or Narcotics Anonymous, and her family has always told her she is a loser who will never be able to make anything of herself.

Suzi is single and lives alone. She is the middle child of three girls and denies any family history of alcoholism. She says that when she sobered up the first time, she started to have trouble having sex with men she dated and she had bad dreams of her father forcing her to have sex with him. She does not remember specific incidents of sexual abuse beyond her dreams. She does not have these dreams when she is drinking (her drug of choice is alcohol, although she says she has tried "everything") and reports being afraid that she will have the bad dreams again when she sobers up for a while. Suzi states that she has problems when she visits her family, which she only does at holidays, when she is sober. She says her father has a habit of french kissing her "hello" and "goodbye," which she does not mind when she is drinking, but did mind that year that she was sober. She is unable to talk at length about what happened during her last visit home over the holidays: She begins to cry uncontrollably when she is asked about it. All she can state is, "This time it was more than french kissing."

As her private therapist, answer the following questions:

1. What are the high-risk situations for Suzi in her addiction recovery?
2. What is her abstinence violation effect?
3. What positive outcome expectancies do you think may precede Suzi's initial use?

4. What may need to change in terms of her coping responses and her environment in order for her to stay sober?
5. Which counseling techniques (10 common dangers, TIPS for coping, decision matrix, mapping) would you use in your work with this client?
6. How might the "observer role" help Suzi learn to stay sober?

CASE STUDY: JEFF

Jeff is a 55-year-old man who admits to being addicted to alcohol and barbiturates. He also admits to being bulimic since his early 20s. He is single, never been married, and has always lived with his mother. He describes his relationship with his mother as a love/hate one: His mother dominates him (which Jeff resents), but Jeff says he does not believe he could live without his mother. Jeff says his mother ignores every assertion or boundary he has made in the relationship. He believes his addiction and his eating disorder are fused: He drinks to avoid the shame of his eating disorder.

Jeff has just entered the halfway house and is open to working on his issues. He says he does not see himself as being able to stay sober because he knows he needs alcohol and barbiturates in order to live with his mother. Due to financial constraints, Jeff will return to live with his mother when he leaves the halfway house in six weeks.

As his primary halfway house counselor, answer the following questions:

1. What are high-risk situations for Jeff?
2. What coping responses might he lack in those high-risk situations?
3. How do you perceive his self-efficacy level in terms of his recovery and how might that be a dangerous match with his positive outcome expectancies of the alcohol and drugs?
4. What are some abstinence violation effects Jeff reports and that you might anticipate?
5. Which of the counseling techniques (10 common dangers, TIPS for coping, decision matrix, mapping) might you use with this client?
6. What positive addictions or substitutes might Jeff look at incorporating into his life?
7. What might be some early warning signals for him in terms of a relapse?

Dual Diagnosis

Dual diagnosis was discussed extensively in Chapter 3; however, it is raised here as a special emphasis in order to discuss relapse prevention techniques with this population. Orlin and Davis (1993) report that a longer time frame may be needed with this population to achieve abstinence due to the presence of two chronic problems. Evans and Sullivan (1990) report high relapse rates with this population and Zimberg (1993) states that relapse may be more common with this population because of how difficult it is to stabilize both problems at the same time. Although these authors make excellent points regarding relapse and dual disorders, once again, the therapist must be careful about not enabling relapse in a dual-disordered client while attempting to create a compassionate atmosphere in which to address recovery issues.

As with other clients, Daley (1995) notes that the causes of relapse (i.e., life-style problems, interpersonal factors, etc.) are often multiple. Daley also recommends similar therapeutic strategies: understanding that relapse is a process; identifying the high-risk factors for the individual; helping the individual cope with cravings, cues, and social pressures; and assisting the individual in developing a recovery network. Daley stresses that a nonjudgmental attitude and a strong therapeutic alliance can make a significant difference in the recovery of a dual-disordered client.

The following case study concerns a client with dual disorders. Following the case study is a list of questions to assist in applying the relapse prevention model. The specific dual diagnosis is not given because sometimes in treatment the behavior indicating a dual diagnosis is present and yet the counselor needs to continue working with the client until an psychological evaluation can be done that clarifies the specific disorder.

CASE STUDY: BOB

Bob is a 50-year-old man who has had a 12-year history of severe alcoholism with four hospital detoxifications and four chemical dependency treatments, none of which had any significant impact on his drinking. He was court-ordered to treatment for his third DUI. After two weeks in the treatment center, it was noted by the staff that Bob rarely was seen sleeping. At night, he would walk up and down the halls of the treatment center. He was also becoming more agitated in group therapy. He alternated in group therapy between being very quiet, yet agitated (unable to sit still) and becoming very hostile when confronted or probed for information about himself by the counselor or other clients. He was the topic of most staff meetings, as counselors complained about how frustrating it was to work with him. There was discussion in the meetings of discharging him. The other clients increasingly refused to associate with him due to his highly critical manner and his tendency to be emotionally explosive.

As his primary therapist, answer the following questions:

1. Without knowledge of his specific mental health diagnosis, how are you limited in helping Bob with regard to relapse prevention?
2. What steps would you need to take to obtain clarification of his mental health problems?
3. What additional information might you want to obtain or explore to ensure that all "dual diagnosis" issues are addressed?
4. Based simply on the behavior he is showing, even though you do not know his mental health diagnosis, what appears to be a high-risk situation(s) for Bob and what appears to be some coping responses he lacks?

Summary

Relapse prevention is a necessary component of the recovery process from addiction. With the reality of fewer therapy sessions being covered by insurance companies and the ongoing process required to break out of an addiction, relapse prevention is a crucial aspect of treatment because it helps the client anticipate problems in advance, thereby reducing the chance of relapse. The use of relapse prevention approaches can increase the efficiency of addiction treatment.

SUGGESTED READINGS

Marlatt, G. A., & Gordon, J. R. (1985). *Relapse prevention: A self-control strategy for the maintenance of behavior change*. New York: Guilford.

National Institute on Drug Abuse. (1994). *Recovery training and self-help: Relapse prevention and aftercare for drug addicts*. NIH Publication No. 94-3521.

Prochaska, J. O., DiClemente, C. C., & Norcross, J. C. (1992). In search of how people change: Applications to addictive behaviors, *American Psychologist, 47*, 1102–1114.

REFERENCES

Annis, H. M. (1986). A relapse prevention model for treatment of alcoholics. In W. R. Miller & N. Heather (Eds.), *Treating addictive behaviors: Process of change* (pp. 407–433). New York: Plenum.

Annis, H. M. (1990). Relapse to substance abuse: Empirical findings within a cognitive-social learning approach. *Journal of Psychoactive Drugs, 22*, 117–124.

Annis, H. M., & Davis, C. S. (1988). Relapse prevention training: A cognitive-behavioral approach based on self-efficacy theory. In D. C. Daley (Ed.), *Relapse: Conceptual, research and clinical perspectives* (pp. 81–103). New York: Hayworth.

Annis, H. M., & Davis, C. S. (1989). Relapse prevention. In R. K. Hester & W. R. Miller (Eds.), *Handbook of alcoholism treatment approaches* (pp. 170–182). New York: Pergamon.

Carroll, K. M., Rounsaville, B. J., & Gawin, F. H. (1991). A comparative trial of psychotherapies for ambulatory cocaine abusers: Relapse prevention and interpersonal psychotherapy. *American Journal of Drug Abuse, 17*, 229–247.

Carroll, K. M., Rounsaville, B. J., & Keller, D. S. (1991). Relapse prevention strategies for the treatment of cocaine abuse. *American Journal of Drug Abuse, 17*, 19–26.

Corey, G. (1995). *Theory and practice of group counseling* (4th ed.). Pacific Grove, CA: Brooks/Cole.

Cormier, S., & Cormier, B. (1998). *Interviewing strategies for helpers* (4th ed.). Pacific Grove, CA: Brooks/Cole.

Daley, D. (1995, October). *Relapse prevention with dual disorder patients*. Paper presented at the meeting of the National Dual Disorder Conference, Las Vegas, NV.

Daley, D. C., & Marlatt, G. A. (1997). Relapse prevention. In J. H. Lowinson, P. Ruiz, R. B. Millman, & J. G. Langrod (Eds.), *Substance abuse: A comprehensive textbook* (3rd ed.) (pp. 458–467). Baltimore: Williams & Wilkins.

DiClemente, C. C., Prochaska, J. O., Fairhurst, S. K., Velicer, W. F., Velasquez, M. M., & Rossi, J. S. (1991). The process of smoking cessation: An analysis of precontemplation, contemplation, and preparation stages of change. *Journal of Consulting and Clinical Psychology, 59,* 295–304.

Evans, K., & Sullivan, J. M. (1990). *Dual diagnosis: Counseling the mentally ill substance abuser.* New York: Guilford.

Gorski, T. T. (1989a). *Passages through recovery: An action plan for preventing relapse.* Center City, MN: Hazelden Educational Materials.

Gorski, T. T. (1989b). *The relapse/recovery grid.* Center City, MN: Hazelden Educational Materials.

Gorski, T. T. (1990). The Cenaps model of relapse prevention: Basic principles and procedures. *Journal of Psychoactive Drugs, 22,* 125–133.

Gorski, T. T. (1992). *The staying sober workbook: A serious solution for the problem of relapse.* Independence, MO: Herald House/Independence Press.

Gorski, T. T., & Miller, M. (1986). *Staying sober: A guide for relapse prevention.* Independence, MO: Harold House/Independence Press.

Mackay, P. W., & Marlatt, G. A. (1990–91). Maintaining sobriety: Stopping is starting. *International Journal of the Addictions, 25,* 1257–1276.

Marlatt, G. A. (1985). Relapse prevention: Theoretical rationale and overview of the model. In G. A. Marlatt & J. R. Gordon (Eds.), *Relapse prevention: A self-control strategy for the maintenance of behavior change* (pp. 3–70). New York: Guilford.

Marlatt, G. A., & George, W. H. (1984). Relapse prevention: Introduction and overview of the model. *British Journal of Addiction, 79,* 261–273.

Marlatt, G. A., & Gordon, J. R. (1985). *Relapse prevention: A self-control strategy for the maintenance of behavior change.* New York: Guilford.

McAuliffe, W. E. (1990). A randomized controlled trial of recovery training and self-help for opioid addicts in New England and Hong Kong. *Journal of Psychoactive Drugs, 22,* 197–210.

McAuliffe, W. E., & Ch'ien, J. M. N. (1986). Recovery training and self-help: A relapse-prevention program for treated opiate addicts. *Journal of Substance Abuse Treatment, 3,* 9–20.

Miller, M., Gorski, T. T., & Miller, D. K. (1982). *Learning to live again.* Independence, MO: Independence Press.

National Institute on Alcohol Abuse and Alcoholism. (1995). *Twelve step facilitation therapy manual: A clinical research guide for therapists treating individuals with alcohol abuse and dependence. Volume 1: Project MATCH monograph series.* NIH Publication No. 94-3722.

National Institute on Drug Abuse. (1994a). *Recovery training and self-help: Relapse prevention and aftercare for drug addicts.* NIH Publication No. 94-3521.

National Institute on Drug Abuse. (1994b). *Relapse prevention.* NIH Publication No. 94-3845.

Orlin, L., & Davis, J. (1993). Assessment and intervention with drug and alcohol abusers in psychiatric settings. In S. L. A. Straussner (Ed.), *Clinical work with substance-abusing clients* (pp. 50–68). New York: Guilford.

Prochaska, J. O., DiClemente, C. C., & Norcross, J. C. (1992). In search of how people change: Applications to addictive behaviors. *American Psychologist, 47,* 1102–1114.

Rawson, R. A. (1990). Cut the crack: The policymaker's guide to cocaine treatment. *Policy Review, 51,* 10–19.

Rawson, R. A., Obert, J. L., McCann, M. J., & Ling, W. (1991). Psychological approaches for the treatment of cocaine dependence: A neurobehavioral approach. *Journal of Addictive Diseases, 11,* 97–119.

Rawson, R. A., Obert, J. L., McCann, M. J., & Mann, A. J. (1986). Cocaine treatment outcome: Cocaine use following inpatient, outpatient and no treatment. *NIDA Research Monograph, 67,* 271–277.

Rawson, R. A., Obert, J. L., McCann, M. J., & Marinelli-Casey, P. (1993). Relapse prevention strategies in outpatient substance abuse treatment. *Psychology of Addictive Behaviors, 7,* 85–95.

Rawson, R. A., Obert, J. L., McCann, M. J., Smith, D. P., & Ling, W. (1990). Neurobehavioral treatment for cocaine dependency. *Journal of Psychoactive Drugs, 22,* 283–297.

Rawson, R. A., Obert, J. L., McCann, M. J., Smith, D. P., & Scheffey, E. (1989). *The neurobehavioral treatment manual: A therapist manual for outpatient cocaine addiction treatment.* Beverly Hills, CA: Matrix Center.

Roffman, R. A., & Barnhart, R. (1987). Assessing need for marijuana dependence treatment through an anonymous telephone interview. *International Journal of Addictions, 22,* 639–651.

Roffman, R. A., Stephens, R. S., Simpson, E. E., & Whitaker, D. L. (1990). Treatment of marijuana dependencies: Preliminary results. *Journal of Psychoactive Drugs, 22,* 129–137.

Shaffer, H. J. (1997). Psychology of stage change. In J. H. Lowinson, P. Ruiz, R. B. Millman, & J. G. Langrod (Eds.), *Substance abuse: A comprehensive textbook* (3rd ed.) (pp. 100–106). Baltimore: Williams & Wilkins.

Wallace, B. C. (1989). Relapse prevention in psychoeducational groups for compulsive crack cocaine smokers. *Journal of Substance Abuse Treatment, 6,* 229–239.

Wallace, B. C. (1990). Treating crack cocaine dependence: The critical role of relapse prevention. *Journal of Psychoactive Drugs, 22,* 149–158.

Wallace, B. C. (1991). *Crack cocaine.* New York: Brunner/Mazel.

Washton, A. M. (1989). Group therapy. In A. M. Washton (Ed.), *Cocaine addiction: Treatment, recovery, and relapse prevention* (pp. 140–161). New York: Norton.

Washton, A. M. (1990a). *Quitting cocaine: The first thirty days.* Center City, MN: Hazelden Educational Materials.

Washton, A. M. (1990b). *Staying off cocaine: Cravings, other drugs, and slips.* Center City, MN: Hazelden Educational Materials.

Washton, A. M., & Gold, M. S. (1987). *Cocaine: A clinician's handbook.* New York: Guilford.

Washton, A. M., & Stone-Washton, N. (1990). Abstinence and relapse in outpatient cocaine addicts. *Journal of Psychoactive Drugs, 22,* 135–147.

Washton, A. M., & Stone-Washton, N. (1991). *Step zero.* Center City, MN: Hazelden Educational Materials.

Zackon, F., McAuliffe, W. E., & Ch'ien, J. M. (1985). *Addict aftercare: A manual of training and self-help.* Rockville, MD: National Institute on Drug Abuse.

Zimberg, S. (1993). Introduction and general concepts of dual diagnosis. In J. Solomon, S. Zimberg, & E. Shollar (Eds.), *Dual diagnosis: Evaluation, treatment, training, and program development* (pp. 4–21). New York: Plenum.

CHAPTER

7 Self-Help Groups

PRETEST

1. What are the names of 12-step programs that help people recover from alcohol/drug addiction?

2. What are five self-help groups other than 12-step groups?

3. Which characteristics of different self-help groups are helpful to some clients?

4. Which characteristics of different self-help groups are not helpful to some clients?

5. How do individual factors such as race and gender affect the effectiveness of some groups?

6. What information would a counselor need to know about a client in order to make an adequate referral to a self-help group?

7. How can a counselor determine if a self-help group is a good match for a client?

8. What characteristics describe a healthy group? An unhealthy group?

9. What characteristics define a healthy sponsor/mentor? An unhealthy sponsor/mentor?

10. What are some self-help group concerns specific to small towns?

This chapter examines the historical development, basic concepts, use in counseling, strengths, and limitations of national self-help groups in the United States. The groups reviewed are 12-step groups (Alcoholics Anonymous, Narcotics Anonymous, Cocaine Anonymous), Women for Sobriety, 16 Steps, Rational Recovery, and Secular Organization for Sobriety. The chapter concludes with a section designed to help counselors match their clients with the self-help group that best meets clients' needs and a listing of major 12-step groups (for both addicts and their families/significant others) and alternatives to 12-step groups. Counselors can contact the groups listed to obtain information on the groups and how to establish a group in their area. Self-help groups for family members and significant others of addicted clients are discussed in Chapter 4. However, the section at the end of this chapter, matching self-help groups to meet client needs, can be used with minor modifications to assist family members and significant others in finding the best self-help group for themselves.

Types of Groups

12-Step Groups

Alcoholics Anonymous

History.   In 1931, American Rowland H. saw Dr. C. J. Jung for his alcoholism and was advised that he needed a religious/spiritual experience in order to overcome his drinking problem. Rowland returned to the United States and joined the New York Oxford Group, a group of nondenominational Christians. In 1934, Rowland introduced Ebby T., another alcoholic, to the Oxford Group; Ebby introduced his friend, Bill Wilson, who later became a cofounder of Alcoholics Anonymous, to the Oxford Group (Judge, 1994). Following his visit with Ebby about the Oxford Group and Ebby's ability to stay sober, Bill was admitted to a hospital under the care of psychiatrist Dr. William Silkworth (Nace, 1997). While in the hospital with his depression worsening, Bill began reading James's (1936) *Varieties of Religious Experience* and realized that his drinking was hopeless (Nace, 1997). Bill began to believe at that time that one alcoholic could help another, as Ebby had helped him (Nace, 1997). In May 1935, Alcoholics Anonymous (AA) began when AA cofounders, Bill Wilson (Bill W.), a failed Wall Street stockbroker, and Dr. Bob Smith (Dr. Bob), a surgeon, met in Akron, Ohio, where Bill Wilson was attempting a stock takeover bid that failed. Afraid he would resume drinking, Bill Wilson contacted a local Oxford Group minister who was listed in a church directory. By contacting the minister and eventually a woman named Mrs. Henrietta Sieberling, Bill obtained the name of another alcoholic in the area, Dr. Bob, who he met at Mrs. Sieberling's house (Nace, 1997). One month after Bill W. and Dr. Bob met, Dr. Bob had his last drink (Judge, 1994) and Alcoholics Anonymous was born on June 10, 1935. The first successful groups of AA were in Akron, New York, and Cleveland (Alcoholics Anonymous World Services, 1953).

From 1935 to 1939, AA attracted 100 members, and in 1939, it received its name "Alcoholics Anonymous" from its book that discussed a theory of alcoholism, the 12 Steps, and stories of alcoholics (Alcoholics Anonymous World Services, 1976). The book is better known in recovering communities as the "Big Book."

The program of Alcoholics Anonymous is based on the concept of one alcoholic helping another, especially during periods of stress (Kurtz, 1988). In the early years of its development, the alcoholics helping one another consisted predominantly of Caucasian, middle-class males who had been professionals (Robertson, 1988).

Basic Concepts. The General Service Office of AA has literature, videos, and meeting directories available. For readers interested in the organizational structure of AA, Robertson (1988) provides an excellent summary. Basically, each group of AA is self-supporting and guided by the 12 Traditions of Alcoholics Anonymous (Alcoholics Anonymous World Services, 1953). The 12 Steps, which were drawn from the Oxford Group concepts (Kurtz, 1988), serve as the backbone of Alcoholics Anonymous for the individual member. These steps are as follows:*

Twelve Steps

1. We admitted we were powerless over alcohol—that our lives had become unmanageable.
2. Came to believe that a Power greater than ourselves could restore us to sanity.
3. Made a decision to turn our will and our lives over to the care of God, *as we understood Him.*
4. Made a searching and fearless moral inventory of ourselves.
5. Admitted to God, to ourselves and to another human being the exact nature of our wrongs.
6. Were entirely ready to have God remove all these defects of character.
7. Humbly asked Him to remove our shortcomings.
8. Made a list of all persons we had harmed, and became willing to make amends to them all.
9. Made direct amends to such people wherever possible, except when to do so would injure them or others.
10. Continued to take personal inventory and when we were wrong promptly admitted it.
11. Sought through prayer and meditation to improve our conscious contact with God, *as we understood Him,* praying only for knowledge of His will for us and the power to carry that out.
12. Having had a spiritual awakening as the result of these steps, we tried to carry this message to alcoholics, and to practice these principles in all our affairs.

The 12 Steps are principles that serve as guidelines for the recovering client; the 12 Traditions are guidelines for the development of the fellowship of AA. They were published in 1946 and confirmed in 1950 at the First International Conference of AA (Alcoholics Anonymous World Services, 1953).

*The Twelve Steps and Twelve Traditions are reprinted with permission of Alcoholics Anonymous World Services, Inc. Permission to reprint the Twelve Steps and Twelve Traditions does not mean that A.A. has reviewed or approved the contents of this publication, nor that A.A. agrees with the views expressed herein. A.A. is a program of recovery from alcoholism *only*—use of the Twelve Steps and Twelve Traditions in connection with programs and activities which are patterned after A.A., but which address other problems, or in any other non-A.A. context, does not imply otherwise.

Twelve Traditions

1. Our common welfare should come first; personal recovery depends upon A.A. unity.
2. For our group purpose, there is but one ultimate authority—a loving God as He may express Himself in our group conscience. Our leaders are but trusted servants; they do not govern.
3. The only requirement for A.A. membership is a desire to stop drinking.
4. Each group should be autonomous except in matters affecting other groups or A.A. as a whole.
5. Each group has but one primary purpose—to carry its message to the alcoholic who still suffers.
6. An A.A. group ought never endorse, finance, or lend the A.A. name to any related facility or outside enterprise, lest problems of money, property, and prestige divert us from our primary purpose.
7. Every A.A. group ought to be fully self-supporting, declining outside contributions.
8. Alcoholics Anonymous should remain forever non-professional, but our service centers may employ special workers.
9. A.A., as such, ought never be organized; but we may create service boards or committees directly responsible to those they serve.
10. Alcoholics Anonymous has no opinion on outside issues; hence the A.A. name ought never be drawn into public controversy.
11. Our public relations policy is based on attraction rather than promotion; we need always maintain personal anonymity at the level of press, radio, and films.
12. Anonymity is the spiritual foundation of all our traditions, ever reminding us to place principles before personalities.

Alcoholics Anonymous inspired the development of numerous self-help groups in the United States (i.e., Narcotics Anonymous, Al-Anon, Overeaters Anonymous, Sexaholics Anonymous, Emotions Anonymous, and Codependents Anonymous). Two of these groups, Narcotics Anonymous and Cocaine Anonymous, will be discussed because of their specific focus in drug use recovery.

Narcotics Anonymous

History.   Narcotics Anonymous (NA) was founded in July 1953 in southern California and opened a World Service Office in Los Angeles in 1972 (Narcotics Anonymous, 1982). It views itself as similar to Alcoholics Anonymous, but its definition of the problem is "addiction" rather than a specific substance "alcohol" (Narcotics Anonymous, 1982).

Basic Concepts.   Narcotics Anonymous essentially uses the same 12 Steps of AA with a few revisions: (1) in Step 1, the word *alcohol* is replaced by *our addiction,* (2) the word *we* is added to the beginning of Steps 2 through 11, and (3) the word *alco-*

holics in Step 12 is replaced by *addicts* (Narcotics Anonymous, 1982). Narcotics Anonymous has its own main book, *Narcotics Anonymous* (1982), which is similar to the "Big Book" of AA in that it has information on addiction and stories of addicts. NA is also guided by 12 Traditions similar to AA's 12 Traditions, with minor alterations: (1) *N.A.* is substituted at times for *A.A.* or *A.A.* is simply deleted and (2) the word *alcoholic* is replaced with the word *addict*.

When referring clients to NA, Gifford (1991) suggests that the time of the organization's formation be taken into account: AA was formed in a more conservative time than NA. The author also suggests that NA has a broader definition of addiction and a more diverse membership. Due to these differences, Gifford (1991) states that NA may work better for adolescents than AA. While these descriptions of differences between the two types of 12-step groups may be accurate, each counselor needs to determine differences between the groups based on the local area information rather than basing perceptions only on tendencies reported in the literature.

Cocaine Anonymous

History. Cocaine Anonymous (CA) was founded in 1982 in Hollywood, California.

Basic Concepts. Cocaine Anonymous uses the text *Alcoholics Anonymous,* and members are encouraged to "translate" the words related to alcohol to include cocaine. A storybook, *Hope, Faith, & Courage,* based on the stories of cocaine addicts, and various literature are available to its members. It uses the 12 Steps of AA, revising Step 1 (*alcohol* is replaced with *cocaine and all other mind-altering substances*) and Step 12 (*alcoholics* is replaced with *addicts*). Cocaine Anonymous also uses the 12 Traditions of AA, replacing the following phrases: *AA* with *CA, alcohol* with *addict, Alcoholics Anonymous* with *Cocaine Anonymous,* and *drinking* with *using cocaine and all other mind-altering substances.*

Types of Meetings
There are different types of 12-step meetings (Johnson & Chappel, 1994) available to clients:

1. In *open* meetings, generally one recovering person speaks to the group about his or her addiction and recovery story and nonaddicts can attend and listen. These meetings are for people who generally want to learn more about addiction.
2. *Closed* meetings are for addicted individuals only.
3. *Discussion* meetings tend to focus on a topic discussed by those addicts in attendance; these meetings are called *participation* meetings in California.
4. In *speaker* meetings, one addicted person speaks to the audience about his or her addiction and recovery story; the speaker meeting may be open or closed.
5. In *step* meetings, the topic for discussion is one of the 12 Steps; typically, these meetings are for addicted individuals only.

6. In *Big Book* meetings, a chapter from *Alcoholics Anonymous* is read and discussed.

Use in Counseling

In a discussion about AA and NA, Humphreys (1993) warns counselors of two main potential difficulties in integrating 12-step groups and counseling: (1) a tendency to view the healthy individual differently (abasement vs. self-responsibility) and (2) a difference in helping responses (community/free/mutual problem vs. individual/paid/ not mutual problem). In spite of these differences, Humphreys urges counselors to find ways to use 12-step programs based on principles of separate yet respectful and cooperative views. For example, the counselor may help the client see that being responsible for oneself includes the capacity to be humble and to see oneself realistically. The counselor may also need to explain the difference between the accessibility and the lay feedback in self-help groups and the process and goals of therapy in order to assist the client in determining the ways in which he or she can appropriately have needs met in the different settings. The following section focuses on ways counselors may use these programs in conjunction with counseling.

Generally, 12-step groups may work well with addicted clients in that they can provide support for recovery (Flores, 1988), reduce a sense of isolation (Talbott, 1990), and develop a sense of self-regulation (Khantzian & Mack, 1994). In addition, they may provide an overall support to therapy (Bristow-Braitman, 1995; Johnson & Phelps, 1991; Riordan & Walsh, 1994).

An effective use of 12-step programs in conjunction with counseling is when the counselor has an intimate knowledge of the workings of such groups. This does not mean, however, that an effective counselor must be recovering from an addiction and attending local self-help groups. An effective counselor is defined here by his or her willingness to work with clients to understand the client's individual reactions to the 12-step groups and literature. As with any philosophy, the 12-step approach is subject to individual interpretation. It is critical, then, that the counselor find out the client's interpretation of the 12-step experience.

Le, Ingvarson, and Page (1995) encourage counselors to remember that AA is not a recovery program that fits all clients. They also encourage counselors to examine their counseling theory and how well AA fits into that theory. It may be helpful for counselors to read materials such as *Alcoholics Anonymous* and *Narcotics Anonymous*, attend open AA and NA meetings, and, if possible, talk with members of these groups who have been involved in the program for a number of years in order to assess the fit between one's counseling theory and the 12-step approach.

The counselor also must be knowledgable about the different types of 12-step groups available in the local community. Knowledge of available local meetings matched to the client's needs can facilitate a referral to a 12-step group.

Strengths

Flexibility. The 12 steps are referred to as "suggested" steps in the How It Works chapters of both *Alcoholics Anonymous* (1976) and *Narcotics Anonymous* (1982).

This notation allows recovering clients the ability to use the steps as they apply to themselves and their lives, avoiding absolute prescriptions against which addicted clients may rebel.

Membership.   The only requirement for membership in AA is a desire to stop drinking (Tradition 3) (and in NA and CA, the desire to stop using). The recovering client can begin and end membership based on his or her desire to change behavior. There are no dues or fees, so help for recovering clients is free and easily accessible. Typically, 12-step groups will "pass the basket" (Tradition 7) at the end of the meeting for costs such as coffee and rental space; individuals are invited to contribute what they can.

Accessibility and Familiarity.   One of the other main strengths of a 12-step program, particularly AA, is that it is widely used for treatment of addiction (Le, Ingvarson, & Page, 1995), making it very accessible for clients. Particularly for clients in rural areas and those clients who travel frequently, knowledge of accessibility to a recovery program may provide the client with a sense of security. In addition to the ease of accessibility is the familiarity of the program for those clients who have received addiction treatment in the United States: Most of the substance abuse treatment programs in the United States use the 12 steps in some capacity in their program (Bradley, 1988). Previous exposure to the program can facilitate the transition from addiction treatment to community support self-help groups. Finally, because of how widespread AA is, there are numerous special-interest groups within AA for sexual orientation (gays/lesbians), professionals (attorneys, physicians, nurses, etc.), gender, and groups such as Two Hatters (recovering counselors).

Limitations

Rigidity.   One of the limitations of a 12-step program is connected to one of the strengths: interpretation and application of the 12 steps. Although the literature discusses the steps as being "suggested," individual AA, NA, and CA groups may interpret the steps as more absolute: They may offer a rigid interpretation of the steps to clients, and "demand" that the client follow the steps as defined by the group or group members. If such experiences arise, the counselor and client may need to discuss ways the client can handle uncomfortable encounters with more rigid interpretations of the steps. For example, a group may interpret *Higher Power* to mean a Christian God and strongly discourage group members from discussing any other form of Higher Power in meetings. The counselor and client may determine together how comfortable the client, who is not Christian, feels in the group: Is it worth it to find a way to stay in the group and how can he or she remain true to his or her own spiritual beliefs? If the client wants to remain in the group, discussion between the counselor and client may focus on how the client shares spiritual beliefs in the meeting in a manner that is respectful to him or her. If it is too uncomfortable for the client, the counselor and client may want to work together to find a group that will be more receptive to the client's spiritual beliefs.

Open Membership.   Because there is no selection criteria for membership, clients need to remember that anyone can be at a self-help meeting. It is important for counselors to stress the *anyone* so that clients approach step meetings with a somewhat protective stance rather than openly and freely trusting individuals simply because they are at the meeting. Clients need to be aware that there are no inherent safeguards against individuals at meetings taking advantage of their vulnerability, such as sexually or financially.

Previous Negative Experience.   Another limitation may be the client's previous treatment and/or self-help group history. Previous exposure to a 12-step program may have been an unpleasant experience or left the client unimpressed, resulting in the client not being open to attending meetings. It is helpful for the counselor to process the client's emotions and experiences in the counseling session in order to determine if the reaction is one that can be resolved or if it is simply more helpful to refer the client to another self-help group. Because of the availability of 12-step meetings, it is important for clients at least to develop a tolerance for these meetings so that, in the event of a recovery crisis, the client has different supports on which to rely. Also, counselors must respect the limits of their clients: If the client simply is not able to draw support from a 12-step group, then exploration of other available self-help groups is necessary.

Limited Applicability.   One criticism of the AA program is its basis in Caucasian, middle-class, male culture, which has resulted in questioning its applicability to other groups. In interviewing some of the critics of AA, Judge (1994) reports two concerns: struggle with the wording of the 12 steps and "isms" experienced in self-help groups. In terms of the wording, both AA and NA use the word *him* when discussing God in the 12 Steps. For some clients, this language may be viewed as sexist and limiting of their concept of God (Higher Power). Another common wording struggle is in the word *powerless* in Step 1: Critics argue that oppressed groups do not need to learn about powerlessness, but need to learn how to own their power (Judge, 1994). For clients who struggle with such wording, the counselor may assist the client in "translating" the word so it is less offensive or may explore alternative self-help groups that are less offensive to the client. An example of translating the 12 Steps for sexual abuse survivors is provided by Miller, Sack, and Simmons (1994). For example, a female sexual abuse survivor may struggle with the concept of powerlessness in Step 1 of AA. Her therapist can help her learn to differentiate between the powerlessness of the sexual abuse and the powerlessness of her chemical dependency: Experiencing the powerlessness of her chemical dependency can free her from its abusiveness. Alternative self-help groups, which may be a better match for clients, are explored later in this chapter.

"Isms."   The second area of concern presented by Judge (1994) is with the "isms" experienced in some 12-step groups. An *ism* is defined as a negative bias and stereotype that discriminate against a certain population. Some examples are sexism, racism, and

homophobia. A group may espouse openness, yet in its own meetings it may only have a select group of individuals who attend (i.e., Caucasian heterosexual males). Because there is no specific selection criteria for membership, clients need to be aware that some "isms" may operate in a group and if those "isms" make the client uncomfortable, he or she may need to find another support group that does not practice discrimination. Some groups even struggle with having clients with "other" problems in their group. For example, an AA group may not want its members talking about the use of other drugs. In order to enhance acceptance by the group, some therapists have recommended that clients identify themselves as other group members identify themselves (Robertson, 1988) and share stories that involve drugs that group members are comfortable discussing. Groups may also have a bias against members taking any medication, including prescribed medication that is not addictive. For clients who have dual disorders, this type of feedback may be hazardous to their recovery.

Spiritual/Religious Emphasis.   A final limitation of a 12-step program, for some clients, is its spiritual/religious dimension. The program of AA has been criticized as being based in Christianity, given its Oxford Group roots (Judge, 1994). The wording in the 12 Steps of both AA, NA, and CA involves the word *God,* which is followed by the phrase *as we understood Him.* This attached phrase sometimes helps clients relax in their reaction (Miller, Simmons, & Sack, 1994). For other clients, though, this phrase, in combination with some self-help groups that begin and/or end meetings holding hands and praying the Lord's Prayer or the Serenity Prayer, may simply be too religious for them. Once again, it is important for the therapist to discuss if the client wants to develop some sort of tolerance for these group tendencies or if another self-help group might be more helpful to the client.

Women for Sobriety

History
Women for Sobriety (WFS), the first national self-help program specifically for alcoholic women, was started in 1976 by Jean Kirkpatrick. Kirpatrick's (1978) book, *Turnabout: Help for a New Life,* describes her recovery process from alcoholism and the evolution of WFS. Kirkpatrick used Emerson, Thoreau, and Unity Church philosophies in conjunction with cognitive-behavioral techniques and emphases on the support of peers and health promotion to develop WFS principles (Horvath, 1997). Women for Sobriety was based on the belief that women alcoholics have problems and needs different from male alcoholics—particularly regarding self-value, self-worth, and reduction of guilt. The shame and stigma of women alcoholics are addressed through positive affirmations to improve self-image.

Kaskutas (1994) states that women who attend WFS describe it as a supportive, nurturing, and safe environment that focuses on emphasizing the positive, building one's self-esteem, and addressing women's issues. Women for Sobriety also advocates individual application of the steps to the members' lives. The program encourages groups to be limited to less than 10 members so that participation and confidentiality are possible. Each group typically has co-moderators who facilitate the group, and a secretary/treasurer. Donations are used to assist the group in functioning. Videos, cassette tapes, literature, and monthly newsletters are available to its members.

Basic Concepts

Women for Sobriety is based on a Thirteen Statement Program designed to assist a woman in addressing her alcoholism and life-style by encouraging her emotional and spiritual growth. Members are encouraged to use the Thirteen Statements in any order they wish to use them. These Thirteen Statements of Acceptance are currently written as follows (Kirkpatrick, 1990):*

1. I have a life-threatening problem that once had me.
2. Negative thoughts destroy only myself.
3. Happiness is a habit I will develop.
4. Problems bother me only to the degree I permit them to.
5. I am what I think.
6. Life can be ordinary or it can be great.
7. Love can change the course of my world.
8. The fundamental object of life is emotional and spiritual growth.
9. The past is gone forever.
10. All love given returns.
11. Enthusiasm is my daily exercise.
12. I am a competent woman and have much to give life.
13. I am responsible for myself and my actions.

Since 1976, the wording of the Thirteen Steps has been changed to assist members in applying the program to their lives. The wording that has changed is as follows: Step 1 (from *drinking problem* to *life-threatening problem*), Step 2 (from *Negative emotions* to *Negative thoughts*), Step 10 (from *returns twofold* to *returns*), Step 12 (from *others* to *life*), and Step 13 (from *sisters* to *actions*).

The Thirteen Statements are formed into the six levels of the "New Life" program (see Figure 7.1). Level I focuses on acceptance of the disorder (Statement 1). Level II emphasizes changing negative thought patterns and tendencies toward guilt by focusing on new problem-solving approaches (Statements 2, 4, and 9). Level III encourages the creation of a new self-image (Statements 5 and 12). Level IV involves the emergence of new attitudes resulting in new behaviors (Statements 3, 6, and 11). Level V stresses the improvement of relationships (Statements 7 and 10). Level VI emphasizes the priorities in one's life, which are spiritual and emotional growth and taking responsibility for self (Statements 8 and 13).

*Source: Reprinted by permission, Women for Sobriety, Inc., PO Box 618, Quakertown, PA 18951-0618.

"New Life" Acceptance Program

1. I have a life-threatening problem that once had me.
2. Negative thoughts destroy only myself.
3. Happiness is a habit I will develop.
4. Problems bother me only to the degree I permit them to.
5. I am what I think.
6. Life can be ordinary or it can be great.
7. Love can change the course of my world.
8. The fundamental object of life is emotional and spiritual growth.
9. The past is gone forever.
10. All love given returns.
11. Enthusiasm is my daily exercise.
12. I am a competent woman and have much to give life.
13. I am responsible for myself and for my actions.

Freedom
Happiness
Liberation

Level VI:
Recognizing life's priorities: emotional and spiritual growth, self-responsibility

The fundamental object of life is emotional and spiritual growth. (8)
I am responsible for myself and for my actions. (13)

Level V:
Improving relationships as a result of our new feelings about self

Love can change the course of my world. (7)
All love given returns. (10)

Level IV:
Using new attitudes to enforce new behavior patterns

Happiness is a habit I will develop. (3)
Life can be ordinary or it can be great. (6)
Enthusiasm is my daily exercise. (11)

Level III:
Creating and practicing a new self-image

I am what I think. (5)
I am a competent woman and have much to give life. (12)

Level II:
Discarding negative thoughts, putting guilt behind, and practicing new ways of viewing and solving problems

Negative thoughts destroy only myself. (2)
Problems bother me only to the degree I permit them to. (4)
The past is gone forever. (9)

Level I:
Accepting Alcoholism as a physical disease

I have a life-threatening problem that once had me. (1)

FIGURE 7.1 **"New Life" Program**

Source: Reprinted by permission, Women for Sobriety, Inc. PO Box 618, Quakertown, PA 18951-0618.

In 1994, Men for Sobriety, a self-help program based on the same Thirteen Statements, was started by Dr. Kirkpatrick at the request of some men (Horvath, 1997). The focus is on issues experienced by men in recovery (Horvath, 1997). Meetings are currently held in major U.S. cities such as Washington and Boston.

Use in Counseling
Women for Sobriety and Men for Sobriety are organizations that can be used effectively to support the recovery process and to complement therapy. In terms of recovery, once again, clients can increase their sense of support, reduce their sense of isolation, and increase their self-regulation through involvement. With regard to therapy, the counselor needs knowledge of the philosophy of the organization, available local groups, and the fit of the philosophy with the counseling approach taken in recovery.

Strengths

Membership.   As with 12-step groups, anyone can call herself or himself a member of WFS or MFS. Once again, then, clients need to be aware of their potential vulnerability with regard to such open membership. There are no dues or fees for membership, so support is easily accessible. It may be especially beneficial for minority individuals who have experienced oppression (e.g., women, ethnic minorities, and gays/lesbians), to have a focus of empowerment. It may also be helpful to those who have unsuccessfully tried other self-help groups.

Spiritual/Religious.   The spiritual dimension, although mentioned in Statement 8, is not as emphasized as in 12-step programs. This deemphasis may make WFS a better match as a recovery program for the client who has religious/spiritual issues or does not see them as a critical component for his or her recovery.

Limitations

Open Membership.   As with any self-help group, clients need to be reminded that because membership is not screened, anyone can be present at the meetings.

Limited Accessibility.   Probably the main limitation of the program is its accessibility to clients. Because it is not as widespread as 12-step groups, there may not be as many meetings available to clients.

Sixteen Steps

History
In 1985, Charlotte Kasl informed her 12-step women's recovery group that she could no longer say the 12 Steps because they did not feel right to her, particularly due to the religious and ego-deflation wording of the steps (Judge, 1994; Kasl, 1992). Kasl (1992) summarized the struggles she and others experienced with the 12 Steps in her

1990 *Ms.* magazine article, "The Twelve Step Controversy." Her book, *Many Roads, One Journey: Moving Beyond the Twelve Steps* (1992), is based on seven years of workshops, projects, and interviews related to addiction recovery.

In the introduction to her book (Kasl, 1992), Kasl states she is writing (1) for women and minorities, who she views as having been historically neglected in addiction recovery approaches; and (2) to support individuals who want to use new healing models in addiction recovery. She describes her model as one based on empowerment and discovery. Her book has four main sections that examine the recovery controversy, the diversity of addiction, the recovery models, and the other healing opportunities such as the 16 Steps.

Basic Concepts
Kasl (1992) reports that she intentionally wrote the 16 Steps in the present tense because she believes healing is a process people go through together. The 16 Steps for discovery and empowerment are as follows:*

1. We affirm we have the power to take charge of our lives and stop being dependent on substances or other people for our self-esteem and security. *Alternative:* We admit we were out of control with/powerless over _____ , but have the power to take charge of our lives and stop being dependent on substances or other people for our self-esteem and security.
2. We come to believe that God/the Goddess/Universe/Great Spirit/Higher Power awakens the healing wisdom within us when we open ourselves to that power.
3. We make a decision to become our authentic Selves and trust in the healing power of the truth.
4. We examine our beliefs, addictions, and dependent behavior in the context of living in a hierarchal, patriarchal culture.
5. We share with another person and the Universe all those things inside of us for which we feel shame and guilt.
6. We affirm and enjoy our strengths, talents, and creativity, striving not to hide these qualities to protect others' egos.
7. We become willing to let go of shame, guilt, and any behavior that keeps us from loving our Selves and others.
8. We make a list of people we have harmed and people who have harmed us, and take steps to clear out negative energy by making amends and sharing our grievances in a respectful way.
9. We express love and gratitude to others, and increasingly appreciate the wonder of life and the blessings we *do* have.
10. We continue to trust our reality and daily affirm that we see what we see, we know what we know, and we feel what we feel.

---

11. We promptly acknowledge our mistakes and make amends when appropriate, but we do not say we are sorry for things we have not done and we do not cover up, analyze, or take responsibility for the shortcomings of others.
12. We seek out situations, jobs, and people that affirm our intelligence, perceptions, and self-worth and avoid situations or people who are hurtful, harmful, or demeaning to us.
13. We take steps to heal our physical bodies, organize our lives, reduce stress, and have fun.
14. We seek to find our inward calling, and develop the will and wisdom to follow it.
15. We accept the ups and downs of life as natural events that can be used as lessons for our growth.
16. We grow in awareness that we are interrelated with all living things, and we contribute to restoring peace and balance on the planet.

Kasl (1992) lists 12 common 16-Step group guidelines that include structure (purpose, format, and length), time sharing, moderator, group focus, collection and dispersion of dues, confidentiality, meeting place and time, member commitments, coping with severe member problems, giving notice of leaving the group, and letting go of individuals who leave the group.

Use in Counseling
As stated previously for other groups, the 16-Step group can also provide the recovering client with additional support, a decreased sense of isolation, and an increase of self-regulation. Again, the counselor needs to have an understanding of how the 16 Steps work, available groups in the area, and how well the philosophy matches the counseling approach.

Strengths

Membership.   The 16 Steps have the common self-help group advantages: Anyone can join without dues or fees, there are no membership requirements, and help can be obtained at times when the counselor may not be available. The empowerment emphasis, which may appeal to those who have experienced oppression, may help clients develop their sense of power and esteem as well as understand the role of the culture in encouraging their addiction. It may also be a helpful program for clients who have had negative experiences with other self-help programs.

Spiritual/Religious.   The 16 Steps may be desirable for clients with spiritual beliefs that are not necessarily Judeo-Christian. Because of the emphasis on different spiritual beliefs, the group may provide a variety of recovery role models. Not only will participants hear Judeo-Christian views at meetings but they will also hear other religious and spiritual perspectives that may be healing. The flexible interpretation encouraged for the steps may assist rebellious clients in "working" the steps in their daily lives.

Limitations

Open Membership.   As with all self-help groups, the counselor needs to remind the client that anyone can be a member of these groups. This strategy may help the client retain healthy boundaries with regard to group members.

Limited Accessibility.   One of the principal limitations of this model is its accessibility. Because of its newness, it may not be available for individuals in terms of location and/or frequency of meetings.

Complicated Language.   The wording of the steps may be too complicated for some clients. Also, clients who come from traditional Judeo-Christian backgrounds may struggle with some of the openness of the spiritual language.

Rational Recovery

History
Rational Recovery groups were started in 1985 by Jack Trimpey; in 1989, he published *Rational Recovery from Alcoholism: The Small Book.* In the preface of his book, he discusses how, as a clinical social worker, he heard clients discuss their difficulties with the AA 12-Step program, how he could not make sense of AA for himself, and how he decided to use his training as a rational emotive therapist to become his own therapist and encourage others to become their own therapists. Trimpey was able to overcome his drinking problem by using a rational approach (Horvath, 1997). Rational Recovery (RR) is based, then, on Albert Ellis's (1962) rational emotive therapy.

Basic Concepts
A client does not have to be abstinent to be a member of Rational Recovery (RR), but the program does encourage the use of a strategy called *addictive voice recognition training (AVRT)* (Rational Recovery, 1992). In this strategy, the client is aware of his or her rational voice and his or her addictive voice (also called the "beast") and learns to control them to make rational choices. Relapses are viewed more as learning experiences than failures. There are no steps, per se, to the program. In the appendix section of *The Small Book,* Trimpey provides an example of 13 steps, but he does not recommend them as steps that should summarize the program for everyone. These statements are not listed here at the request of Rational Recovery because the organization views them as obsolete (L. E. Trimpey, personal communication, November 25, 1997). Because RR is not a step program, Trimpey suggests that the reader make up his or her own RR ideas. The same flexibility is applied to meetings (Rational Recovery, 1992): Members are encouraged to attend meetings for 6 to 12 months as they learn

to be their own therapists. There are no fees for membership, although collections may be taken for meeting expenses. Rational Recovery has literature, videos, and a meeting directory available as well as its own journal, the *Journal of Rational Recovery.*

A group is facilitated by a trained counselor, who becomes less directive as the group develops, possibly serving later as a consultant to the group for special problems. In Chapter 13 of *The Small Book,* Trimpey (1989) offers 16 ground rules for individuals in RR groups, which include sharing and socializing at the individual's comfort level (sponsorship is not recommended); keeping conversations confidential and focused on addiction; making own decisions regarding usage and attendance at meetings; reading RR literature; supporting the group with donations of money, time, and energy; contacting the consultant when necessary; and refusing to allow observers to be present at meetings. Meetings focus on learning AVRT, where the member learns to recognize his or her addictive voice (Horvath, 1997). Trimpey believes that AVRT can help people without treatment or groups; therefore, since 1993, Rational Recovery focuses more on educating people about AVRT (Horvath, 1997). Current views on Rational Recovery are summarized in *Rational Recovery: The New Cure for Substance Addiction* (Trimpey, 1996).

Use in Counseling
As stated with the previous self-help groups, RR can provide the client with recovery support, thereby decreasing isolation and increasing self-regulation. The counselor making a referral to RR would best serve clients by being aware of the philosophy of the group, knowledge of local groups available, and the match of RR with the counselor's counseling philosophy.

Strengths

Membership.   Similar to the other self-help groups, RR allows anyone to become a member and it does not charge fees. It may be a helpful referral for clients who have negative experiences with other self-help groups. Galanter, Egelko, and Edwards (1993) write that the majority of members they studied were men who had previously attended AA. Finally, the use of a professional to develop, guide, and/or consult with the group may assist the group in developing and maintaining healthy group norms as well as monitor the type of members present.

Focus.   Rational Recovery makes help available to individuals struggling with addiction issues and may appeal to individuals who are unsure if they want to abstain, since a person can be attending meetings before deciding to stop using. The program may especially appeal to individuals who value looking at issues logically and rationally.

Spiritual/Religious.   Rational Recovery may appeal to clients who do not want to focus on a spiritual or religious dimension of recovery. No mention is made of this area as a necessary aspect of recovery.

Limitations

Limited Accessibility.   One of the prime limitations with RR may be its accessibility for clients in terms of location. Rational Recovery groups may not be available in as many areas as 12-step groups.

Limited Guidance.   Rational Recovery encourages clients to read RR literature, make their own interpretations of recovery, and trust their own logic. Therefore, RR may not be helpful to those who require more guidance in their recovery and those who are well defended about their addiction and/or other personal problems.

Secular Organization for Sobriety

History
James Christopher is the founder of Secular Organization for Sobriety/Save Our Selves (SOS). In his own addiction recovery process, he wrote "Sobriety without Supersti-tion," a 1985 *Free Inquiry* magazine article (Kasl, 1992), and in 1986, he began SOS, which was originally called Secular Sobriety Groups (SSG) (Christopher, 1997).

Basic Concepts
The groups are open to anyone struggling with any type of addiction problem and his or her family members and friends (Kasl, 1992). Through attending meetings, family members and friends, as well as the addict, can learn about the addiction cycle (Chris-topher, 1997). Addiction is viewed as a cycle involving a physiological need, a learned habit, and the denial of both; the sobriety cycle involves recognizing and accepting the addiction and making sobriety the top priority of one's life (Christopher, 1992). The philosophy is one of empowerment and esteem building based in abstinence and secularism. The SOS program (Christopher, 1988) offers six guidelines:*

1. To break the cycle of denial and achieve sobriety, we first acknowledge that *we are alcoholics.*
2. We *reaffirm* this truth daily and accept without reservation—one day at a time—the fact that, as sober alcoholics, we cannot and do not drink, *no matter what.*
3. Since drinking is not an option for us, we take whatever steps are necessary to continue our sobriety priority lifelong.
4. A high quality of life—the good life—can be achieved. However, life is also filled with uncertainties; therefore, we do not drink regardless of feelings, cir-cumstances, or conflicts.
5. We share in confidence with each other our thoughts and feelings as sober alco-holics.

Source: How to Stay Sober: Recovery without Religion by James Christopher (Amherst, NY: Prometheus Books). Copyright 1988. Reprinted by permission of the publisher.

6. Sobriety is our priority, and we are each individually responsible for our lives and our sobriety.

Meetings are organized according to the group members. There are no rigid guidelines or procedures. The organization offers a newsletter, which is printed four times a year, as well as literature, audiotapes, videotapes, a meeting directory, and a yearly national conference. Sponsorship is not encouraged because SOS does not believe in one person telling another how to live his or her life. Current information on SOS is available in the *Sobriety Handbook: The SOS Way* (SOS, 1997).

Use in Counseling
As with other self-help groups, SOS can provide support for recovery while decreasing social isolation and increasing self-regulation. Again, the counselor needs to be familiar with the philosophy of the group, how it matches his or her counseling philosophy, and knowledge of available groups in the area.

Strengths

Membership.   Secular Organization for Sobriety allows anyone to be a member and does not charge any dues or fees, so help is available to anyone who chooses to attend. It encourages empowerment and self-esteem building, which may be helpful to clients who have little or no experience "owning their power" and who have poor self-concepts. It may also be appealing to individuals who have had negative experiences with other self-help organizations.

Spiritual/Religious.   The program may be helpful to clients who do not feel as though they have spiritual or religious needs that require addressing in their addiction self-help program. A spiritual/religious focus to recovery is not encouraged.

Limitations

Open Membership.   As with other self-help groups, anyone can attend SOS meetings. In addition, the openness of who may attend (addicts as well as their family members and friends) may be uncomfortable for some clients.

Limited Accessibility.   These group meetings are likely to be held in major metropolitan areas, so SOS may also have the problem of limited accessibility for clients in certain areas. It is not as widespread as some of the 12-step programs.

Limited Guidance.   Secular Organization for Sobriety does not offer sponsorship and encourages flexibility in recovery interpretation and at meetings. As a result, SOS may not offer enough structure for some clients.

Self Management and Recovery Training

History

Self Management and Recovery Training (SMART) became a nonprofit organization in 1992 under the Rational Recovery Self-Help Network in order to oversee Rational Recovery support groups (Horvath, 1997). Disagreement between Jack Trimpey, RR founder, and the organization with regard to management and focus resulted in the two groups separating (Horvath, 1997). SMART was started in August 1994 by Dr. Joseph Gerstein, Dr. Tom Horvath (current president of SMART), and 12 other SMART Recovery board members throughout the United States. It evolved from Rational Recovery when the SMART Board of Directors voted to end their connection with Rational Recovery's founder, Jack Trimpey (Orr, 1996). The organization is headquartered in Cleveland, Ohio. Dr. William Knaus published *SMART Recovery: A Sensible Primer* in 1995. SMART, like Rational Recovery, is based on Albert Ellis's (1962) rational emotive therapy.

Basic Concepts

The SMART organization focuses on cognitive-behavioral approaches to changing self-destructive behavior: Controlling thoughts and emotions can result in empowerment to abstain. The emphasis of SMART is on motivation, coping skills, rational thinking, and life-style. The basis of the program is that in order to recover from chemical dependency, a person needs to be motivated, learn to resist urges as well as learn new ways to cope, and develop a positive life-style. The SMART organization stresses the present and the change of self-destructive behaviors in the present. It does not believe that addiction is a disease, but it does encourage abstinence. Sobriety is viewed as a choice and relapse is seen as a learning opportunity. Religion and spirituality may be helpful to an individual, but are not viewed as a part of the SMART program. SMART does not have any steps to follow, but it advocates the following ideas:*

1. I'm not "powerless" over alcohol or drugs, or other addictive behavior. I can certainly use some help, but I believe I can beat this problem, like millions of other people have.
2. Booze and other drugs don't jump into my body. I choose to use them, so I can choose not to and make it stick.
3. My substance use hurts me and others. I may feel good for a short time, but I suffer more in the long run. It is the "buy now—pay later" plan of life.
4. SMART can help me achieve my goal of sobriety, but I gain power by accepting personal responsibility for my life and what I put into my body.
5. Getting drunk or high is a way of indulging myself and trying to cope with stress, frustration, and anger. It's just not worth it!

*Source: Reprinted by permission, S.M.A.R.T. Recovery® Self-Help Network, 24000 Mercantile Road, Suite 11, Beachwood, OH 44122.

6. There are better ways of coping with life than intoxicating myself. Once I learn these, I will be willing to give up my addictive behavior permanently.
7. It makes sense to seek help to learn new approaches because whatever I've been doing hasn't been working.
8. I can learn from others and enjoy their support without depending on the group for the rest of my life.
9. Once I have mastered the proven methods of self-management offered by SMART, I can recover, graduate from the program and get on with my life.

Groups meet one or two times a week for about 90 minutes. Coordinators of the groups are lay professionals who have been trained by SMART. Some of them have a history of chemical dependency problems and some do not; SMART says it is not necessary for the coordinators to be in recovery, since the focus of the program is educational mental health. Most groups have a volunteer advisor who is a mental health professional to help with crisis or special situations. Donations are welcomed but not required for attendance. Individuals are not expected to attend the groups for the rest of their lives; they can attend for as long as they want, however.

Through dialogue, group members look at their drinking problem as well as their personal problems. One person presents one problem at a time and the group attempts to help the person solve the problem. One format suggestion for a group is PACES (Knaus, 1995):

1. (P) Problem identification (what happened)
2. (A) Active examination (feelings and actions of the person)
3. (C) Clarification of the problem (self-talk about drinking or using)
4. (E) Effect a measurable result (problem-solving actions that will reduce or eliminate drinking or using)
5. (S) Seek follow-up information (person gives a follow-up report at the next meeting)

Use in Counseling

Like the other self-help groups discussed, SMART can provide a client with a sense of belonging and encouragement to change addictive behavior. This self-help group's philosophy would be an excellent match for a counselor comfortable working within a cognitive-behavioral framework. Once again, a counseling referral needs to account for its philosophy and availability of the group for the client.

Strengths

Membership.   As with the other self-help groups, SMART allows people simply to say they are members; fees are not charged. It may be a good referral for clients who have had negative experiences with other self-help groups. Also, having trained lay professionals and possibly a mental health professional advisor would possibly screen out individuals who do not belong in the group or may contribute to poor health in the group.

Focus.   This program may appeal to clients who like to look at life rationally and focus on a problem. The structure of the meetings may be beneficial to some clients.

Spiritual/Religious.   Individuals who do not want to have religious or spiritual beliefs as a part of their recovery program may do well in this program. However, SMART does not prohibit people from having these as a part of their recovery program.

Limitations

Limited Accessibility.   The main limitation with SMART is that it may be available only to clients who live in a large metropolitan area.

Matching Self-Help Groups to Meet Client Needs

Helping a Client Find a Self-Help Group

Humphreys and Rappaport (1994) describe a *self-help group* as a voluntary group where each member is both the helper and helpee. All of the self-help groups reviewed seem to have some additional common factors: Each encourages (1) individuals to examine the need for a behavior change, (2) education of oneself regarding the addictive process as interpreted by the specific program, (3) some contact with others in similar situations, and (4) a personalization of the recovery process.

Helping a client find a group requires knowledge of one's own theoretical orientation, knowledge of the self-help group's philosophy and availability, and a knowledge of the client. Counselors are encouraged to spend some time determining the match of their theoretical orientation with the various self-help group philosophies. The availability of the various self-help groups, both nationally and locally, may temper the use of them in counseling. The counselor and client may develop a mix-and-match approach in terms of combining various literature with available meetings. The caution here is that the counselor not overwhelm the client with recovery options and information.

Prior to asking questions to understand a client better, a sensitive therapist may experience empathy for a client attending a new self-help group by imagining the following scenario: You walk into a room of strangers and, simply by entering the room, you are admitting that you have a problem that everyone in the room knows you have because you are there and this problem is one with which you have tried to address and failed. This sense of vulnerability and openness to strangers is commonly felt by individuals who are breaking an addictive pattern. In order to facilitate a match to such a group, all counselors need to be sensitive to clients' self-help group experiences, life-styles, and values in order to make the best match possible.

Questions to Ask

The following questions may be used directly in an interview with a client or can be used as a mental checklist by the counselor in terms of making a referral:

1. *What types of self-help groups are available where you live and/or work?* The counselor needs a list of all of the different types of self-help groups available in the client's community. This list needs to be shared and reviewed with the client. In some cities, lists of self-help groups are quite specific (nonsmoking, gay/lesbian, etc.) in their descriptions. In this situation, the client can review the descriptors of the group and determine the type of group he or she wants to try. Even if the therapist believes that the client is being too particular about the type of group, it is important that the client choose a group where he or she will anticipate feeling the most comfortable. After attending the chosen group, the individual may be more open-minded about attending another group. In the location where a list of groups is not very descriptive about the groups, the client will simply need to try the group and determine if it is one where he or she feels comfortable.

If the client is being treated in one location and lives in another, it is important that the client attend groups in the area where he or she plans to attend both during and after addiction treatment. If this is hard to arrange (e.g., the client is in a different state for treatment), it is critical to provide the client with a link in his or her hometown community for a similar self-help group. Sometimes, individuals will not want to attend groups near their homes for anonymity reasons. Some therapists may take issue with this approach; however, it is most important that clients attend groups in a setting where *they are comfortable* rather than one where their therapist believes they would or should be comfortable.

If a client has an extremely hectic schedule, it may be easier to attend a meeting during a work lunch hour or before or after work. Some work environments may allow meetings to be held in the workplace, and if a client is comfortable, he or she may be able to meet someone who can be supportive in the work environment. Some clients have also had employers participate actively in their treatment program, and these employers may work with the clients regarding lunch-hour extensions or connections with other recovering individuals in the company. For clients with child-care responsibilities, fitting their recovery meetings with their work schedule may assist them in attending meetings. Finally, an individual who travels frequently may need to obtain a national and/or international directory of self-help groups in order to locate a meeting in the area where he or she is traveling. Many groups have a contact person listed who can be reached prior to travel.

2. *When you look at your life, where and how is it easiest to fit in meetings?* The feasibility of meetings is critical for clients. Given their values, life-styles, and commitments, it is important that the counselor find a position between enabling clients to miss meetings (e.g., believing all of the reasons they cannot attend) and insisting that they attend meetings in spite of their life situation (e.g., expecting a single parent with children to attend 90 meetings in 90 days). If the client cannot attend any meetings in a week for numerous reasons, the therapist can tentatively assume that the client is being resistant. In this case, the therapist needs to explore the resistance with the client. Possibly the client is afraid to go to a meeting alone, angry at being required to attend meetings, or overwhelmed with life responsibilities. Encouraging clients to express their feelings regarding attendance at self-help group meetings can result in enhanced counseling. A discussion of apparent resistance may also encourage clients to discuss pragmatic recovery roadblocks (e.g., no babysitter available).

Some counselors may believe that a person needs to spend most of his or her recovery time in self-help meetings. This viewpoint is fitting with regard to particular circumstances. First, early in a person's recovery, attendance at as many self-help meetings as possible may be necessary to build supports for making a change. Also, attending meetings may provide the client with a "time filler" because he or she is no longer involved in securing and using alcohol or drugs. Finally, attending various meetings helps clients become exposed to different groups, different individuals, and different ways of being sober. However, the counselor needs to remember that clients did not necessarily sober up to spend all of their free time in meetings; they also need to build or rebuild relationships with significant others in their lives and learn to have fun without alcohol and drugs. Overall, clients need to attend as many recovery meetings as needed in order to stay sober. A minimum self-help group meeting of once a week is a good guideline to use.

3. *How comfortable are you with giving out your phone number to members of the self-help group?* Often, members of self-help groups share their phone numbers with one another. Those who are attending a group for the first time should think about the comfort level with sharing their phone numbers and then rehearse responses to such a request with their counselors if they do not want to share their numbers. Usually, individuals share only their first names and their phone numbers.

4. *How comfortable are you with being touched in a self-help group?* In some self-help groups, it is very common for members to hug each other and/or hold hands at the closing of the meeting. The new member in a group may need to consider how to respond to being touched in a group. This area may be of significant concern to the recovering person who has been physically and/or sexually abused.

Assessing a Group's Personality

Self-help groups, like individuals, have unique personalities. Often, clients need to attend the same group for five or six meetings to learn how the group tends to operate and the types of individuals in the group. Attending a meeting more than once can assist a client in developing a commitment to the recovery process, enhancing tolerance toward others, and developing impulse control.

After attending a meeting for the first time, there are a series of questions that can help the counselor and client assess the health of the group. The counselor can approach this area by asking the client to "walk me through the meeting step by step":

1. What was the meeting like overall? (Friendly? Hospitable?)

2. What was the meeting like physically? (Safe part of town? Easy parking? Comfortable room? Too much smoke in the room?)
3. How were you greeted? (Respectfully? Friendly?)
4. Was there anyone in the group with whom you felt particularly comfortable? (Potential sponsor/mentor?)
5. What was the topic of the meeting? (Relevant to recovery?)
6. Did everyone participate in the meeting? (Everyone spoke?)
7. Did you feel comfortable with the person (people) who seemed to direct the meeting? (Reasonable leader?)
8. Did you go early and/or stay late at the meeting? (Visit informally with others?)

These questions provide examples of how a group's health can be assessed. Some meetings are simply more open to newcomers, individuals who are in treatment, or those court-ordered to self-help groups. Note that some meetings, because of their location or openness to new members, may in time become overwhelmed with new individuals in recovery and have few members who can serve as recovery role models for clients. The overall atmosphere of the meeting might help the client determine that he or she needs to seek a meeting in a different location or one that is more compatible with his or her needs. For example, some meetings may be held in an undesirable part of town, and if the client needs to park some distance away from the building, this may increase the chances that the client will not attend or will not feel safe. An example of a difficult meeting room condition is that some meetings allow smoking, and it may be very difficult for the client to tolerate cigarette smoke.

Even though many self-help groups are committed to anonymity, it is quite legitimate for the client to describe individuals at the meeting without using names. For example, a client may describe a meaningful discussion at a meeting by saying, "A divorced woman with two children said she has a hard time trusting a Higher Power because of her life experiences." Finding out who greets the newcomers and how may help the counselor determine the appropriateness of the meeting for the client. Many types of people attend self-help groups; clients must understand that they cannot automatically trust all individuals who attend them. Some group members may approach new members with the intention of using them somehow (i.e., financially or sexually); self-help groups are not free from the social influences that exist at any social gathering.

Also, finding out who felt trustworthy to the client may indicate client issues as well as strengths. A female client, for example, may trust only males and may need to be encouraged to trust some women in the group. The questions that focus on topic, participation, and leaders in the group will assist the client in determining the norms of the group. This may be difficult to assess after one meeting, but these questions will heighten the client's awareness of the meetings attended and provide clues as to which groups are more comfortable for the client than others. A self-help group that gently but firmly encourages all members to participate can assist recovering clients in developing skills such as reading (if they read materials at the meeting), public speaking (if they need to introduce themselves), and social skills (conversing with others, setting boundaries, etc.). The final question about going early and/or staying late may also assist a client in fitting in with the group. Going early and/or staying late may allow the individual to participate in preparing the room for the meeting and provide him or her with both a sense of ownership in the meeting (assembling and disassembling the meeting room) and a chance to visit informally with others.

Guidelines for Healthy and Unhealthy Groups

These guidelines, in part, are determined by the comfort level of the client in the group. However, some general rules may be applied based on the previously stated questions. The following indicators of an unhealthy group are based on observations of more than one meeting:

1. An unwelcoming sense to the group
2. No greetings for newcomers or greetings that seem manipulative in nature
3. An unhappy, negative tone to the majority of the group members
4. An unwillingness by group members to discuss practical, optimistic approaches to recovery issues
5. Dominance by one or a few individuals who do not encourage participation by others
6. A general lack of participation and/or interest in the meeting

Kasl (1992) describes unhealthy groups as those that limit outside involvement, reading material, disagreement within the group, members from having different group roles, member discussion ("robot talk" or "jargon"), and member choices (on involvement in the group). She also describes these groups as grandiose, paranoid, lacking self-reflection, and having sexual needs met within the group.

By contrast, a healthy self-help group leaves the newcomer feeling like his or her presence was both wanted and needed by the group. This begins with genuine greetings by the group and continues with an optimistic, how-to recovery approach in the meeting, which involves the participation of everyone in the group who wants to participate. Individuals who belong to a healthy recovery self-help group are enthusiastic about the meeting and very willing to be supportive to one another.

Kasl (1992) describes healthy groups as flexible, open to self-scrutiny, having a clear focus, using conflict management approaches, and retaining a sense of humor. She also states that members in these groups want to participate at a personal level through regular attendance and to feel respected as a whole person, not exploited.

Helping a Client Find a Sponsor/Mentor

Some self-help groups (e.g., Alcoholics Anonymous) strongly encourage sponsorship, whereas others (e.g., Rational Recovery) do not believe it is necessary. Because self-help groups do not keep track of who sponsors who, sponsorship is an option for group participation, whether the group endorses it formally or not. Sponsorship is helpful in terms of providing a recovery role model for the client and someone the client has permission to contact if recovery issues surface. Because it is not necessary to have a sponsor to be in a self-help group, it is truly an option for the client. Regardless of whether a client formally asks a person to be his or her sponsor, the client can watch for an individual (or individuals) in self-help groups who seem to be living the recovery life the client aspires to live. The counselor can encourage conversations and activities with this individual who may provide the client with a strong role model, a recovery mentor. Fagan (1986) indicates that sponsors may be a significant component in the recovery process, especially early in recovery.

Some groups recommend same-sex sponsors in order to help the individual learn about recovery. However, this recommendation may also exist to discourage sexual relations in such an intimate relationship, and such a recommendation assumes a heterosexual bias. It may be best for the counselor to help the client choose a sponsor based on the qualities of the potential sponsor and to assist the client in considering the possible impact of gender on his or her choice of a sponsor.

The process of sponsor selection can be approached in a number of ways. For instance, a sponsor can be either temporary or permanent. If the counselor is familiar with different individuals in recovery in the local community, a temporary sponsor can be arranged for the client. This is a sponsorship where it is understood by both individuals that the relationship is only a tentative one that will stop as soon as the individual obtains a permanent sponsor. The danger of a counselor arranging for a sponsor is twofold: The sponsor may be linked with the client's treatment and the client may learn a passive approach to recovery. Understanding the client's history can assist the counselor in facilitating a discussion regarding effective sponsorship for the client, allowing the client to choose the most appropriate sponsor.

Asking an individual to be a temporary sponsor can be helpful to both the client and the sponsor. It allows both individuals to "try on" the relationship and determine if the match is a good one. At some point, the client can then ask the sponsor to be a permanent sponsor, or, if the match was not a good one, the relationship can simply dissolve and does not have to be addressed unless the client so desires.

Questions to Ask
If a client decides to obtain a sponsor, there are some questions he or she may find helpful to ask the potential sponsor:

1. Would you be willing to sponsor me in the self-help program?
2. What do you think it means to be a good sponsor?
3. What expectations would you have of me if I were your sponsee?
4. How often could I contact you about recovery questions?
5. Are there certain times of the day or week that you would not want me to contact you?
6. Have you ever sponsored anyone before?

Questions such as these may prevent misunderstandings and conflicts about the sponsor/sponsee relationship. The client can discuss the potential sponsor's answers with the counselor in order to determine the quality of the match. Even though the client may obtain appealing answers from the potential sponsor, it is important that the client watch the behavior of the sponsor over time to see if the verbal responses match the sponsor's behavior, at least most of the time. For example, a sponsor who promises accessibility to a client and then is usually unavailable for recovery support can be both frustrating and discouraging to the client. The counselor can use the following guidelines in helping the client find a match.

Guidelines for a Healthy/Unhealthy Sponsor/Mentor

Once again, there are no absolute guidelines for a healthy sponsor/sponsee relationship because recovering clients have very different needs. An appropriate sponsor for one client may be inappropriate for another. There are some tendencies, however, that may discourage a client's recovery process. An unhealthy sponsor may be:

1. An individual who promises *always* to be available for the person
2. An individual who views sponsorship as a legitimate means to control another person.
3. An individual who uses sponsorship as a means to use a person in recovery (i.e., for sexual or financial gratification)
4. An individual who discourages the person to think for himself or herself; rather, the individual tells the person what to think and how to act
5. An individual who has unrealistic expectations of the person's recovery
6. An individual who is unavailable to the person
7. An individual who is highly critical and judgmental of the person
8. An individual who has a relatively short recovery time (less than a year sober)

By contrast, the healthy sponsor is realistic in the expectations of himself or herself as well as the sponsee and views sponsorship as a role modeling of recovery. Firm, clear boundaries are set between the sponsor and the sponsee, preventing the sponsee from being used by or using the sponsor. A healthy sponsor is also one who is willing to explore the options facing the sponsee rather than approaching problem solving simplistically. Finally, a healthy sponsor is one who is available and supportive to the sponsee, and one who has some significant time in recovery so that the sponsee can draw on the sponsor's experiences.

Special Issues

Small-Town Concerns

A number of issues arise in relation to small-town recovery concerns. First, there may be a limited number of types of self-help groups and a limited number of self-help meetings in general. With regard to limited types of groups, small towns may only have Alcoholics Anonymous meetings available. For the client to whom this self-help type of group does not seem an option, the counselor can work with him or her at developing a tolerance toward the philosophy and "translate" it into a "language" that makes sense to the client. For the counselor unable to do the so-called translation, it may be helpful to suggest that the client approach the most "open" individual at a meeting for assistance with the program; this would be a person who has been sober a few years and views the recovery process as unique to each individual. Attendance at meetings can also be supplemented with readings from another type of self-help group.

When a counselor in a small town makes a referral to a self-help group, it is important to warn the client that meetings may be listed as active, but meetings may have stopped due to a small number of participants. This warning may be helpful to the client who attends a meeting at a listed site and then discovers no one is there. Also, if a client attends one meeting in a small town and presents a list he or she has been given of potential meetings, typically a member of the self-help group can let the client know which groups are still active.

Another small-town concern is the amount of anonymity provided by the meeting. Generally, people in a small town know one another's business. This may include where and when the self-help groups are held. All clients referred to self-help groups in small towns need to keep this fact in mind. Some clients may prefer to drive to a different location or a larger city for self-help meetings in order to preserve their anonymity.

Finally, the topics discussed in a small-town meeting may need to be discussed between the counselor and the client before the client brings them up in a meeting. Even general discussions of individuals and organizations in a small town may cause others to know exactly who and what is being discussed at the meeting. It may be more helpful to the client who does not want others to know his or her specific concerns to talk in the meeting about general themes and save the details of the recovery struggle for their sponsor and/or their counselor.

Anonymity

Generally, members of self-help groups make a commitment not to talk specifically about who is present at a meeting. This encourages people to share freely in a group. Clients need to understand that there is no guarantee of anonymity in a group and that what they say may be talked about outside of a meeting. Although this may inhibit clients in their speech, it is critical that they are informed of the nonregulatory function of self-help groups.

Summary

This chapter has reviewed 12-step groups (AA, NA, CA), and four alternatives to 12-step groups (WFS, 16 Steps, RR, SOS) in terms of their history, basic concepts, strengths, and limitations. Each group has in common a desire to help people break out of their habitual patterns with alcohol and drugs. Each group also varies in terms of its development and philosophy. Counselors referring clients to these groups need to be aware of the strengths and limitations of each group in order to assist clients in locating a group that meets the clients' idiosyncratic recovery needs.

DISCUSSION EXERCISE 1

Match the following individual descriptors with the most appropriate self-help groups by making an *X* under the group heading.

Descriptor	12 Steps	WFS	16 Steps	RR	SOS	SMART
Has desire to stop using						
Travels frequently						
Lives in a small town						
Is an ethnic minority						
Is female						
Is nonreligious/aspiritual						
Is nonreligious/spiritual						
Likes structure/order						
Is highly self-critical						
Has high shame/guilt						
Has low self-esteem						
Has little sense of power						
Is cognitive focused						
Does not like 12 steps						

DISCUSSION EXERCISE 2

Your client has difficulty with each of the following life problems. Which step for each of the respective programs would you suggest your client work on and why?

Life Problem	12 Steps	WFS	16 Steps	RR	SOS	SMART
"Knows-it-all"						
Relapsed						
Ashamed/guilty						
Oversensitive						
Mistrustful						
Future-anxious						
Drug denial						
Defensive						
Secretive						
Proud						
Angry						

ADDICTION SUPPORT GROUP INFORMATION

12-Step Programs

1. Adult Children of Alcoholics
   Central Service Board
   P.O. Box 3216
   Torrance, CA 90510
   (310)534-1815
   www.recovery.org/acoa/acoa.html

2. Al-Anon Family Group Headquarters
   1600 Corporate Landing Parkway
   Virginia Beach, VA 23454-5617
   (757)563-1600

3. Alcoholics Anonymous
   World Services Inc.
   P.O. Box 459
   Grand Central Station
   New York, NY 10163
   (212)870-3400
   www.alcoholics-anonymous.org

4. Cocaine Anonymous
   3740 Overland Avenue
   Suite C
   Los Angeles, CA 90034-6337
   (310)559-5833
   (800)347-8998 (referral line)
   www.ca.org
   cawso@ca.org

5. Co-Dependents Anonymous
   (602)277-7991
   www.ourcoda.org
   info@ourcoda.org

6. Nar-Anon Family Group
   Headquarters World Service Office
   P.O. Box 2562
   Palos Verdes Peninsula, CA 90274
   (310)547-5800

7. Narcotics Anonymous
   World Service Office
   P.O. Box 9999
   Van Nuys, CA 91409
   (818)773-9999
   www.wsoinc.com
   info@wsoinc.com

Alternatives to 12-Step Programs

1. Rational Recovery Systems (RR)
   Lotus Press
   P.O. Box 800
   Lotus, CA 95651
   (916)621-4374
   (800)303-CURE
   (916)621-2667 (voice and fax)
   http://www.rational.org/recovery
   rrc@rational.org

2. Secular Organizations for Sobriety
   5521 Grosvenor Boulevard
   Los Angeles, CA 90066
   (310)821-8430
   (310)821-2610 (fax)
   http://www.codesh.org/sos/
   sosla@loop.com

3. SMART Recovery (SMART)
   24000 Mercantile Road
   Suite 11
   Beachwood, OH 44122
   (216)292-0220
   (216)831-3776 (fax)
   www.smartrecovery.com
   SRMail1@aol.com

4. Women for Sobriety (WFS)
   P.O. Box 618
   Quakertown, PA 18951-0618
   (215)536-8026
   http://www.mediapulse.com/wfs
   WFSobriety@aol.com

5. Sixteen Steps (16 Steps)
   Many Roads, One Journey PACKET
   362 N. Cleveland Avenue, Suite 1
   St. Paul, MN 55104
   (608)249-9076
   members.aol.com/empower16/steps.htm
   empower16@aol.com

6. American Self-Help Clearinghouse
   Northwest Covenant Medical Center
   25 Pocono Road
   Denville, NJ 07834
   (201)625-7101 (group information)
   (201)625-9565 (administration)
   (201)625-8848 (fax)

SUGGESTED READINGS

Alcoholics Anonymous World Services. (1953). *Twelve steps and twelve traditions.* New York: Author.

Alcoholics Anonymous World Services. (1976). *Alcoholics Anonymous* (3rd ed.). New York: Author.

Christopher, J. (1988). *How to stay sober: Recovery without religion.* Buffalo, NY: Prometheus Books.

Christopher, J. (1992). *SOS sobriety.* Buffalo, NY: Prometheus.

Cocaine Anonymous. (1993). *Hope, faith, & courage.* Los Angeles: Author.

Kasl, C. D. (1992). *Many roads, one journey: Moving beyond the 12 steps.* New York: HarperCollins.

Kasl, C. (1995). *Yes, you can: A guide to empowerment groups.* USA: Author.

Kirkpatrick, J. (1978). *Turnabout: Help for a new life.* New York: Doubleday.

Kirkpatrick, J. (1981). *A fresh start.* Dubuque, IA: Kendell-Hunt.

Kirkpatrick, J. (1990). *Stages of the "new life" program.* Quakertown, PA: Women for Sobriety.

Knaus, W. (1995). *SMART Recovery: A sensible primer.* United States: SMART.

Narcotics Anonymous (1982). *Narcotics Anonymous.* United States: C.A.R.E.N.A..

Secular Organizations for Sobriety/Save Our Selves (SOS). (1997). *Sobriety handbook: The SOS way.* Oakland, CA: LifeRing Press.

Trimpey, J. (1989). *Rational Recovery for alcoholism: The small book.* New York: Delacorte.

Trimpey, J. (1996). *Rational recovery: The new cure for substance addiction.* New York: Pocket.

REFERENCES

Alcoholics Anonymous World Services. (1953). *Twelve steps and twelve traditions.* New York: Author.

Alcoholics Anonymous World Services. (1976). *Alcoholics Anonymous* (3rd ed.). New York: Author.

Alcoholics Anonymous World Services. (1991). *Twelve steps and twelve traditions.* New York: Author.

Bradley, A. M. (1988). Keep coming back. *Alcohol Health & Research World, 15,* 194–199.

Bristow-Braitman, A. (1995). Addiction recovery: 12-Step programs and cognitive-behavioral psychology. *Journal of Counseling & Development, 73,* 414–418.

Christopher, J. (1988). *How to stay sober: Recovery without religion.* Buffalo, NY: Prometheus Books.

Christopher, J. (1992). *SOS sobriety.* Buffalo, NY: Prometheus.

Christopher, J. (1997). Secular organizations for sobriety. In J. H. Lowinson, P. Ruiz, R. B. Millman, & J. G. Langrod (Eds.), *Substance abuse: A comprehensive textbook* (3rd ed.) (pp. 396–399). Baltimore: Williams & Wilkins.

Ellis, A. (1962). *Reason and emotion in psychotherapy.* New York: Lyle Stuart.

Fagan, R. W. (1986). The use of volunteer sponsors in the rehabilitation of skid-row alcoholics. *Journal of Drug Issues, 16,* 321–337.

Flores, P. J. (1988). Alcoholics Anonymous: A phenomenological and existential perspective. *Alcoholism Treatment Quarterly, 5,* 73–94.

Galanter, M., Egelko, S., & Edwards, H. (1993). Rational recovery: Alternative to AA for addiction? *American Journal of Drug and Alcohol Abuse, 19,* 499–510.

Gifford, P. D. (1991). A.A. and N.A. for adolescents. *Journal of Adolescent Chemical Dependency, 1,* 101–120.

Horvath, A. T. (1997). Alternative support groups. In J. H. Lowinson, P. Ruiz, R. B. Millman, & J. G. Langrod (Eds.), *Substance abuse: A comprehensive textbook* (3rd ed.) (pp. 390–396). Baltimore: Williams & Wilkins.

Humphreys, K. (1993). Psychotherapy and the twelve step approach for substance abusers: The limits of integration. *Psychotherapy, 30,* 207–213.

Humphreys, K., & Rappaport, J. (1994). Researching self-help/mutual aid groups and organizations: Many roads, one journey. *Applied and Preventive Psychology, 3,* 217–231.

James, W. (1936). *The varieties of religious experience.* New York: Modern Library. (Original work published 1902).

Johnson, P. N., & Chappel, J. N. (1994). Using AA and other 12-step programs more effectively. *Journal of Substance Abuse Treatment, 11,* 137–142.

Johnson, P. N., & Phelps, G. L. (1991). Effectiveness in self-help groups: Alcoholics Anonymous as a prototype. *Family and Community Health, 14,* 22–27.

Judge, M. G. (1994). Recovery's next step. *Common Boundary, 12,* 16–24.

Kaskutas, L. (1994). What do women get out of self-help? Their reasons for attending Women For Sobriety and Alcoholics Anonymous. *Journal of Substance Abuse Treatment, 11,* 185–195.

Kasl, C. (1990). The twelve step controversy. *Ms., 1,* 30–31.

Kasl, C. D. (1992). *Many roads, one journey: Moving beyond the 12 steps.* New York: HarperCollins.

Khantzian, E. J., & Mack, J. E. (1994). How AA works and why it's important for clinicians to understand. *Journal of Substance Abuse Treatment, 11,* 77–92.

Kirkpatrick, J. (1978). *Turnabout: Help for a new life.* New York: Doubleday.

Kirkpatrick, J. (1990). *Stages of the "new life" program.* Quakertown, PA: Women for Sobriety.

Knaus, W. (1995). *SMART recovery: A sensible primer.* United States: SMART.

Kurtz, E. (1988). *A.A.: The story.* San Francisco: Harper and Row.

Le, C., Ingvarson, E. P., & Page, R. C. (1995). Alcoholics Anonymous and the counseling profession: Philosophies in conflict. *Journal of Counseling and Development, 73,* 603–609.

Miller, G., Sack, T., & Simmons, K. (1994). Sexual abuse and alcohol: Women survivors [Summary]. *Proceedings of the Fourth International Counseling Conference.* Vancouver, British Columbia.

Nace, E. P. (1997). Alcoholics anonymous. In J. H. Lowinson, P. Ruiz, R. B. Millman, & J. G. Langrod (Eds.), *Substance abuse: A comprehensive textbook* (3rd ed.) (pp. 383–390). Baltimore: Williams & Wilkins.

Narcotics Anonymous. (1982). *Narcotics Anonymous.* United States: C.A.R.E.N.A..

Orr, A. D. (1996, August/September). SMART Recovery: A new approach to self-help. *Epikrisis:* North Carolina Governor's Institute on Alcohol and Substance Abuse.

Rational Recovery. (1992). *Self-empowered recovery from substance dependency.* Lotus, CA: Rational Recovery.

Riordan, R. J., & Walsh, L. (1994). Guidelines for professional referral to Alcoholics Anonymous and other twelve step groups. *Journal of Counseling and Development, 72,* 351–355.

Robertson, N. (1988, February 21). The changing world of Alcoholics Anonymous. *The New York Times Magazine,* pp. 40, 42–44, 47, 92.

Secular Organizations for Sobriety/Save Our Selves (SOS). (1997). *Sobriety handbook:*

The SOS way. Oakland, CA: LifeRing Press.

Talbott, G. D. (1990). Commentary on "Divine intervention and the treatment of chemical dependency." *Journal of Substance Abuse, 2,* 46–471.

Trimpey, J. (1989). *Rational Recovery from alcoholism: The small book.* New York: Delacorte.

Trimpey, J. (1996). *Rational recovery: The new cure for substance addiction.* New York: Pocket.

CHAPTER

8 Brief Therapy and Addiction Counseling

PRETEST

1. What is brief therapy?
2. What are some of the attitudes for and against brief therapy?
3. How does brief therapy affect screening?
4. How does brief therapy affect interviews?
5. What are some of the different theoretical orientations of brief therapy?
6. What are some interventions used in these different theoretical orientations?
7. What are some of the obstacles in working with brief therapy?
8. What are some forms of resistance with brief therapy?
9. What are some difficult clients with regard to brief therapy?
10. How can a counselor evaluate failures and successes of brief therapy?

This chapter will present a definition of *brief therapy* as well as its historical development. Attitudes of counselors toward brief therapy and the impact of brief therapy on screening and interviewing clients will be examined. The chapter then reviews various theoretical orientations and interventions of brief therapy and discusses difficulties with brief therapy in terms of obstacles, resistance, and types of clients. Finally, suggestions on how counselors can evaluate treatment effectiveness will be provided. Although counseling in general will be discussed, addictions counseling will be highlighted throughout the text.

Overall, brief therapy focuses on specific goals within a limited number of counseling sessions to enhance a client's coping abilities so he or she can manage future situations in an improved manner (Nugent, 1994). This type of therapy is also labeled *solution-focused therapy* and *planned short-term psychotherapy*. The differences in terminology have been influenced by managed health care and the different theoretical orientations (Bloom, 1997). In this type of therapy, the following aspects are common (Koss & Shiang, 1994):

1. Intervention is prompt and early.
2. Therapists are active and directive.
3. Goals are specific and time limited.

4. Therapy focus is on the here and now.
5. Limited goals are to reduce symptoms and enhance coping.
6. Therapists remain focused on goals, quickly assess problems and resources, obtain necessary information to work with the situation, and have a flexible intervention approach.

Historical Development

Although brief therapy may be amenable to counseling work due to current counseling constraints by mental health or managed health care systems, brief therapy did not emerge due to these influences. Bloom (1997) reports that *planned* short-term psychotherapy began in the early and mid-1960s along with the community mental health movement: Treatment was planned to achieve therapeutic outcomes within a limited period of time. In the 1960s, there was a need to provide efficient, effective, and prompt counseling to as many individuals as possible, and it was found that short time spans of counseling could result in significant changes for clients. Brief therapy also became important in the late 1980s because of an interest by counselors and insurance companies in efficient and less expensive counseling due to fewer financial resources, higher costs, and an increase in demand for counseling (Nugent, 1994). In the 1990s, short-term counseling has become even more appealing because it is viewed as efficient, effective, and less costly (Nugent, 1994).

Currently, addiction counselors may be more open to using brief therapy theories and techniques for a variety of reasons. First, as discussed in Chapter 1, the reality of mental health agencies' and managed health care systems' financial constraints (e.g., a limited number of sessions) may encourage counselors to consider such a model. Second, counselors who have large caseloads or who work with clients only interested in having a few counseling sessions may use brief therapy because it helps them retain a professional balance and realistic perspective of therapy with their clients. Third, counselors use this therapy because they believe that if goals can be achieved in a shorter period of time, they should be.

Attitudes

Often, counselors who are not specifically trained in brief therapy techniques will approach this type of counseling as though it is of less quality and less effective. Bloom (1997) contrasts the views of long-term counselors with short-term counselors. Long-term counselors view therapy as a forum in which to change basic character, believe that client complaints represent deeper problems, maintain that there cannot be too much therapy, and see therapy as centrally important to the client's life. By contrast, short-term counselors focus on more limited interventions with the individual, which can occur in daily life, see the complaints as legitimate in and of themselves, believe that therapy can be too long; and view therapy as just one important aspect of someone's life. Traditional counselor training may condition counselors to be biased against the use of brief therapy, which could be beneficial for their clients.

In training, counselors may be encouraged to equate length of counseling with the strength of the therapeutic alliance; increased resolution of client resistance, transference, and countertransference issues; more sensitive addressing of termination; and improved life functioning (Talmon, 1990). Counselors may need to reexamine these attitudes, however, in order to avoid waiting lists and to provide treatment for clients who may not otherwise receive it (Bloom, 1997). At the same time, counselors need to remember that brief therapy may not work with all individuals from all cultural settings. Steenbarger (1993) cautions that brevity and diversity in counseling may not be a good match. For example, effective brief therapy work with clients who are not empowered may depend not only on the health of the client but also on that of the environment and culture of the client.

In terms of shifting perspectives toward brief therapy, Talmon (1990) suggests that counselors see therapy as beginning from the moment of first contact with clients and that assessment and therapy overlap throughout the counseling process. The blending of assessment and therapy may assist the counselor in more readily adapting a brief therapy approach: Treatment begins when contact begins rather than an assessment period followed by a treatment period. Also, a here-and-now therapy focused on changing client perceptions of one issue may result in both the client and counselor experiencing less pressure to produce extensive change. Rather, the client may be more willing to change and celebrate small victories with the counselor (Talmon, 1990). As a result, counseling can be viewed as a series of small changes leading to larger change. When counselors do not know that they will see their clients from session to session, each session needs to be viewed as a one-time opportunity to have some impact on the clients' lives: Counselors need to make the most out of the sessions with their clients. Therefore, a shift in self-view by counselors needs to occur. Counselors must see themselves as consultants to clients: Consultation about problems occurs in sessions, whereas the main therapy work may happen outside of the sessions, during the clients' day-to-day lives. Counselors are teaching clients to be their own therapists.

Counselors working with addicted clients may legitimately ask, How can I use brief therapy with such a long-standing, deeply entrenched problem as addiction? The answer is that the approach requires a shift in perspective. Changing habits requires small, successive changes over time with support for such changes to occur. The counselor, as consultant, can help the client make changes with the addiction (avoid using alcohol/drugs) while assisting the client in creating a support network to change through education (bibliotherapy), treatment (relapse prevention), and community support (self-help groups). Addiction therapy may be brief in that a number of sessions may occur within a short period of time with follow-up visits or that sessions may be spread out over a longer period of time.

Screening and Interviewing

Screening

Brief therapy may not work for every client; therefore, screening is an important aspect of this type of therapy. Bloom (1997) indicates that there are basically two ways to look at selection criteria. In the first view, every client can begin therapy within a time-limited focus. In the second view, counselors may select clients according to the client's motivation, ability to establish a working alliance, history of relationships, ability to experience thoughts and feelings and reflect on them, and ability to focus. Typically, clients with severe, chronic pathology, history of treatment failure, problems with reality, and poor motivation would not benefit from this short-term form of therapy, although this type of client may be difficult to treat within any therapy context.

Counselors working with addicted clients may treat all of their clients initially with a brief therapy focus. As stated previously, the counselor would be active and direct in sessions, intervene promptly and early in treatment, focus on the here-and-now with specific time-limited goals to reduce addiction symptoms, and enhance coping abilities to stay sober. The counselor assesses the client's problems and resources regarding the addiction, obtains necessary information to treat the addiction, and is flexible in treatment, particularly with regard to relapse. This approach may be appealing to counselors who are comfortable in the brief therapy focus or who are required to work within this framework given the work setting or the client's situation (motivation, financial assets, etc.).

Counselors who are working in a setting where they can screen their clients need to determine the type of clients they can best serve given the setting. Facts such as level of addiction, reality problems, motivation, as well as number of previous treatments and responses to treatment need to be considered. By setting limits as to the type of clients who can be treated in therapy, the counselor can be more effective and possibly find the work with addicted clients more rewarding. Setting limits with the types of addicted clients the counselor is willing to treat will require that the counselor have an extensive referral list of other counselors and agencies who can be helpful to the addicted client.

The counselor begins the screening and counseling process by approaching the initial contact with an openness to his or her own perceptions of the situation. If the client contacts the counselor by phone or through an intake session, the counselor can begin brief therapy by suggesting that the client become aware of the problem even more intensely and think of how he or she wants the situation to be different in the future. This encouragement to be aware may help the client shift from a present to a future focus (Talmon, 1990). A client's willingness to participate in such a process will indicate his or her level of commitment to counseling and can enhance the beginning aspects of counseling.

Interviewing

The information covered in the interview, as well as who is present in the interview, will be determined by a combination of who referred the client to counseling and why, who was able to attend the session or who was asked, and the counselor's orientation to counseling. Talmon (1990) suggests that the counselor examine three areas in the interview to facilitate the brief therapy screening process. These three areas focus on if the counselor is the best counselor for the client, who the client is, and if there is a hidden agenda. Answers to these self-directed questions may assist the counselor in determining if brief therapy is the best approach with this client or what goals can be realistically achieved within the context of brief therapy.

Talmon (1990) also suggests that historically focused questions be minimized and that not much time be spent on the event that facilitated the referral for counseling. Rather, in the interview, the counselor should have a familiarity with mental status exams, client expectations, and matching counselor style and client need.

Good screening criteria in combination with a thorough interview may be beneficial for both counselor and client even if a referral cannot be made. The screening criteria and the interview process will assist the counselor in establishing realistic goals with the client. Such a realistic treatment focus may reduce frustration levels for both counselor and client, assist them in avoiding power struggles, and benefit both in terms of the goals they attempt to achieve. For example, the counselor working at an agency who is assigned a court-ordered client who is not interested in being sober as a long-term goal can use this screening information to develop a realistic treatment plan. While the client may be ordered to be abstinent during the treatment, the counselor can focus on educating the client about addiction and motivating him or her in terms of remaining abstinent. This realistic focus may prevent power struggles regarding their different views about addiction and recovery and may actually result in the client being more motivated to seek treatment.

Theoretical Orientations and Interventions

The acronym FRAMES represents six aspects in brief therapy treatment (Miller & Sanchez, 1994): feedback, responsibility, advice, menu, empathy, and self-efficacy. Hester and Bien (1995) clarify these aspects of counseling in terms of the substance-abusing client. Therapeutic *feedback* may be needed because the client may not have noticed the negative feedback of his or her alcohol/drug usage. Hester and Bien (1995) explain that addicts may not be aware of negative consequences because they are delayed while the positive effects of using alcohol/drugs are more immediate. Also, some clients may receive feedback on their usage, but not absorb the information because it is given in a negative and judgmental manner. Giving feedback in a nonjudgmental manner allows the client to learn about the negative aspects of the alcohol/

drug usage. For example, by using the words *addiction* and *disease,* the counselor makes the client responsible for his or her current usage, but not for the development of the substance abuse problem (Friedman & Fanger, 1991). With regard to *responsibility,* the client needs to be aware that he or she is responsible for the choice to use or not use, thereby avoiding power struggles. *Advice* from the counselor needs to be avoided in order to encourage the client's choice to act in ways that will either facilitate or inhibit recovery. *Menu* means that the client is presented with options to choose from with regard to changing his or her substance-using behavior. The *empathy* conveyed by the therapist listening to the client's story is helpful in the establishment of a collaborative relationship in counseling. The counselor needs to encourage a sense of *self-efficacy,* where the client can view himself or herself as able to change the substance-using pattern. Regardless of the counselor's brief therapy theoretical orientation, the FRAMES model can be used to guide the brief therapy approach with the addicted client.

Bloom (1997) divides the theoretical approaches to planned short-term psychotherapy into psychodynamic, cognitive and behavioral, and strategic and systemic. A few of these theories will be chosen from each of these categories for application to addictions counseling.

Psychodynamic

Marmor (1968) states that there are five common beliefs to psychodynamic approaches:

1. Human behavior is motivated.
2. The person is not aware of this type of motivation.
3. Biology and experiences shape a person's personality.
4. Disturbances in thoughts, feelings, and behaviors result from contradictory feedback.
5. Early experiences play an important role in later reactions.

Two psychodynamic approaches—Bloom's focused single-session therapy (1997) and Davanloo's broad-focus psychotherapy (1980)—will be examined.

Bloom's (1997) overall objectives are to help clients uncover something significant and to help them begin a therapeutic process. In order to assist clients in learning about themselves, Bloom suggests the following guidelines for the counselor:

1. Focus on a problem.
2. Present simple ideas.
3. Be active in the latter part of the session (avoid self-disclosure, ask open-ended questions, learn the language the client speaks, provide simple information, and have the responsibility of the communication lie with the client).
4. Explore and present tentative interpretations.

5. Use empathy.
6. Be aware of the time.
7. Minimize factual questions.
8. Do not focus too much on the event that brought the client to counseling.
9. Avoid side issues.
10. Do not overestimate what the client knows about himself or herself.

These approaches may assist the addicted individual in obtaining clarity about his or her addiction as well as assist the counselor in making the assessment and possible referral for the client.

A few of Bloom's (1997) objectives need to be emphasized in working with addicted clients. The counselor has a ready-made focus on the client's problem: It is an addiction. However, depending on the reasons the client is referred for counseling (e.g., referred by another rather than self-referred), the counselor may need to help the client develop a problem focus that is appealing to both the referral source and the client. Learning the language spoken by the client can also facilitate a problem focus. Metaphors used by the client or interests or values expressed can be used by the counselor to communicate information about addiction recovery. For example, the client who is in treatment only because a court order states he must get counseling may, in conversation, express an interest in car racing. The counselor may use this interest as a way to provide information about recovery: Like a car needs oil to run, an addict needs to attend treatment and self-help groups in order to stay sober. Simple information and ideas are also important in counseling. A person new to the recovery process may be overwhelmed by the consequences of use and intense emotions, so the simpler the information is presented, the more likely it will be remembered. Finally, avoidance of side issues may be necessary, especially with individuals who have been referred to counseling by others.

To begin a chain reaction of a therapeutic process, Bloom (1997) suggests that the interview focus on the myths the client has about self and others. In addition, Bloom (1997) suggests that the counselor (1) acknowledge the work the client has already done outside of the session, (2) be aware of the client's strengths, (3) help build social supports, (4) educate the client when necessary, (5) add additional therapy sessions if necessary, and (6) have a follow-up plan.

To develop a chain reaction of therapy, the counselor needs to help the client examine the ways he or she has tried to stop using and how these strengths can be used at this point in recovery. The importance of social networks, especially with a recovering community that makes sense to the client, can help the client stay sober. The development of a solid relapse prevention plan is also necessary to determine when future counseling will occur and what other ingredients are necessary in the client's life to help recovery occur. This chain reaction of therapy may be especially helpful with addicted clients in terms of breaking their denial of addiction and helping them explore what recovery may mean for them.

The theoretical concepts from Davanloo's theory (Bloom, 1997; Davanloo, 1980) may be of most assistance with addicted clients who are in the triangle of conflict or the triangle of person. The *triangle of conflict* has one of the following items at each point on the triangle: impulse, anxiety, and defense. The client experiences an unacceptable impulse, which increases his or her anxiety, which results in a defensive reaction. For the addicted client, the defense would be the addiction. The counselor needs to assist the client in determining the impulses leading to the anxiety that results in the chemical usage behavior. For example, a recovering addicted client may have a lot of difficulties with his father. When he has contact with his father, his impulse is to get high, which may increase his anxiety, which may result in him using alcohol/drugs to defend against the anxiety.

The second triangle is the *triangle of person.* At each point on the triangle is one of the following: past, present, and therapist. In this triangle, significant people are considered to be a part of each of these, and the client's reactions toward the therapist are similar to those he or she experienced in the past or in the present. This triangle may assist the counselor in understanding the client's transference and enable the counselor to work more effectively with the transference. For the addicted client, issues with a significant female in his or her life (e.g., mother, intimate partner) may be projected on to a female counselor. A counselor with this understanding can assist the client in breaking out of these interactional patterns by pointing them out to the client and encouraging the client to try out different behaviors.

Although Davanloo's theory (Bloom, 1997; Davanloo, 1980) does not suggest the triangle be used in this manner, the concept of the triangle can also be used to help the client determine supportive individuals in his or her life. Counseling can assist the client in determining which people were significant in the past as well as in the present so any useful connections can be enhanced in counseling. For the addicted client who may have severed or scarred relationships with others, an examination of these relationships may assist the client's recovery process by determining if some of these relationships can be built into the client's current support network as well as the types of individuals the client finds supportive so he or she can more actively seek them out.

Cognitive and Behavioral

Cognitive and behavioral planned short-term therapy focuses primarily on the present, with an assessment of current problems, establishment of goals, reduction of pressure from problems, and increase of client's self-efficacy (Bloom, 1997). Two theoretical approaches will be examined here: Ellis's rational emotive psychotherapy (1962) and Beck's cognitive restructuring therapy (1976).

Ellis's theory (Bloom, 1997; Ellis, 1962) is anchored in the view that actions are the results of beliefs. The goal of this form of counseling is to help the client accept himself or herself through direct, active therapy, which may involve homework assignments and bibliotherapy. The counselor confronts the cognitive, emotional, behavioral problems of the client by examining the beliefs that occur between the experience and the emotion. This brief therapy approach can be very useful with addicted clients because they may hold highly irrational beliefs about what their chemical usage does for them and how it affects others. Ellis (1992) states that when working with a problem drinker, he focuses on the drinking and the dysfunctional beliefs causing the drinking, and then uses rational emotive therapy (RET) techniques to intervene.

Similarly, Beck (Beck, 1976; Bloom, 1997) examines the relationship between thoughts and feelings. Specifically, Beck (Beck, 1976; Bloom, 1997) views depression as a result of distortions of oneself, the world, and the future. These schemas, or ways of viewing the world, emphasize failure while minimizing success. This form of therapy examines the client's automatic thoughts, explanations of life events, assumptions of the world, and development of new responses from new assumptions. Beck (Beck, 1976; Bloom, 1997) states that the counselor needs to be trustworthy, communicate well, and have confidence that the client's situation can change. In terms of specific techniques, the counselor needs to help the client identify his or her automatic thoughts (identify what occurs between the event and the client's reaction to it by use of something such as a record of reactions to events), identify the client's underlying assumptions, use questions to increase awareness, and involve homework assignments that may assist in increasing awareness.

This form of therapy may be especially beneficial for the addicted client because it focuses on addressing hopelessness, which many addicts experience. It also provides the addicted client with a sense of control and self-observation, underscoring the reality that the addict has choices about his or her life. For example, when an addicted client wants to use, the counselor may help the client determine what his or her automatic thoughts were in the situation where the urge was experienced ("Oh, no. I didn't think they would be serving alcohol at a work function"), what underlying assumptions may be present ("I will never be able to live through this situation sober"), and help the client through questions ("How have you been able to stay sober before in previous situations?") and homework ("Watch yourself the next time you have an urge and become aware of the thoughts and feelings you have during the experience. Keep a log of these experiences and we will review them in your next session").

An example of cognitive-behavioral strategies with addiction counseling can be seen in the area of relapse prevention. (Chapter 6 discussed a relapse prevention model in detail.) Relapse prevention treatment involves techniques of homework, bibliotherapy, guided imagery, role-play, and self-monitoring (Giannetti, 1993). Clients need to identify situations that may trigger a relapse, avoid triggers to relapse, substitute rewards, test new skills, picture themselves in a relapse-provoking situation and develop a coping plan, and develop realistic long-term goals.

Strategic and Systemic

The theory focused on here is de Shazer's solution-based brief therapy (Bloom, 1997; de Shazer, 1985), which began in the mid-1970s. This form of therapy emphasizes solutions rather than problems in marriage and family therapy. There are three main objectives: change clients' perceptions, change clients' behavior, and help clients access their strengths. The focus is on finding an exception to the problem—that is, discovering when the problem does not exist. The counselor looks at the symptoms, the exceptions, and then applies interventions. Specification of goals is viewed as critical to the process. Often, in the first session, the miracle question is asked: "If a miracle occurs tonight while you are asleep and the problem is eliminated, how will you know the next morning? How will others know? What will you be doing differently or saying differently?" This question stresses healthy functioning and the client determining his or her own solutions to the problem (Kingsbury, 1997). It is also important that the sessions involve homework to help the client determine what is a successful solution to the problem (Huber & Backlund, 1992).

Berg and Miller (1992) outline steps for using this form of therapy with substance abusers. These steps emphasize the importance of a good therapeutic relationship; development and implementation of treatment goals; and focusing on interviews, treatment interventions, and maintenance of change. The overall goal is to help the client use available resources and strengths to increase the frequency of times when drugs are not used by studying exceptions to the client's use (Stevens-Smith & Smith, 1998). Berg (1995) points out that clients often have periods when they do not use, so this information about what they do that helps them stay sober is already available, whether these exceptions are deliberate (the client intentionally tries to stay away from using and can explain the steps taken to attain abstinence) or random (the client cannot explain the steps taken to achieve abstinence). In the case of deliberate exceptions, the counselor can help the client plan to retake the same steps, and with random exceptions, the counselor can help the client learn to predict times of recovery in order to enhance a sense of control (Berg, 1995). In this type of philosophy, the client does not need to fix what works, does need to do more of what does work, and has to do something different if he or she tries something that does not work (Berg & Miller, 1992).

The treatment can be one session or a series of brief sessions that occur over time in the individual's recovery (Berg, 1995). Whether in individual or group counseling, the miracle question is used to establish goals. Scaling questions (scales of 1 to 10 or 1 to 100 are used to describe the intensity of the clinical issues experienced) are used to determine progress, and behavioral tracking is done to determine what steps have helped the client stay sober (Berg, 1995). For example, after asking the addicted client the miracle question, scaling questions could be used as follows: "On a scale of 1 to 10, 10 being the highest point, in what settings do you have the greatest urge to use and what point on the scale would you assign to each of those settings?" and "In the last week, using a scale of 1 to 10 again, scale the most stressful interaction you had with someone and describe that experience." These techniques can aid the counselor in determining the extent of the difficulty of the clinical issues of the client.

Difficulties: Obstacles, Resistance, and Types of Clients

Obstacles

Various obstacles for both clients and counselors may appear through the brief therapy process. Clients may view their situation as stable, they may not believe there is anything they have not tried, and they may look at their particular situations as uncontrollable (Huber & Backlund, 1992). For clients who view their situations as stable, the counselor can focus on helping them recognize exceptions to the stability and then reinforce a successful solution to the problem (Huber & Backlund, 1992). As stated previously, addicted clients who believe they can never be sober need to look at times they have been able to stay sober and build on the successful components of those attempts at sobriety. For clients who believe they have tried everything to cope with the situation, they may be encouraged to try something different; follow-up with them can determine how successful that change was (Huber & Backlund, 1992). Clients who believe they have done everything to stay sober may need to try something different (e.g., attending Women for Sobriety rather than AA) to see if it is helpful. For clients who feel as though their situations are uncontrollable, it may be helpful to focus on what they did to try to make a difference in their situations, again focusing on the successful aspects of their solutions (Huber & Backlund, 1992). Addicted clients who believe they cannot have an impact on their recovery may need to carefully examine attempts at sobriety in terms of one day rather than a lifetime.

Walter and Pellar (1992) state that there are not as many resistant clients as there are inflexible therapists. Therefore, counselors may also have habits that are obstacles for them in this type of therapy. Counselors may not set goals well (vague goals or forgetting goals), may repeat unsuccessful solutions, or may focus on problems rather than solutions (Huber & Backlund, 1992). The addiction counselor may set a goal of abstinence but not state how the client may achieve this goal or how progress toward this goal will be monitored. The counselor may also neglect to review goals set for the client, thereby losing the guidelines for the counseling. Because brief therapy necessitates the counselor to be focused on the goals that have been set, a counselor who has difficulty with this aspect of counseling may want to talk with his or her supervisor or colleagues for suggestions on how to improve goal-setting practices. With regard to repetition of unsuccessful solutions, the counselor may encourage a client to use the same coping behaviors ("Don't drink," "Go to meetings," "Read the Big Book") in spite of the client's continuing relapses, thereby missing underlying problems such as a dual diagnosis. In this situation, the counselor can ask clients what has and has not been helpful in previous counseling and help them avoid repetition of these patterns (Huber & Backlund, 1992). An example of focusing too much on problems rather than solutions is when the counselor focuses on the relapse rather than the days the client was able to stay sober prior to the relapse. If the tendency is to focus on problems rather than solutions, the counselor may need to make a studied attempt to focus on exceptions, strengths, and resources, with an emphasis on interrupting the client's process (Huber & Backlund, 1992).

Resistance

Resistance is basically the client's attempt to avoid discussion of a topic. It can show up in various behaviors, such as those reported by Morrison (1993): tardiness; forgetfulness; inconsistent, exaggerated, or omitted information; topic changing or other distractions such as joking, smoking, bathroom use, counselor-focused questions; silence or hesitation before responding; and behaviors such as difficulty maintaining eye contact, watching the clock, shifting physically, blushing, yawning, and swallowing excessively. These behaviors are only possibly indicative of resistance. They may also reflect cultural differences, habits of the individual in anxiety-producing situations, or physical problems. While the counselor needs to be aware of signs of resistance, he or she also needs to be aware that these behaviors can be reflective of something other than resistance.

It is also necessary for the counselor to remember that resistance may not simply be an indication of the client not wanting to obtain counseling or change behavior. It may also be a reflection of feelings (embarrassment, fear of criticisms or labels, mistrust, anger, etc.), protection of someone else, minimization of the importance of one's experiences or thoughts, and unconscious testing of the counselor (Morrison, 1993).

In order to work effectively with the resistance, the counselor needs to be aware that resistance may be present and that it may be motivated by different reasons. Depending on the counselor's style, the approach to resistance may vary. He or she may directly confront the behavior as being symbolic of resistance or may want to ask the client to explain the reason for the behavior in the context of resistance. With addicted clients, the counselor may want to work with resistance both directly and flexibly. Signs of resistance need to be raised directly with clients, yet power struggles need to be avoided. It may be most useful to put the responsibility for explaining the resistance on the client, such as stating, "You say you want to be sober, yet you do not follow your treatment goals. How do you explain this behavior?"

Morrison (1993) also suggests that the counselor attempt to prevent resistance by learning as much as possible about the client prior to the session, using conversational topics to reduce the stress, individualizing the history-taking aspects of the session, describing mental status questions as routine ones, and monitoring his or her own reactions to the client. These suggestions of personalizing the counseling process may assist in establishing rapport with the addicted client. Knowing the client's usage and life history, treating the client as a human being, and obtaining information in a manner comfortable to the client will help the client trust the counselor and the counseling process. Looking for signs of dual diagnosis can also prevent the counselor from mislabeling mental health problems as resistance. Finally, examining oneself for countertransference can reduce resistance in sessions, allowing the client the opportunity to be seen as himself or herself and understood in sessions.

Because of the short-term nature of this form of counseling, the counselor needs to minimize the presence of resistance. The less resistance present in the session, the more effective and efficient counseling can be.

Types of Clients

In addition to those clients discussed previously who might not be good candidates for brief therapy, there may be clients who would do well in brief therapy, but some of their behaviors prevent them from doing so. Morrison (1993) discusses a number of these client behaviors and makes suggestions for how counselors may handle them. For clients who are vague (unfocused, overgeneralized, approximate, etc.), the counselor needs to determine what is causing the vagueness, provide structure for being specific, and help them learn to generalize. For clients who are confused, it is important to obtain information and complete a mental status exam where the counselor is friendly, has a slow, careful approach, and chooses words carefully. With clients who lie, the counselor once again needs to determine the motivation for the lying and ask the clients to restate their answers, find the truth somewhere else, or confront the clients with the discrepancy.

For behavioral problems, various strategies may be applied. For seductiveness, the counselor needs to be distant and formal. For the client who talks too much, the counselor needs to direct the topic of the session and set limits on the conversation. If the client uses humor, the counselor can listen for the pain it is covering. If the client is tearful, a touch, silence, or offering of a tissue may show support.

If the client is hostile, the counselor needs to determine the source of the hostility and then address it through calm confrontation while monitoring one's own feelings. In terms of violence, the counselor needs to look at the past behavior of the client in terms of violence and impulse control as well as being aware of the physical situation (who is closest to the door, location of the security guard or panic button, if the door is to be left open, proximity of one's colleagues, etc.).

Clients who are older may need more time in an interview and a slower pace during the sessions. For clients who are physically challenged, various approaches may be used. For the blind, awareness of voice tones is important as well as notification of movements. For the deaf, or hearing impaired, lips should be visible and talking "down" to the client should be avoided. For the mute, be certain that paper and pencil are available as well as be prepared to do further evaluation regarding the cause of the muteness.

Clients who are addicted and have these difficulties may require adaptive, sensitive behaviors of the therapist to facilitate the counseling process. Although a counselor may not be inherently knowledgeable about how to address all the difficulties that can be present, the counselor can make a commitment to consult with other professionals who specialize in working with individuals with those difficulties and apply those approaches.

Evaluation of Effectiveness

The evaluation process of counseling hinges on both the client's and counselor's perceptions of the work. The most important indicator is the client's contentment regarding the counseling (Huber & Backlund, 1992). The client needs to be asked throughout counseling, as well as at its completion and follow-up, to evaluate how helpful counseling was. In addition to dialogue about counseling effectiveness, the counselor may find it helpful to use forms that are easy to complete (scaled items) and allow for written comments.

The counselor can evaluate the progress by looking at the degree that the client is using successful solutions and is more rational (Huber & Backlund, 1992). Both in-session self-reports and a frequent review of treatment plans and progress reports can also provide a form of measurement of counseling effectiveness.

Huber and Backlund (1992) also suggest that the counselor learn from treatment failures (e.g., no progress or worsening of symptoms, treatment not viewed as sufficient or satisfactory, etc.). Some possible explanations for failures are termination too soon, premature intervention, perceived abandonment, rejection of the therapist, and too many sessions. If a counselor is able to catch a treatment failure quickly, it is possible that this mistake can be addressed in counseling. If the client has already ended counseling and is no longer interested in receiving treatment from the counselor, the counselor can enhance further work with clients by carefully reviewing the clients' records and learning from the mistakes of therapy for the benefit of future clients.

CASE STUDY: ROGER

Roger, in his mid-30s, was referred for an assessment of his addiction because of an argument with his girlfriend: She says if he does not cut out all of his chemical use, she is breaking up with him. He has come to the session quite defensive, claiming that he does not have a drinking or drug problem. Roger says he normally does not drink alcohol, but when he feels a lot of stress in his life with work and his girlfriend, he drinks more than he should. He is divorced and has three children by his previous two marriages. His father was a heroin addict and his mother a "pothead." His parents are still married and use marijuana a few times a week. Roger reports he uses marijuana with them and the three of them strongly believe that marijuana is not addicting and should be legalized. He says he does not plan on changing any of his using behavior because he rarely uses alcohol (maybe once every six months) and he does not see his daily use of marijuana as a problem. He admits to having used too much alcohol, speed, and cocaine in the past, but views himself as having cut back successfully to the point where he does not currently experience negative consequences of his use.

1. Would you see Roger as a good candidate for brief therapy? Why or why not?
2. How would you approach Roger in the interview?

3. What context of therapy (individual, couple, family, or group) would you see as most helpful to him and why?
4. Which theoretical orientation of brief therapy would be most comfortable for you in working with this client?
5. Which different theoretical techniques would you use to help Roger?
6. How would you evaluate if brief therapy was helpful to Roger?

Summary

Brief therapy can be helpful within different addiction treatment contexts (individual, couple, family, and group) and different stages of addiction treatment (assessment, treatment, and relapse prevention). The counselor using this form of therapy needs to have some training in this area, or at least be supervised by someone who has been trained in these techniques, as well as know the clients with whom this therapy may be most beneficial. Although brief therapy may not be able to serve the needs of all addicted clients in all situations, it may be beneficial to those who do not need or who are unable or unwilling to have longer-term counseling.

SUGGESTED READINGS

Berg, I. K. (1995). Solution-focused brief therapy with substance abusers. In A. M. Washton (Ed.), *Psychotherapy and substance abuse: A practitioner's handbook* (pp. 223–242). New York: Guilford.

Berg, I. K., & Miller, S. D. (1992). *Working with the problem drinker: A solution-focused approach.* New York: Norton.

Bloom, B. L. (1997). *Planned short-term psychotherapy: A clinical handbook* (2nd ed.). Boston: Allyn and Bacon.

Giannetti, V. J. (1993). Brief relapse prevention with substance abusers. In R. A. Wells & V. J. Giannetti (Eds.), *Casebook of the brief psychotherapies* (pp. 159–178). New York: Plenum.

REFERENCES

Beck, A. T. (1976). *Cognitive therapy and the emotional disorders.* New York: International Universities Press.

Berg, I. K. (1995). Solution-focused brief therapy with substance abusers. In A. M. Washton (Ed.), *Psychotherapy and substance abuse: A practitioner's handbook* (pp. 223–242). New York: Guilford.

Berg, I. K., & Miller, S. D. (1992). *Working with the problem drinker: A solution-focused approach.* New York: Norton.

Bloom, B. L. (1997). *Planned short-term psychotherapy: A clinical handbook* (2nd ed.). Boston: Allyn and Bacon.

Davanloo, H. (1980). A method of short-term dynamic psychotherapy. In H. Davanloo (Ed.), *Short-term dynamic psychotherapy* (pp. 75–91). Northvale, NJ: Aronson.

de Shazer, S. (1985). *Keys to solution in brief therapy.* New York: Norton.

Ellis, A. (1962). *Reason and emotion in psychotherapy.* New York: Stuart.

Ellis, A. (1992). Brief therapy: The rational-emotive method. In S. H. Budman, M. F. Hoyt, & S. Friedman (Eds.), *The first session in brief therapy.* New York: Guilford.

Friedman, S., & Fanger, M. T. (1991). *Expanding therapeutic possibilities: Getting results in brief psychotherapy.* Lexington, MA: Lexington Books.

Giannetti, V. J. (1993). Brief relapse prevention with substance abusers. In R. A. Wells & V. J. Giannetti (Eds.), *Casebook of the brief psychotherapies* (pp. 159–178). New York: Plenum.

Hester, R. K., & Bien, T. H. (1995). Brief treatment. In A. M. Washton (Ed.), *Psychotherapy and substance abuse: A practitioner's handbook* (pp. 204–222). New York: Guilford.

Huber, C. H., & Backlund, B. A. (1992). *The twenty minute counselor.* New York: Continuum.

Kingsbury, S. J. (1997, April). What is solution-focused therapy? *The Harvard Mental Health Letter.*

Koss, M. P., & Shiang, J. (1994). Research on brief psychotherapy. In A. E. Bergin & S. L. Garfield (Eds.), *Handbook of psychotherapy and behavior change* (pp. 664–700). New York: Wiley.

Marmor, J. (1968). New directions in psychoanalytic theory and therapy. In J. Marmor (Ed.), *Modern psychoanalysis: New directions and perspectives* (pp. 237–243). Northvale, NJ: Aronson.

Miller, W. R., & Sanchez, V. C. (1994). Motivating young adults for treatment and lifestyle change. In G. Howard (Ed.), *Issues in alcohol use and misuse by young adults* (pp. 55–81). Notre Dame, IN: University of Notre Dame Press.

Morrison, J. (1993). *The first interview.* New York: Guilford.

Nugent, F. A. (1994). *An introduction to the profession of counseling* (2nd ed.). New York: Macmillan.

Steenbarger, B. N. (1993). A multicontextual model of counseling: Bridging brevity and diversity. *Journal of Counseling and Development, 7,* 8–14.

Stevens-Smith, P., & Smith, R. L. (1998). *Substance abuse counseling: Theory and practice.* Upper Saddle River, NJ: Prentice-Hall.

Talmon, M. (1990). *Single session therapy.* San Francisco: Jossey-Bass.

Walter, J. L., & Pellar, J. E. (1992). *Becoming solution-focused in brief therapy.* New York: Brunner/Mazel.

9 Treatment of Addiction

Special Issues

PRETEST

1. What is multicultural counseling?
2. What are four environmental aspects to consider when working with someone from a different culture?
3. What role does dialogue play in multicultural counseling?
4. How can a counselor create a dialogue-friendly atmosphere?
5. What are some barriers women face in treatment?
6. What are some cultural considerations that may affect treatment for African Americans? Asian Americans? Hispanics? Native Americans?
7. What are six main barriers to treatment for the clients who are hard of hearing or deaf?
8. What components are needed for effective treatment for adolescents?
9. How do stereotypes affect the assessment of the elderly in terms of addiction?
10. What are some suggestions in working effectively with the homeless population?

Multicultural Approaches

Multicultural counseling involves counseling strategies to build bridges between the cultural differences between counselor and client. This type of counseling can be very difficult because it is difficult to understand the world from a completely different viewpoint. One's culture is often fused with who one is as an individual. Even for those who have had different cultural experiences from those with whom they were originally exposed, it is still difficult at times to understand how individuals think and act the way they do.

Multicultural counseling, then, involves specific challenges to the counselor. It requires the counselor to have an awareness of self, others, and different cultures, as well as to be flexible, open, perceptive, and willing to learn in order to build a bridge between the differences. It does not require counselors to personally give up their value systems in order to work with clients, but it does require counselors to know their limitations and be willing to refer clients with whom they cannot work.

Because each person is a product of the culture in which he or she was raised, all people need to learn to work with individuals different from themselves. No one can be all things to all people. Three items are important to keep in mind with regard to multicultural counseling. First, it may be more comfortable to work with people of some cultures than with others. No therapist can work with all individuals from all cultures equally well. Second, the clients need to speak to counselors from the clients' own cultural experiences. There is a danger that when a counselor learns things about different cultures, he or she will end up stereotyping individuals based on what was learned about that culture. It is most important that the therapist hears the individual's story of what it was like for him or her to grow up in the United States, and then work within that viewpoint. Finally, therapists need to remember that some individuals are more comfortable going beyond the limits of their culture than others. When working with culturally different individuals in counseling, then, the therapist must determine the clients' comfort levels for trying something different from what they have known. Initially, it may be more comfortable for clients to be exposed to counseling theories and techniques that fit well with their traditional cultures, but as they proceed in counseling, they may be willing to try something different. For example, a female client from an Asian culture may initially be most comfortable with client-centered counseling techniques in an individual setting, but as she progresses in counseling, she may become comfortable with joining a counseling group that is more confrontational in its style.

This chapter examines different aspects of multicultural counseling. The first section of the chapter presents an overview on multicultural counseling, followed by an examination of the impact of drug abuse and addiction on different groups. A word of caution is needed before reading this chapter: Be wary about finding a pat formula for multicultural counseling. It is more feasible to develop a counseling approach that encourages an adaptive counseling style.

Defining Multicultural

One of the difficulties with multicultural counseling is that even the definitions vary. Here, *multicultural* is defined as working with differences. Differences may be in ethnicity or sexual orientation; whatever the context of the differences between client and counselor, the emphasis is on the fact that there are differences between client and counselor.

One approach to developing multicultural counseling methods is to develop a culturally sensitive environmental framework. Koss-Chionio and Vargas (1992) provide a framework of four environmental aspects that are important to take into account when working with individuals from different cultures: poverty, racism (or "isms") and prejudice, acculturation, and normative behavior. These aspects are reviewed in the following section, with some adaptations for working with addicted individuals.

Social-Environmental Aspects

Poverty

Sometimes, different groups experience oppression along with their different cultural experiences. For example, women, people of color, and gays and lesbians may be oppressed as well as come from a different culture than that of the counselor. Women, for instance, who in their oppression have a different cultural experience than men, often experience poverty as a part of their oppression. Oppressed groups of individuals will often experience different struggles in conjunction with their societal status, such as poverty. This experience of poverty may have a significant impact on their treatment. For example, for a recovering individual to be referred to self-help groups in the community, the issue may arise of not having transportation to such groups due to a lack of money. The reality of their poverty may have a significant affect on their treatment plan and recovery process.

A counselor needs to be aware of these social-environmental aspects and the impact they may place on counseling. When someone is from a different culture, the counselor needs to be careful not to assume that the client has the same cultural advantages as the counselor. It is equally important for the counselor to avoid assuming that the client has had fewer cultural advantages than the counselor. Extreme assumptions of clients must be avoided.

Isms and Prejudice

Individuals from different cultural groups may also experience an "ism" or prejudice regarding their status in the society. *Isms* is a term used here to summarize the prejudicial biases of individuals toward others. Oppressed individuals may be directly attacked physically or verbally for who they are or they may experience systematic attacks on them by a system being organized around values that are unfamiliar to them. Experiencing these isms and prejudices may cause an individual to approach those considered "mainstream" with anger, bitterness, and distrust. If the counselor is considered mainstream by the client (e.g., by look, dress, or speech), then the counselor may find need to "stretch" to assist the individual in trusting him or her. The same may be true if the client is the one who is considered mainstream and the counselor is of the oppressed group.

Acculturation

Individuals who are considered outside the mainstream may also have difficulty adjusting to the predominant cultural values to which they are exposed. It may be helpful to ask these individuals who they identify with in order to understand how they may be feeling alienated. Even individuals who have "made it" may struggle with these issues, because they may believe that somehow they have sold out and/or that there are specific things they have missed because of their standing outside the mainstream culture.

Normative Behavior

Acculturation also brings up the issue of normative behavior. What is normal? What is typical for the environment in which one lives? How much of an adjustment should a person be required to make in order to fit in? These are questions that need to be examined at the onset of counseling. What are the differences between what the client and the counselor consider as normative behavior? The counselor needs to assist the client in being aware of these issues and then determine at what level the client wants or needs to adjust to these pressures. Some clients may be more flexible in terms of adjusting to different environments, whereas others will refuse to do so.

Cultural Aspects

American History of Cultural Diversity

Murphy (1995) discusses the possible need for a scapegroup. He reports that the American Jewish Committee once included a group called Wisians (a nonexistent group) in a attitude survey they were doing. About 40 percent of survey respondents gave opinions on this nonexistent group. This humorous article underscores how easily one may form opinions based on ignorance.

Schwarz (1995) reports that the United States has a diversity myth that it promotes internationally. This is the myth that there is a long history of tolerance and harmony in the United States regarding different cultures. Schwarz attacks this myth with examples regarding race, ethnicity, and North/South differences. This history of oppression toward specific cultural groups, such as racial minorities and gay and lesbian populations (Vacc, DeVaney, & Wittmer, 1995), has resulted in negative experiences among specific U.S. cultural groups. Therefore, counselors working with different cultural groups need to understand the history of that group's experience in the United States in order to provide some perspective for the struggles of different individuals in counseling.

Breakdown of Communication

If an individual is from an oppressed group, then it may be more difficult to establish sincere communication lines between the client and the counselor. The history of negative experiences may make it much easier to distrust than to work on a relationship with one another. This may be the case regardless of whether the counselor or the client is from an oppressed group.

The breakdown of communication often seems to be based on schemata. *Schemata* means the systems of knowledge one has about certain areas, such as types of people and situations (Mook, 1987). One type of schemata is person schemata, where the impressions of a group of people are overly simple, rigid, and generalized (e.g., stereotypes). Personal and social experiences are used as the sources of information about a group of individuals and then that fixed knowledge of information is used to judge current experiences with individuals from that group (Fiske & Taylor, 1983). Simply stated, when a person is caught in stereotypes of individuals, that person organizes his or her information about a group of individuals and then applies it to all individuals from that group.

Multicultural counseling requires the therapist to examine his or her perceptions of others and listen carefully to their stories to determine if he or she is typecasting them. In order to prevent the limitation of stereotypes, therapists must accommodate their beliefs about an individual to new information received about the person.

Multicultural Competence

Atkinson, Morten, and Sue (1993) report that in order to develop cross-cultural competence, counselors must examine their own attitudes, beliefs, knowledge, and skills in terms of awareness of their own cultural values and biases, awareness of the client's world view, and intervention strategies that fit the client's culture. Cross, Bazron, Dennis, and Isaacs (1989) developed a similar framework where the counselor can be culturally incompetent, culturally sensitive, or culturally competent in terms of cognitive, affective, and skills dimensions, with overall effects ranging from destructive, neutral, and constructive, respectively. In this latter framework, the culturally competent counselor is knowledgeable (cognitive), committed to change (affective), highly skilled (skill), and has a constructive effect on the counseling.

Whichever theoretical framework is adopted to encourage a multicultural counseling approach, the goal is for the counselor to develop a capacity to work with individuals who are different from him or her. The following section discusses some pragmatic approaches to facilitate multicultural counseling.

Dialogue

Friere (1989) describes dialogue as different from a communique where one person is above another without empathy; rather, dialogue is a horizontal relationship between two people who are empathically joined in a search. Burbules (1993) describes the necessary components of dialogue as respect, concern, interest, commitment, open participation (nonauthoritarian), continuous, developmentally sequenced, and exploratory and interrogative in nature. Oakeshoff (1991) describes dialogue as conversation that lacks debate, does not attempt to discover the truth, is taken at face value, is unrehearsed, and is intellectual as well as rich in both seriousness and playfulness.

All of these definitions of dialogue combined indicate that it is a process where two individuals are involved. A counselor attempting to work within a multicultural context needs to be able and willing to create a dialogue-friendly atmosphere so schemata and stereotypes do not dominate the direction of the sessions.

Creation of Dialogue-Friendly Atmosphere

How can a counselor create a dialogue-friendly atmosphere? Initially, it is helpful for the counselor to be aware of differences between oneself and the client. As stated previously, it is beneficial if the therapist has knowledge of the culture in which the client lives and the impact of that culture on his or her life. This awareness of potential or explicit differences will assist the counselor in maintaining an openness to learning about the client rather than relying on stereotypes.

Also, there is the importance of interpersonal factors such as genuineness, empathy, and unconditional positive regard (Rogers, 1987). These factors can establish a solid baseline from which the therapist can work in counseling. If a client believes the counselor is genuine, empathic to his or her struggles, and holds a positive view of him or her, many differences can be bridged.

Another important factor is the role the counselor takes at a critical moment in therapy: Is the counselor a compassionate authority individual or a critical one? In multicultural counseling, there will invariably be places of conflict and differences. What is important is the approach taken by the counselor at those times. Rather than focusing the blame on someone for the event, which is the stance of the critical authority individual, it is more important that the counselor focus on what has occurred and its impact on the client and the counseling relationship. A sincere apology for the misunderstanding between the counselor and client can deeply facilitate the therapeutic relationship. In addition, a careful, thoughtful, respectful processing of the event can assist the client in trusting the counselor in therapy and learning about patterns of his or her own behavior.

So-called common-sense approaches are also helpful in therapy. Asking a client "What would you like to be called?" in terms of identification of ethnicity, or sexual orientation, or whatever, and then remembering to call the client by that title is respectful. Also, gently and respectfully asking a client who is the only member of a specific group or culture "What is it like to be the only ____ in this place?" is helpful. Finally, when there is a disagreement or conflict of some type, the counselor may not know what occurred that caused the client to withdraw; however, the counselor may feel a qualitative shift in the therapeutic relationship. This experience can be described as a glass wall that drops down between the counselor and the client. The client may or may not appear engaged with the counselor, but it feels to the counselor that he or she has been shut out. At that point, it is necessary for the counselor to ask, "What happened here?" in order to learn what may have been offensive or alienating to the client.

The danger for all counselors in multicultural counseling is experiencing a lack of compassion based on ignorance and fear. To operate out of ignorance and fear will not only limit the counseling but it will also be hurtful to the client. When counseling struggles appear to be based in cultural differences, the counselor needs to process the struggle carefully with the client. It is helpful to take a deep breath and then proceed into the dialogue about the conflict with honesty, setting limits, and taking time to discuss the issues. The conflict and discussion needs to be personal. At this point in the encounter, the counselor needs to show his or her humanness. The amount of disclosure required may vary from counselor to counselor, but what is most necessary is that the client feel the counselor's willingness to hear about the conflict.

General Counseling Suggestions

The counselor who desires to be sensitive and effective with individuals from other cultures needs to be aware of a number of areas. First, the counselor must be aware of his or her own culture and how that affects his or her life. Second, the counselor needs to be aware of the social environmental aspects that may be experienced by some groups, including the history of treatment of these groups in the United States. Third, the counselor needs to work at continually creating a dialogue-friendly atmosphere in order to facilitate counseling across different cultures. Some specific multicultural counseling suggestions follow:

1. Provide a respectful, open environment, particularly with regard to cultural differences.
2. Be flexible.
3. Be an expert in the field of counseling, but not in the clients' lives.
4. Establish a relationship of trust with a client. Do not pretend you know what you do not know.
5. Remember that a person can be a part of several cultures at one time.
6. Say, "I do not know what it is like to be . . . ."
7. Ask clients to teach you what you do not know.
8. Do not create issues, but address them if they arise.
9. Do not fight with people, but respond to their statements; do not let things go by.
10. Share your own experience of a communication breakdown if it occurs.
11. Apologize when wrong.
12. Learn how to deal with people who do not like you.
13. Turn to other counselors for support.
14. Remember the commonalities between all people.

Assessment, Treatment, and Aftercare Issues

Gender

Prior to discussing the different ways which assessment, treatment, and aftercare need to shift in order to enhance treatment of addicted women, it is necessary to review research on women's ways of relating to others. Miller (1976) describes a woman's sense of self as being organized around her relationships: making and maintaining them. It is precisely this sense of connectedness that leads to a woman's sense of herself as well as her moral views (Surry, 1985). A woman's self, then, is organized and developed within important relationships in her life (Surry, 1985). Furthermore, it is as important for a woman to be understood by the significant others in her life as much as it is important for her to understand them. The mutuality of relationships is the basis for the individual woman's growth and awareness (Surry, 1985). McClelland (1979) defines power for women as having the strength and capacity to care for and give to others in her life.

Keeping in mind this viewpoint of women's development, a woman at the different phases of treatment needs to be viewed with an awareness of her relationships with others in terms of her self-development and her sense of power. A woman may have difficulty during an assessment, for example, telling the truth about her chemical usage for fear that it may have an impact on the raising of her children. During the treatment phase, she may have difficulty concentrating on treatment concerns because she is worried about loved ones in her life. Finally, during aftercare, a woman may have difficulty thinking about what is best for her because she is concerned about the well-being of those she loves.

Also important, in terms of treatment, is the sense of helping the woman organize her recovery. The recovery process needs to be made personal for her in a manner that makes sense to her. She may not see a reason for sobering up for herself, but she may see a reason in sobering up for the sake of those individuals she loves. She may be able to stay with the recovery process more if she is both confronted as well as supported by her counselor. (This can assist her in looking at her issues within the context of a supportive relationship with her counselor.) She may also be able to stay involved in the recovery process better if she develops a social network of important relationships with individuals who are meaningful to her and to her recovery.

Some therapists believe that a woman needs to connect with other women as early as possible in order to stay sober. This type of connecting is important for women in recovery in order to address the issues of sexism that arise. Blume (1997) states that chemically dependent women are stigmatized because they (1) are alcoholic, therefore they are immoral or their addiction is their fault; (2) are measured against higher moral standards than men; and (3) experience sexual stigma related to their chemical usage (e.g., they are promiscuous). Such stigma may be best understood by another recovering chemically dependent woman. However, sometimes women sober up with such a high mistrust of other women that the only individuals who they will listen to are males. This mistrust may emerge from negative experiences with other women due to competing with them for drugs, money, or intimate partners, or negative experiences in general with other women. A counselor, then, needs to reflect on the importance of whether the woman hears the message of recovery no matter who delivers it or if the individual delivering it is more important than the message. It may be more pragmatic to engage the woman in a therapeutic relationship where she trusts the individual, male or female, and then during her recovery process, encourage her to rely on the support of other females who will understand the sexism she may face in the general culture and/or in the recovering community in which she lives.

Assessment

The National Institute on Alcohol Abuse and Alcoholism (NIAAA, 1990) reports that 4.6 million of 15.1 million addicted individuals are women. Pape (1993) states that addiction is a serious problem among women who are often treated disparagingly for becoming addicted. Some of the known facts about women and addiction are as follows:

1. Because women have more fat, they absorb alcohol faster and become intoxicated more quickly on the same amount of alcohol as a male (Johnson, 1991).
2. Just before menstruating, women are able to become intoxicated easier (Jones & Jones, 1976; Sutker, Goist, & King, 1987).
3. Women taking birth control pills have higher blood alcohol levels when drinking, because the liver metabolizes both the pills and the alcohol (Jones & Jones, 1984).
4. Women have more pure alcohol enter their bloodstream because of differences in the stomach's capacity to oxidize alcohol (Frezza, DiPodova, Pozzato, Terpin, Baraona, & Lieber, 1990).
5. Women develop alcohol dependency more quickly than men (telescopic effect) (Hill, 1981, 1984).
6. Women do not need to use as much alcohol for as long a time as men in order to develop alcohol related physical consequences (Pape, 1993).
7. Alcoholic women have more gynecological problems than nonalcoholic women (Wilsnack, 1973).
8. Women may begin drinking alcohol heavily due to a specific circumstance or stressor; they may use to self-medicate (Straussner, 1985).
9. Women are more likely to come from families with a history of alcoholism (Pape, 1993).
10. Many women who abuse alcohol have a history of sexual abuse (Hurley, 1991; Orrok, 1992).
11. Women are more likely to attempt suicide (Pape, 1993).
12. The majority of tranquilizers, antidepressants, and amphetamines are prescribed for women (Davis, 1990).

Spelman (1988) states that gender is mixed with race, class, and sexual orientation: "All women are women, but there is no being who is only a woman" (p. 102). Pape (1993) summarizes the findings of Wilsnack (1990) and Straussner (1985). In terms of class, women who have a higher income tend to drink more, but that does not mean that they are more likely to become dependent. In terms of race, African American women abstain more than Caucasian women, and Hispanic women are more likely to abstain and drink less than non-Hispanic women; it is important to note, though, that Hispanic women who are more acculturated may have higher rates of alcoholism (Eden & Aguilar, 1989). Native American women have higher rates of alcohol-related deaths and fetal alcohol syndrome in comparison with African American or Caucasian women. Drinking problems appear to be more common among divorced, separated, or single women than married or widowed women.

This knowledge of the impact of alcohol/drugs on women can be used in the assessment process. The counselor needs to make sure that a thorough physical examination is done, as well as an assessment that involves the use of prescription drugs, the usage pattern, and the consequences experienced (Pape, 1993). Assessment of dual diagnosis is also important. The counselor needs to be aware of the higher susceptibility of women to alcohol addiction, the tendency for women to begin using due to a specific circumstance, and the possible impact of race on the use process. In addition, this information can be used during the treatment and aftercare process to educate the woman about her addiction.

Treatment and Aftercare

Women may face specific barriers to treatment that men do not face. One barrier is that women may not be identified as readily by others (legal system employees, employee assistance counselors, etc.) as men. Also, women tend to have higher levels of guilt and shame regarding their addictions, resulting in them hiding their usage. When women do come in for counseling, they may present other problems as their issues rather than their chemical usage. Women who are in treatment may not respond well to traditional high-confrontation addiction treatment programs due to low self-esteem. Finally, women may not go to treatment due to lack of child-care resources (Pape, 1993).

If a woman does make it into treatment in spite of these barriers, she may have numerous practical problems as well as common issues related to family of origin, current family, and history of experiencing violence (Pape, 1993). Because of the importance of relationships to a woman's life, the alcohol/drug usage of other individuals important to her must be done either informally with the woman when discussing relapse prevention issues or formally when the individuals are involved in some part of the treatment program. Women also need to look at their career goals, because they may need to make more money than they are currently earning or they may want to find a more fulfilling career. To enhance her success in treatment, specific areas need to be examined for each woman. These areas include a thorough assessment (physical abuse, sexual abuse, physical problems, psychiatric problems, family usage of alcohol/drugs, etc.), opportunities for needed services (child care, couples or family therapy, medications, etc.), and education (parenting skills, self-esteem building, sexism, etc.).

In addition to a thorough assessment and a holistic treatment plan, all women in treatment should receive reproductive information, including how she and significant others think and feel about different forms of contraception and the impact of alcohol and drug use on the fetus (Mitchell, 1993). For the pregnant client, services need to include health care and survival-related issues (e.g., housing, psychosocial problems, parenting/family skills, etc.). These services need to be available both during and after addiction treatment (Mitchell, 1993).

Women who are pregnant and abusing alcohol and drugs may experience even more ostracism than women in general. Geller (1991) points out that pregnant women who use alcohol/drugs may be unaware of the impact on the fetus or they may be addicted and cannot stop using. Counselors working with this population need to be able to give women information about the consequences of the alcohol/drugs on the fetus in a firm, clear, but nonjudgmental manner.

More is known about the impact of alcohol than illegal drugs on pregnant women (Center for Substance Abuse Treatment [CSAT], 1994). Fetal alcohol syndrome (FAS) or fetal alcohol effects (FAE) are the result of alcohol abuse. The child may have low birthweight as well as physical, cognitive, or behavioral limitations (CSAT, 1994). In FAS, there are deficiencies in growth, problems with the central nervous system, deformities in the face, and malformed organs (Clarren, 1981). In FAE, babies have less severe effects (Pape, 1993). Some of the neonatal effects of drugs are as follows:

1. Heroin usage may result in low birth weight, sexually transmitted diseases, abstinence syndrome (the child experiences withdrawal symptoms that accompany abstinence from the drug), subacute withdrawal, and an increase in sudden infant death syndrome (SIDS) (Mitchell, 1993).
2. Cocaine usage may result in lower birth weight, smaller head circumference, premature birth, central nervous system dysfunction (e.g., tremors), and an increase in sudden infant death syndrome (SIDS) (Mitchell, 1993).
3. Sedative/hypnotics during pregnancy may result in toxicity, withdrawal, and morphologic and/or behavioral teratogenicity (Miller, 1995).

Finally, pregnant addicts find a variety of treatment barriers that counselors need to assist them with in order to treat their addiction effectively. Some of these barriers include lack of child care, insurance, money, and transportation; fear that their children will be removed from them as well as fear of homelessness if they admit to an addiction; and problems with depression, denial, and shame regarding their addiction (Hayes, 1997).

CASE STUDY: DEBBIE

Debbie is a 28-year-old, Caucasian female who is single and lives alone with her 3-year-old daughter. She is the sole supporter of her child. Her parents do not have any contact with her due to her drug usage (she has stolen money from them and lied to them) and the father of her child is in prison for drug dealing. Debbie has not had any contact with him since the birth of her daughter. She is a flight attendant and has contacted you, an employee assistance counselor, for assistance after her last binge of alcohol and cocaine. She became frightened because after coming off of her three-day binge, she realized she had no money left from her paycheck and did not know how she was going to pay her bills. She has low self-esteem, in part, due to her involvement with the father of her child. During their involvement, she was a prostitute for him in order to obtain her drugs. Debbie quit being a prostitute when she became pregnant, but she still runs into individuals who know her from those days.

1. What life-style or value differences might make it difficult for you to work with Debbie?
2. What types of behavior would you need to show Debbie in order to develop a therapeutic environment?
3. What interventions might you need to take with regard to Debbie's child? How might such interventions harm the therapeutic relationship?
4. What are possible issues underlying Debbie's drug addiction that need to be addressed in counseling?
5. How would you best approach obtaining information about possible underlying issues?

Race

African Americans

Prior to discussing assessment and treatment of African Americans, it is important to remember that African Americans are a heterogeneous group and there are limitations on the scientific drug abuse research with this population (John, Brown, & Primm, 1997). Substance use in African Americans appears connected to value conflicts with the dominant culture (Harvey, 1985) and as a way to cope with the stresses of daily living (Gary, 1986; Harvey, 1985; Richardson & Williams, 1990). Alcohol abuse is negatively correlated with life span this population (Brown & Tooley, 1989). For example, approximately twice as many African Americans die of cirrhosis of the liver as Caucasians (Herd, 1985). Also, African American men are killed through homicide five times more often than Caucasian men and alcohol is involved in at least half of the offenses (Gary, 1986; Harvey, 1985).

Assessment.   Bell (1990) states that African Americans tend to enter treatment later in the addiction process due to a higher emotional pain tolerance, which is a result of experiencing racism; an awareness of the failures of treatment experiences; fewer treatment resources; and lack of clarity regarding appropriate alcohol and drug use. Bell (1990) elaborates that later entry often means African Americans are court-referred, have more problems due to their addiction, require more expensive treatment, and are less likely to be successful.

Treatment and Aftercare.   During the treatment process, it is critical for the counselor to discuss race and culture with the African American client (Bell, 1990). The related issues must be acknowledged, experienced, and worked through as a part of counseling. These issues can be understood more fully by knowing the level of acculturation of the client (Bell, 1990).

The church and spirituality or religion are often important for African Americans (Hudson, 1986) and can serve as a support system for their recovery (Dembo, Burgos, Babst, Schmeidler, & Le Grand, 1978); however, the church may view addiction as a sin (Bell, 1990; Gordon, 1994). The counselor, then, needs to assess the comfort of each African American with his or her sense of spirituality and if that sense of spirituality involves a church, it is necessary to find out how that church views addiction in order to determine the level of support it can provide. Also, effective treatment and aftercare will assist the African American client in developing some support for recovery within the African American community, which may or may not include the church.

CASE STUDY: CHRIS

Chris is a 45-year-old African American male who has never been in treatment for alcohol and drug addiction. He has always lived at home with his mother and relies on her and odd handyman jobs to support himself. Chris began developing a drinking and drug problem when he returned from the service at age 20. Since that time, he has not had a steady job or girlfriend.

His mother has been his biggest enabler because she feels sorry for what the war did to her son and she has never been able to set consistent consequences for him. His father died when Chris was an adolescent and he is an only child. In the last few years, he has become increasingly violent when drunk or high and his mother has been more frightened about being left alone with him. Recently, she confided her fears to a woman in her church who shared her story about helping her son sober up. After their conversation, Chris's mother decided to call the police when he became violent again. She did and Chris was taken to detox.

1. What differences are there between you and Chris that might make it difficult for you to trust one another?
2. What might you do to bridge such differences?
3. What stereotypes might you hold of Chris and his mother that could interfere with hearing his story?
4. What issues may underlie Chris's alcohol and drug addiction and how might you find out about them?
5. What facts do you need to know about this client's use history and its consequences in order to be helpful to him? How might you approach obtaining such sensitive information, taking into account the differences you share?

Asian Americans

Typically, Asian Americans have one of the lowest alcohol use rates of ethnic minorities (Rebach, 1992); however, the more acculturated they become, the more their use reflects that of the dominant culture (Sue, 1987). This population may experience a flushing response when drinking alcohol (i.e., skin color changes, as well as warmth and tingling sensations) (Rebach, 1992). Sensitivity to alcohol and cultural values regarding its use may explain their lower overall use of alcohol and incidence of alcoholism (Ho, 1994). As with other minority groups, value conflicts with the mainstream culture seem related to substance use (Yee & Thu, 1987).

Assessment, Treatment, and Aftercare.   Once again, it is important to remember that many different cultures make up the group of Asian Americans (Westermeyer, 1997). Asian Americans typically do not enter treatment (Sue, 1987). If they do enter treatment, they may enter it late in their addiction due to shame-related issues, such as admitting a loss of control over their use, putting oneself before one's family, and admitting that the family could not take care of the problem (Westermeyer, 1997). If Asian Americans do come to a counselor for assessment, treatment, and/or aftercare for an addiction problem, there are some culture traits that would be helpful for the counselor to consider.

Some of the traditional Asian values are to obey one's parents and take care of the family (Sue & Sue, 1995). These values may run counter to the dominant culture value and create conflict for the Asian American client. Typically, there is an emphasis on education and emotional restraint (Sue & Sue, 1995). Because Asian Americans tend to view counseling as bringing shame to their families, those who come in for counseling tend to be more disturbed and more likely to talk about somatic rather than emotional problems (Sue & Sue, 1987).

The counselor, then, needs to arrange the assessment, treatment, and aftercare with an awareness of the traditionalism of the client and/or the significant others in his or her life. The Asian American client may come to counseling with more severe problems, have more difficulty with expressing emotion openly, and may have a greater sense of shame, particularly with regard to their families. Sue and Sue (1995) recommend a subtle, less confrontive counseling approach for both individual and group counseling. With regard to aftercare, it may be important to assess the individuals and systems that will be supportive to the recovery of the Asian American. For example, the client may have a difficult time speaking about concerns in a group setting, particularly when strong, direct confrontation may be used. The counselor working with an Asian American client in this group setting may want to make a point of processing the group experience with the client initially to determine the fit of the group with the client's need and comfort level.

CASE STUDY: FRANK

Frank is a 30-year-old Asian American who teaches at a university in the United States. He moved here from China to attend school as an undergraduate and then remained in the country through his degrees until he obtained a doctorate in business. He decided to become a U.S. citizen and teach at a research university. He has an American Caucasian wife and one child who is 2 years old. Frank graduated with his doctorate and began teaching two years ago. During his doctoral training, he began to feel more stress than he could handle. Because he was viewed as such a success to his family, he did not want to tell them, including his wife, of his problems. The stress was affecting his ability to sleep and concentrate. He began taking muscle relaxers and minor tranquilizers, which he obtained from a physician friend. Frank believes he experiences a lot of racism predominantly from Caucasian males in his department. He is afraid that the racism will keep him from being reappointed to his teaching position next year. Recently, his friend told him that he would not be able to continue writing prescriptions for him because he is afraid that Frank is becoming addicted. He gave Frank the name of a counselor to see. Frank is in your office for the first time to obtain help for his stress.

1. What will Frank notice about your office when he enters the room? Will it be an atmosphere that is open and inviting?
2. What cultural assumptions might you make about Frank in terms of the information just given?
3. How would you invite Frank to discuss his concerns with you?
4. What cultural differences might you anticipate that would make counseling a difficult process between the two of you?
5. How would you invite Frank to discuss his drug usage with you?

Hispanics

Hispanics, which include individuals of Mexican, Puerto Rican, Spanish, Central and South American, and Cuban descent, are the fastest growing racial minority in the United States (Eden & Aguilar, 1989). They tend to use alcohol most frequently, followed by marijuana, cocaine, and heroin (Eden & Aguilar, 1989). Historically, Mexican and Central/South American communities used alcohol as a way to come together culturally (Madsen & Madsen, 1969) and used drugs in their religious ceremonies, which may facilitate a cultural tolerance toward the use of alcohol/drugs (Eden & Aguilar, 1989). Machismo, the behavior of Hispanic men, may be viewed as including the use of alcohol (Eden & Aguilar, 1989).

Assessment.   Lawson, Ellis, and Rivers (1984) suggest that three areas be examined for risk: sociocultural, psychological, and physiological. An elaboration of these three areas is provided by Eden and Aguilar (1989). Sociocultural risk factors include using alcohol to connect with others, experiencing difficulties and stresses in adapting to U.S. culture, and having problems becoming or staying employed. The psychological risk factors involve self-esteem, a sense of personal control, isolation as connected to acculturation difficulties, and less frequent use of counseling services. Physiological risk factors, such as genetic predisposition, may be exacerbated by the sociocultural stressors they experience. Because of the frequency of alcohol use, it is important in the evaluation to ask the Hispanic client exactly how much is being used (Rebach, 1992).

Treatment and Aftercare.   Treatment of Hispanics needs to include bilingual/bicultural professional staff so that the cultural needs of the clients are better met (Ruiz & Langrod, 1997). Eden and Aguilar (1989) suggest that treatment take into account the frequent use of alcohol in the Hispanic community, the power of women in the Hispanic community, and the possibility that being alcoholic may elicit a sense of failure and guilt. This sense of failure and guilt may result in a shame that delays the addressing of the addiction problem (Rebach, 1992). Treatment that is less confrontive, but stresses areas such as family support, may be a better fit for the Hispanic client (Arredondo, Weddige, Justice, & Fitz, 1987). Aftercare that draws on other sober Hispanic individuals, the importance of being sober to take care of the family, and an understanding of the process of addiction may reduce the relapse potential of the Hispanic client.

CASE STUDY: ROBERT

Robert is a 56-year-old Hispanic male who has been arrested for a DUI. This is his first arrest and you are the DUI assessor who has been appointed to evaluate him. You have been told that Robert has been in the United States for about six months and that his English is fair, but in case of translation difficulties, an interpreter is present. When you enter the room with the interpreter, Robert makes eye contact with the interpreter, but not with you. In answer to your questions, Robert seems friendly, but brief.

1. How would you help Robert feel more comfortable in the session?
2. How would you use the interpreter to facilitate the session discussion?
3. What kinds of approaches would you take to facilitate Robert's answering your questions about his drinking?
4. Are there any other individuals you may need to contact regarding Robert's drinking? If so, who might they be and how might you contact them?

Native Americans

Rebach (1992) reports that there are approximately 300 Native American tribes in the United States and each has its own culture. As a result, the generalizations made regarding this population need to be made with these cultural differences in mind. Furthermore, about 650,000 of these 1,000,000 Native Americans are on or near a reservation (Anderson & Ellis, 1995). The difference in location of being on or off the reservation may have an impact on the types of stresses Native Americans experience. For example, there is higher alcohol use among urban Native Americans (Young, 1988).

Another important fact to note regarding this population is that Native Americans have the highest alcohol absorption rates of any minority population, resulting in a higher blood alcohol level (Reed, 1985). In a comparison of Native Americans with the general population, May (1986) found higher death rates, more deaths caused by cirrhosis of the liver, and more incidents of suicide and homicide. Young (1988) reports that 75 percent of the deaths in this ethnic population are related to alcohol.

Assessment.   In the assessment process, it may be important to determine the acculturation level of the Native American client and his or her comfort with being acculturated. There are many value conflicts between the dominant Caucasian culture and Native American ways. For example, success of the individual and competitiveness may be commonly valued in the dominant culture, but not the Native American culture (Rebach, 1992). Also, alcohol use may be involved in trying to cope with the stresses of being oppressed, which affects Native Americans' income and day-to-day living (Beauvais & LeBoueff, 1985). In addition, alcohol may be used by some to self-medicate a dual disorder especially if they live in an area (rural or ghetto) where psychiatric help may not be accessible (Westermeyer & Peake, 1983). These factors need to be taken into account when assessing the abuse problem of the Native American.

Treatment and Aftercare.   Frequently, Native Americans enter treatment at a chronic stage of addiction without family or job resources (Westermeyer, 1997). Flores (1986) reports that differences in values between treatment staff and Native American clients may result in mutual stereotyping and increased dropout rates. Anderson and Ellis (1995) recommend that treatment counselors look for the reinforcements for drinking that exist within the individual and the culture. In terms of outside influences, both family and culture can have a significant impact on the drinking behaviors of Native Americans (Weisner, Weibel-Orlando, & Long, 1984). Treatment and aftercare need to fit with the values of this population. Typically, these values include a present-time focus, a harmony within and outside of oneself, and a priority of group needs over individual needs (Hill, 1989). The counselor needs to examine meaningful value systems and support systems for the Native American who wants to remain sober.

CASE STUDY: TOM

Tom is a 35-year-old Native American who was raised on a reservation until he was 6 years old and was then raised by a Caucasian foster family off the reservation and in another state until he completed high school. He returned to his reservation when he was age 18. Both of his parents were alcoholic and his father died 10 years ago of alcoholism. Tom has a 6-year-old boy by his ex-wife. He is currently on probation for a fight in a bar, where he almost killed another Native American man who said negative things about his wife at the time. He was in prison for the crime, was on probation, relapsed from his recovery program, had another fight in a bar, and returned to prison. Tom is currently on probation again, living at a halfway house, and involved in a local self-help program. He has told the staff he is most comfortable talking with other Native Americans from his tribe.

1. What potential counseling problems do you anticipate between yourself and Tom and why?
2. How would you approach Tom in terms of inviting him to trust you?
3. How would you handle a communication problem with Tom when you felt a "glass wall" appear?
4. What issues do you believe Tom may need to address in his recovery and how would you facilitate these discussions?

Disability

Disability means that an individual is limited in functioning (physical, mental, and/ or emotional) because of an impairment that affects his or her life performance activities (Albrecht, 1992). There is a lack of research on alcohol and drug use (Tyas & Rush, 1993) and on alcohol and drug abuse treatment with the disabled population (Glow, 1989). Yet, it is estimated that 15 to 30 percent of those who are disabled abuse alcohol and drugs (Nelipovishc & Buss, 1991). The substance abuse among the disabled may, in part, have caused the disability, may have an impact on rehabilitation through behavioral or cognitive changes or medical problems, and may affect vocational rehabilitation (Heinemann, 1997). Although it has been recommended that the disabled population be treated within a typical alcohol and drug treatment program (*The Seed,* 1987), this approach would require treatment programs to look at the specific disability and then what the individual with that disability requires (Glow, 1989). Unfortunately, many treatment programs would prefer to not serve the disabled population (Tyas & Rush, 1993). Glow (1989) recommends that the counselor not focus on the disability, but focus on the alcohol/drug problem while keeping the disability in mind. Three disabled populations—the deaf and hard of hearing, the blind and visually impaired, and the physically injured—will be discussed in this section.

Deaf and Hard of Hearing

Some of the best information on the alcohol/drug abuse treatment of this population has emerged from the Minnesota Chemical Dependency Program for Deaf and Hard of Hearing Individuals, located in the Fairview University Medical Center in Minneapolis. It has noted six main barriers to treatment and recovery for this population (1994):

1. *Recognition of a problem.* There is a general lack of awareness of the problem and a stigma about having such a problem.
2. *Confidentiality.* There is a close communication network among individuals who are deaf that may concern someone who wants to examine their problems with alcohol/drugs. For example, this population may be concerned that an interpreter may not respect the confidentiality of the counseling process and will share information with individuals in their deaf community.
3. *Lack of resources.* Resources for providing information and services on alcohol and drug addiction are not often accessible to individuals who are deaf or hard of hearing.
4. *Enabling.* Alcohol and drug use behaviors may be excused by family members and friends as a result of the disability; therefore, they may continually rescue these individuals from the consequences of their behavior.
5. *Funding concerns.* Often to receive treatment, people who are deaf or hard of hearing need to travel a distance to receive assistance from staff that are specially trained.
6. *Lack of support in recovery.* It is often difficult for people who are deaf or hard

of hearing to receive support for their recovery, due to both the small numbers of individuals in their local deaf or hard-of-hearing community and the even smaller number who are in a recovery process.

Assessment.   Assessment of this population is similar to that with other addicted populations. Examination of physical, work, school, social, legal, financial, emotional, and spiritual aspects of the person's life that show a pattern of alcohol/drug-related problems warrant a thorough assessment. In the assessment process, it is important to remember that about 75 percent of Americans who are deaf use American Sign Language (ASL) as their preferred mode of communication (Vernon, 1990). The individual completing the addiction assessment with this population needs to be fluent in ASL or utilize a qualified interpreter to ensure accurate communication. The assessor also needs to be aware that alcohol/drug abuse education is not equivalent to that provided to the hearing population (Rendon, 1992). Because the deaf community's lack of general education on addiction, the assessor may need to avoid commonly used addiction slang terms (e.g., blackouts). Rather, the assessor may communicate better by using descriptions of behavior, such as, "Have you ever had a period of time when you were drinking that you cannot remember what you said or did?" Also, it is important when assessing an individual who is deaf or hard of hearing to look at the individual when speaking even when an interpreter is present.

Treatment and Aftercare.   Access to treatment can be enhanced for this population through telecommunication devices (TDD), presence of sign language use (interpreters as well as counselors), collaboration with vocational rehabilitation personnel, and contact with the deaf community (outreach, community organizations, etc.) (McCrone, 1982). In treatment, it is recommended that time be spent addressing defenses, educating and discussing feelings, attending a special focus group on deaf issues, working with the 12 Steps of Alcoholics Anonymous, addressing self-esteem issues, and involving families (Guthmann, Swan, & Gendreau, 1994). In addition to an overall treatment evaluation of the individual, it is also recommended that treatment involve an assessment of communication skills, education of chemical dependency, coping skills and decision-making skills, and the need for occupational and recreational therapy (Guthmann, 1994).

Finally, aftercare planning is important in working with this population. Vocational rehabilitation counselors or other professionals providing services to people who are deaf or hard of hearing may be able to provide information about resources in the client's community. This individual may be able to help the client advocate for himself or herself and educate the community of recovery about what is needed to assist the individual (Sandberg, 1994).

Blind and Visually Impaired

Too much isolation, time, and lack of employment are risk factors for substance abuse in this population (Nelipovich & Buss, 1989). Glass (1980–81) reported two kinds of blind and visually impaired drinkers: the client who drank before acquiring the disability (Type A) and the client who drank after the disability occurred (Type B). Glass states that the Type-A client uses drinking as a main coping mechanism and requires substance abuse treatment. The Type-B client may be able to stop abusing alcohol if the underlying stressors are examined in combination with skills to assist the person in coping with his or her disability.

Continuing to use Glass's categorization system, the Type-A client needs psychological or psychiatric help to assist with life problems that existed prior to the disability. This treatment has a skills training component to assist the individual in coping more effectively with his or her problems (Glass, 1980–81). The Type-B client needs to learn skills to be able to be more independent. Either abstinence or controlled drinking may be recommended for this individual.

Physically Injured

Traumatic brain injuries (TBI) are one of the major causes of disability, and half of those injuries are caused by motor vehicle accidents, many of which involve the presence of alcohol (Heinemann, 1997). Another disability, spinal cord injury (SCI), is often related to the use of alcohol and drugs, which means that clinicians need to be aware of how alcohol/drugs can affect these clients medically and in terms of rehabilitation and independence. Individuals with these types of physical problems may self-medicate their pain as well as use drugs to cope with their feelings of anxiety and depression. Screening for problems with alcohol and drugs as well as careful assessment and appropriate referrals are a necessary part of general treatment for individuals with these conditions (Heinemann, 1997).

CASE STUDY: BRENDA

Brenda is a 32-year-old Caucasian woman who is deaf. She has been referred to you for an evaluation because she was found passed out in her apartment by her landlady. The landlady contacted 911 and Brenda was taken to the emergency room. While being detoxed in the hospital, the attending physician referred her for an alcohol/drug evaluation. A qualified interpreter is available for the evaluation.

1. What would you need to talk with the interpreter about prior to the evaluation?
2. How would you approach Brenda in order to facilitate her communicating with you?
3. What types of questions would you ask of Brenda in order to facilitate her trust in you?
4. What would you do if Brenda refused to talk with you about her personal history, including her drug use?

Adolescents

Assessment

One of ten adolescents has a problem with alcohol and drugs (Hird, Khuri, Dusenbury, & Millman, 1997); therefore, careful assessment is necessary with this population. Assessing adolescents in terms of their chemical use history is difficult for a number of reasons. First, there is often a shorter use history on which an assessment is based. Second, adolescents may be acting out family system issues or psychiatric problems through their chemical use. Yet, accuracy in the assessment of adolescent chemical usage is important because of the end results of the two extremes (Doweiko, 1990): (1) adolescents may be overly diagnosed as addicted due to the fears of their parents and/or the greed of institutions and (2) adolescents may be underdiagnosed, resulting in suicide (Crumley, 1990) or physical problems.

Margolis (1995) reports six characteristics that specifically pertain to working with this population in terms of chemical usage:

1. Problem behaviors are indicators of drug abuse.
2. The addiction cycle is more rapid in this population than in the adult population.
3. Adolescents often use more than one drug.
4. Adolescents often have stronger denial.
5. Adolescents tend to have stronger enabling systems.
6. Drug use developmental delays are common.

Specific criteria can be examined for indications of dependency. First, the counselor needs to examine the consequences of chemical usage in terms of legal, social, educational, and vocational problems. In particular, if there has been a marked change in appearance, emotional expression, social group, or grades, there is legitimate cause for concern. Also, if the adolescent shows a preoccupation with usage and loss of control or using at inappropriate times, there may be a problem with alcohol/drugs.

The assessing counselor also needs to be aware of any history of physical or sexual abuse that may be leading the adolescent to using chemicals in order to cope with the trauma. Also, the counselor needs to assess the family system to determine if the adolescent seems to be acting out family struggles. In addition, the counselor needs to assess the adolescent for psychiatric problems that may be leading to alcohol/drug abuse.

The assessing counselor needs to determine the stages of use that the adolescent may be in (Jones, 1990). The first stage, which is called the learning stage, is where the adolescent learns how to use and to interpret the effects of the mood swing (the impact of the drug on emotional states). In the second stage, the adolescent seeks the mood swing, resulting in friendship, school, mood, and behavioral changes. In the third stage, the adolescent is preoccupied with the mood swing and changes friends, has more severe problems with family and school and work, and may be using daily. In the final stage, the adolescent may be using to feel normal and, as a result of use, may have some physical, memory, or emotional problems.

It may be difficult to engage the adolescent in the treatment process due to a distrust for authority (i.e., the assessing counselor may be viewed as another adult authority) and a tendency to be brought in for an assessment involuntarily by parents, school personnel, or legal system employees. It is important for the counselor to know state laws governing confidentiality of adolescent use and treatment. Some counselors report finding it helpful to tell the parents at the beginning of an interview that the counselor will not give the specifics of the adolescent's use, but they will tell them their diagnosis, recommendation, and general level of concern regarding the adolescent's use. When done in the adolescent's presence, this may increase the adolescent's degree of trust in the counselor and facilitate the disclosure of the chemical history. It is sometimes helpful also to interview the parents regarding the concern for the adolescent in the presence of the adolescent. This, too, may facilitate the trust and an atmosphere of openness, so it does not seem to the adolescent that the adults are talking behind his or her back. Finally, obtaining information from any additional adults is helpful. In particular, school counselors and teachers can be excellent resources for the assessing counselor when the adolescent is in school. If the adolescent is employed or in legal trouble, the authorities involved with these systems may be helpful.

One group of drugs that may be missed in the assessment process is inhalants. Of the three types of inhalant users described by Beauvais and Oetting (1987), two involve adolescents: young inhalant users (ages 12 and 13) and polydrug users (mid- to late adolescence). The first group does not use inhalants extensively or have severe physical problems, whereas the second group tends to use them moderately to severely. Inaba and Cohen (1991) report that 10- to 20-year-olds are most likely to use inhalants to the point of intoxication, and Miller and Gold (1990) report that the most common usage occurs between ages 10 and 15. Children seem most likely to be introduced to inhalants by their peers and are encouraged to stop their usage when, later in adolescence, their peers view it as "kid stuff" (Miller & Peele, 1995).

Inhalants provide a quick high with little hangover effects, although intense use within a brief period of time may result in a headache (Sharp & Rosenberg, 1997). Miller and Peele (1995) report inhalant abuse is prolific and dangerous because inhalants are legal, cheap, and accessible; children typically do not understand their vulnerability to the dangers of inhalants, which can cause death, even at first usage. Although some signs of inhalant abuse are similar to the previously listed consequences of chemical use, there are other signs specific to the use of inhalants. Assessing counselors need to be aware of (1) chemical odors, paint stains, and cold symptoms (Miller & Peele, 1995); (2) nausea, headaches, memory loss, and inability to concentrate (Davis, 1993); and (3) empty spray cans, plastic bags, and school supplies at home (Davis & Baker, 1990).

Treatment and Aftercare

Ross (1994) reviews and elaborates on Dr. Forest Richeson's four recovery dimensions. The first plateau is *admitting*. In this dimension, the adolescent has reached a place of admitting to an alcohol/drug problem. In the second plateau, *submitting*, the adolescent asks for assistance in addressing his or her alcohol/drug problem. During the third dimension, *committing*, the adolescent begins to take action steps to go along with the new beliefs he or she has about his or her alcohol/drug usage. In the fourth stage, *transmitting*, the adolescent realizes that in order to maintain recovery, he or she must consistently work on habit changes.

Effective treatment with adolescents involves a team approach made up of the different environments in which the adolescent is involved: school and/or employment, family, and peers. The adolescent needs to find a support group with individuals of similar age who can serve as role models for staying sober. The adolescent also needs to learn some aspects of adulthood in treatment (e.g., being responsible, setting limits on oneself, etc.) as well as aspects of childhood (e.g., allowing oneself to play). During treatment, the counselor needs continuously to assess family and psychiatric problems that may have been masked by the chemical usage. Overall, the treatment counselor for the adolescent needs to have an awareness of rebelliousness and power struggles as well as the common developmental issues present at this stage.

Aftercare for adolescent treatment is similar to treatment for addicts in general in that it involves applying the treatment goals to the posttreatment environment. In order to assist the adolescent in staying sober, it is important to involve the family, school and/or work environment, and other systems in relapse prevention as well as assist the adolescent in understanding his or her own "soft spots" with regard to relapse. An example of another system might be a church or a social group in the community. It is helpful to the adolescent to have an aftercare plan of recovery and to remain in contact with the primary treatment source (Schonberg, 1993).

CASE STUDY: SAMANTHA

Samantha is a 16-year-old female who has been referred to her school counselor for an alcohol/drug assessment. She was caught smoking marijuana on school grounds during morning classes the previous week. She has a C average and has never seen a school counselor before. Samantha is the oldest of five children, and her parents are influential in the local community. Upon entering the counseling session, she tells you that she has no interest in seeing a counselor and you better be careful because her dad is a "big deal around here and he wouldn't want anybody messing with me."

1. How would you establish a trusting, respectful atmosphere with Samantha?
2. What about Samantha's behavior might you find offensive and how would you handle that?

3. What would you need to know about confidentiality limitations with regard to this client, the school, and her parents? How would you communicate those limitations to Samantha?
4. How would you handle Samantha's implicit threats about her being carefully handled by you in terms of her father, the school administration, and liability issues?

Elderly

Assessment

Historically, alcohol and drug problems have not been addressed very often in the elderly population due to low problem rate estimations (Graham, Saunders, Flower, Timney, White-Campbell, & Pietropaolo, 1995). Graham and colleagues (1995) indicate that this problem has received more focus in the last decade due to awareness that surveys may not accurately assess the problem level; evidence that alcohol and drug problems may differ for this group; knowledge that the human body has a diminished capacity to process drugs with age, so it takes less for the elderly to experience the effects of alcohol/drugs; statistics showing the elderly have the highest prescription drug use; and requests from health care clinicians on how to work effectively with this population.

Alcoholism and addiction among the elderly may be missed due to stereotypes held of older people and/or because of uncertainty about how to treat the problem, the lack of hopefulness about treatment effectiveness, and discrimination about the elderly (Foster, 1995). Physicians may have difficulty with diagnosis due to the aging process presenting similar symptoms (Blake, 1990). Significant others may not intervene because of feelings such as shame and guilt (Peluso & Peluso, 1989; Vandeputte, 1989). In addition, older alcoholics tend to be hidden (Duckworth & Rosenblatt, 1976); that is, consequences related to alcohol/drug abuse may not be present due to more limited social functioning and no or limited employment (Abrams & Alexopoulos, 1987).

Although causal factors for alcoholism in this population have been difficult to determine (Graham et al., 1995), Lawson (1989) reports some common risks: stresses that accompany the aging process, and loss, bereavement, depression, isolation, retirement, and sex-related issues. Also, problems with depression, loneliness, and social support appear to precipitate drinking (Schonfeld & Dupree, 1991).

In order to assess addiction in the elderly, a classification system is helpful. Zimberg (1978) offers one kind of classification system for older alcoholics: late onset alcoholics and early onset alcoholics. *Late onset alcoholics,* about one-third of elderly alcoholics, are defined as those elderly who develop drinking problems later in life and may be using in response to stresses common to aging. *Early onset alcoholics,* about two-thirds of elderly alcoholics, are those who either continued a chronic problem of drinking all of their adult lives or developed a more chronic problem as they aged. The early onset alcoholic may also be using due to stresses and problems related to aging and he or she may have more medical problems resulting from alcohol.

Gambert (1997) recommends using "red flags" such as daily use of alcohol, times of drinking-related amnesia, refusal to stop using alcohol after warnings, physical problems related to usage, as well as changes in cognitive capacity and physical problems (anemia, liver abnormalities, frequent falls, seizures, etc.). Also, because the elderly often use medication for physical problems and experience depression and anxiety, their risk for addiction with prescribed medication is high (Gambert, 1997). Another sign of substance abuse can be the extensive usage of commonly misused prescription medications by the elderly: sedative-hypnotics, anti-anxiety, and analgesics (Gambert, 1997). A resource for individuals who want to approach the topic of a possible substance abuse problem with this population is the Hazelden pamphlet, *How to Talk to an Older Person Who Has a Problem with Alcohol or Medications* (1996).

Treatment and Aftercare

Even though the elderly may be as likely to recover from addiction as younger clients, treatment designed to meet the specific needs of the elderly may enhance their chances at recovery (Gambert, 1997). Adequate treatment requires knowledge about both addiction and the aging process (Graham et al., 1995). With regard to their chemical usage, they may require a longer withdrawal and a more structured environment while they are involved in treatment (Dunlop, Manghelli, & Tolson, 1989). Elderly patients require a thorough medical exam (including neurological testing) as well as a psychiatric exam in terms of the impact of the chemical usage on their bodies and the aging process on their bodies. Their treatment program also needs to be based on and adapted to a comprehensive assessment (Rathbone-McCuan, 1982). Also, social and emotional problems may need to be assessed to determine any causal problems underlying the chemical usage. This population needs to develop a social network that is sensitive to the needs of the elderly and that provides adequate recovery role models. Attendance at self-help meetings such as Alcoholics Anonymous may be one way to reduce social isolation (Clay, 1996). The addiction counselor may also need to be more involved in organizing social service networks to provide services for the elderly individual. Rathbone-McCuan and Bland (1975) suggest treatment center on three areas: the symptoms of their drinking problems, their health problems, and their social problems.

Because U.S. culture seems biased against older people, it is helpful for the elderly to have the option of counseling to work on struggles they have with ageism and the losses that go along with old age. Their children, church, and other community agencies may provide them with a sense of meaningfulness about their lives, which can facilitate their recovery. Lawson (1989) recommends that treatment be accessible to the elderly in places they naturally attend and in their homes. In addition, Corey and Corey (1982) recommend that the counselor have a respect for the elderly, a history of positive experiences with them, and knowledge of their age-related needs.

CASE STUDY: EVELYN

Evelyn is a 78-year-old woman who lives alone in her own home. She was referred to a community counselor for a drug/alcohol assessment because her Meals-on-Wheels delivery people and her home health aide noticed that she seemed to be "out of it" when they would try to talk with her, and they noticed that she had a lot of prescription medication on her dining room table as well as beer in the refrigerator. You have gone to her home to evaluate her and you notice the home is quite messy. Evelyn begins to cry shortly after you introduce yourself and ask if she has any close family or friends in the area. She seems unable to stop crying.

1. How would you help Evelyn begin to trust you with information about herself?
2. Would a messy home make it difficult to do an assessment of Evelyn's usage?
3. What stereotypes of the elderly do you hold that might make it difficult to hear Evelyn's life story, including her alcohol/drug history?
4. If an intervention on her usage is necessary, what factors would make it hard for you to intervene on Evelyn's life?

Homeless

Homeless clients may be difficult to treat because of the high rates of mental illness and substance abuse (Koegel, Burman, & Baumohl, 1996) in combination with their state of homelessness. Programs that focus on their homelessness may be reluctant to treat these individuals due to their mental health and/or substance abuse problems, and the state of homelessness may complicate working with them in mental health and substance abuse programs (Oakley & Dennis, 1996). Also, the homeless often have practical problems (i.e., housing, food, money, etc.), are mobile, and have a general mistrust of helping agencies (Schutt & Garrett, 1992). In addition, they often have health problems, are unemployed, have criminal histories (both as victims and perpetrators), are cross-addicted, and are socially isolated (Stahler, 1995). These numerous problems may cause counselors not to view them as "good" patients (Stahler, 1995). Often, they are placed at the end of waiting lists for treatment due to a lack of money and identification (Joseph & Paone, 1997).

Assessment

Homeless clients often provide misinformation about their alcohol/drug use (Schutt & Garrett, 1992). Counselors attempting to obtain information from homeless clients regarding their alcohol/drug usage need to do the following (Schutt & Garrett, 1992):

1. Ask the client questions that make him or her think about use history.
2. Ask a cluster of questions with regard to the usage rather than relying on only one.
3. Remember that long-term effects of usage and withdrawal from the substance(s) may affect the recall of the client.

4. Establish good rapport and practice patience because of the high possibility that the client may have both substance abuse and mental health problems.
5. Be aware of the tendency to be duped into believing the client has more awareness of his or her substance abuse problem than he or she actually does.

Treatment and Aftercare

Detoxification centers were started as alternatives to incarceration for publicly intoxicated individuals because of the 1971 Hughes Act (Uniform Alcoholism and Intoxication Treatment Act) to decriminalize public intoxication. Although sometimes jail is the only place available for publicly intoxicated individuals, when they are placed in detoxification centers, they have a safe, respectful place where they can withdraw and the chance for others to intervene on their usage. Intervention with the homeless can be difficult for reasons stated previously (their numerous problems) as well as their tendency to miss appointments and referrals, their high recidivism rates, and difficulty in connecting them with helping agencies (Schutt & Garrett, 1992). Schutt and Garrett (1992) recommend that counselors enhance the intervention process by doing the following:

1. Carefully match the client and the agency.
2. Give the client pertinent information about the referral, especially by giving the name of a contact person.
3. Make sure they have all necessary documents for the referral.
4. Arrange transportation to the referral agency.
5. Follow up with the referral agency once the intake has been done.

Beginning in the 1980s, the National Institute of Alcohol Abuse and Alcoholism (NIAAA) and the National Institute on Drug Abuse (NIDA) researched the treatment of homeless clients with substance abuse problems. Stahler and Stimmel (1995) review 14 of these funded projects in terms of their treatment effectiveness, service dosage effects, and client characteristics with regard to treatment effectiveness. Overall, the research results indicate that traditional abstinence-based programs are not as effective with this population as ones that have a harm-reduction emphasis, a careful assessment of the client and his or her needs, flexibility to meet a variety of needs and motivational levels, and a counseling style that allows for relapse (Oakley & Dennis, 1996). The findings also indicate that addiction treatment needs to include the meeting of the client's basic needs, high dropout rates should be expected, clients tend to improve over time even with small amounts of treatment (e.g., the control groups), clients need longer-term treatment, and clients who have more education and less severity in terms of substance abuse, criminal trouble, and social isolation have more positive treatment results (Stahler, 1995).

Oakley and Dennis (1996) make a number of recommendations for both counselors and agencies who work with the homeless population. First, counselors need to address both substance abuse and mental health issues at the same time. Second, systems such as mental health, social services, and legal agencies need to work together, since many of the clients have interaction with all of them. Next, agencies need to reach out to these clients in a nonthreatening manner that cultivates their motivation for help. Fourth, agencies also need to bring services to these clients over time and be flexible in terms of types services and styles of service delivery. Finally, general treatment strategies should include:

1. Involving clients in their assessment and treatment process
2. Educating clients on their conditions
3. Using peer groups for support and role-modeling
4. Cautiously discussing medication with them
5. Emphasizing harm-reduction techniques (decrease substance use, change to less dangerous ingestion mode, switch drugs, have a more healthful life, etc.)
6. Using case managers to arrange care
7. Helping them find jobs or meaningful activities
8. Providing treatment sensitive to their culture
9. Being suspicious of easy solutions to the problems of homelessness

Counselors working with this population need to be cognizant of all the struggles their clients may be experiencing. Viewing recovery from substance abuse problems as a process may facilitate a compassion that results in increased motivation with the homeless client.

CASE STUDY: RAY

Ray is a 40-year-old male who has come to a local homeless shelter. He has a bulbous nose, tremulous hands, and appears quite disheveled. During the intake process, he rarely looks at the interviewer and instead focuses his eyes on the floor. His answers are short and lack detail. Ray says he cannot remember the last time that he had something to drink or how much he normally drinks. He seems suspicious and defensive with regard to the questions about his drinking.

1. What would you focus on as a top priority with Ray?
2. How would you attempt to establish rapport with Ray?
3. What concerns might you have regarding the accuracy of Ray's substance use history and why?

Summary

This chapter surveyed special multicultural issues that can emerge in addiction counseling in assessment, treatment, and aftercare: gender, race, disability, adolescents, elderly, and homeless. Every counselor needs to be able to bridge differences with clients in order to develop treatment rapport. Awareness of how these different areas may affect assessment, treatment, and aftercare with these populations can help the counselor be sensitive to their issues and thereby facilitate the development of a personalized recovery plan that fits the client.

SUGGESTED READINGS

Albrecht, G. L. (1992). *The disability business: Rehabilitation in America.* Newbury Park, CA: Sage.

Atkinson, D. R., Morten, G., & Sue, D. W. (1993). *Counseling American minorities: A cross-cultural perspective* (4th ed.). Madison, WI: Brown & Benchmark.

Brown, F., & Tooley, J. (1989). Alcoholism in the black community. In G. W. Lawson & A. W. Lawson (Eds.), *Alcoholism and substance abuse in special populations.* Rockville, MD: Aspen.

Eden, S. L., & Aguilar, R. J. (1989). The Hispanic chemically dependent client: Considerations for diagnosis and treatment. In G. W. Lawson & A. W. Lawson (Eds.), *Alcoholism and substance abuse in special populations* (pp. 205–222). Rockville, MD: Aspen.

Geller, A. (1991). The effects of drug use during pregnancy. In P. Roth (Ed.), *Alcohol and drugs are women's issues: A review of the issues (Volume One)* (pp. 101–106). Metuchen, NJ: Scarecrow.

Glow, B. A. (1989). Alcoholism, drugs, and the disabled. In G. W. Lawson & A. W. Lawson (Eds.), *Alcoholism and substance abuse in special populations* (pp. 65–93). Rockville, MD: Aspen.

Graham, K., Saunders, S. J., Flower, M. C., Timney, C. B., White-Campbell, M., & Pietropaolo, A. Z. (1995). *Addictions treatment for older adults: Evaluation of an innovative client-centered approach.* New York: Haworth.

Hill, A. (1989). Treatment and prevention of alcoholism in the Native American fam-

ily. In G. W. Lawson & A. W. Lawson (Eds.), *Alcoholism and substance abuse in special populations* (pp. 247–272). Rockville, MD: Aspen.

Hill, S. Y. (1984). Vulnerability to the biomedical consequences of alcoholism and alcohol-related problems among women. In S. C. Wilsnack & L. J. Beckman (Eds.), *Alcohol problems in women.* New York: Guilford.

Johnson, S. (1991). Recent research: Alcohol and women's bodies. In P. Roth (Ed.), *Alcohol and drugs are women's issues (Volume One)* (pp. 32–42) Metuchen, NJ: Scarecrow.

Koegel, P., Burnam, M. A., & Baumohl, J. (1996). The causes of homelessness. In J. Baumohl (Ed.), *Homelessness in America* (pp. 24–33). Phoenix, AZ: Oryx.

Margolis, R. (1995). Adolescent chemical dependence: Assessment, treatment, and management. *Psychotherapy, 32,* 172–179.

Oakley, D., & Dennis, D. L. (1996). Responding to the needs of the homeless people with alcohol, drug, and/or mental disorders. In J. Baumohl (Ed.), *Homelessness in America* (pp. 179–186). Phoenix, AZ: Oryx.

Pape, P. A. (1993). Issues in assessment and intervention with alcohol- and drug-abusing women. In S. L. A. Straussner (Ed.), *Clinical work with substance-abusing clients* (pp. 251–269). New York: Guilford.

Schutt, R. K., & Garrett, G. R. (1992). *Responding to the homeless: Policy and practices.* New York: Plenum.

Sue, D. (1987). Use and abuse of alcohol by Asian Americans. *Journal of Psychoactive Drugs, 19,* 57–66.

REFERENCES

Abrams, R. C., & Alexopoulos, G. (1987). Substance abuse in the elderly: Alcohol and

prescription drugs. *Hospital & Community Psychiatry, 38,* 1285–1288.

Albrecht, G. L. (1992). *The disability business: Rehabilitation in America.* Newbury Park, CA: Sage.

Anderson, M. J., & Ellis, R. (1995). On the reservation. In N. A. Vacc, S. B. DeVaney, & J. Wittmer (Eds.), *Experiencing and counseling multicultural and diverse populations* (pp. 179–198). Bristol, PA: Accelerated Development.

Arrendondo, R., Weddige, R. L., Justice, C. L., & Fitz, J. (1987). Alcoholism in Mexican-Americans: Intervention and treatment. *Hospital and Community Psychiatry, 38,* 180–183.

Atkinson, D. R., Morten, G., & Sue, D. W. (1993). *Counseling American minorities: A cross-cultural perspective* (4th ed.). Madison, WI: Brown & Benchmark.

Beauvais, F., & LaBoueff, S. (1985). Drug and alcohol abuse intervention in American Indian communities. *The International Journal of the Addictions, 20,* 139–171.

Beauvais, F., & Oetting, E. R. (1987). Toward a clear definition of inhalant abuse. *The International Journal of the Addictions, 22,* 779–784.

Bell, P. (1990). *Chemical dependency and the African-American* [Brochure]. Center City, MN: Hazelden.

Blake, R. (1990). Mental health counseling and older problem drinkers. *Journal of Mental Health Counseling, 12,* 354–367.

Blume, S. B. (1997). Women: Clinical aspects. In J. H. Lowinson, P. Ruiz, R. B. Millman, & J. G. Langrod (Eds.), *Substance abuse: A comprehensive textbook* (3rd ed.) (pp. 645–654). Baltimore: Williams & Wilkins.

Brown, F., & Tooley, J. (1989). Alcoholism in the black community. In G. W. Lawson & A. W. Lawson (Eds.), *Alcoholism and substance abuse in special populations.* Rockville, MD: Aspen.

Burbules, N. C. (1993). *Dialogue in teaching.* New York: Teachers College Press.

Center for Substance Abuse Treatment (CSAT). (1994). *Practical approaches in the treatment of women who abuse alcohol and other drugs.* (DHHS Publication No. (SMA) 94-3006). Rockville, MD: Author.

Clarren, S. K. (1981). Recognition of Fetal Alcohol Syndrome. *Journal of the American Medical Association, 245,* 2436–2439.

Clay, R. (1996, December). Older alcoholics isolated, yet in need of treatment. *APA Monitor, 38.*

Corey, G., & Corey, M. S. (1982). *Groups: Process and practice* (2nd ed.). Monterey, CA: Brooks/Cole.

Cross, T. L., Bazron, B. J., Dennis, K. W., & Isaacs, M. R. (1989). *Towards a culturally competent system of care: A monograph on effective services for minority children who are severely emotionally disturbed.* Washington, DC: Child and Adolescent Service System Program Technical Assistance Center, Georgetown University Child Development Center.

Crumley, F. E. (1990). Substance abuse and adolescent suicidal behavior. *Journal of the American Medical Association, 263,* 3051–3056.

Davis, D. D. (1993). Inhalants: Know the facts. *The Next Step, 6,* 7.

Davis, D. J. (1990). Prevention issues in developing programs. In R. C. Engs (Ed.), *Women: Alcohol and other drugs* (pp. 71–77). Dubuque, IA: Kendall/Hunt.

Davis, L. (Discussion Guide Writer), & Baker, S. (Editor). (1990). *Inhalant abuse: Kids in danger/Adults in the dark* [Film]. (Available from Media Projects, Inc., 5215 Homer Street, Dallas, TX 75206).

Dembo, R., Burgos, W., Babst, D. U., Schmeidler, J., & Le Grand, L. E. (1978). Neighborhood relationships and drug involvement among inner city junior high school youths: Implications for drug education and prevention programming. *Journal of Drug Education, 8,* 231–252.

Doweiko, H. E. (1990). *Concepts of chemical dependency* (2nd ed.). Pacific Grove, CA: Brooks/Cole.

Duckworth, G. L., & Rosenblatt, A. (1976). Helping the elderly alcoholic. *Social Casework: The Journal of Contemporary Social Work, 57,* 291–301.

Dunlop, J., Manghelli, D., & Tolson, R. (1989). Senior alcohol and drug coalition statement of treatment philosophy for the elderly. *Professional Counselor, 4,* 39–42.

Eden, S. L., & Aguilar, R. J. (1989). The Hispanic chemically dependent client: Considerations for diagnosis and treatment. In G. W. Lawson & A. W. Lawson (Eds.), *Alcoholism and substance abuse in special populations* (pp. 205–222). Rockville, MD: Aspen.

Fiske, S. T., & Taylor, S. E. (1983). *Social cognition.* Reading, MA: Addison- Wesley.

Flores, P. J. (1986). Alcoholism treatment and the relationship of Native American cultural values to recovery. *The International Journal of the Addictions, 20,* 1707–1726.

Foster, S. (1995, November). Alcoholism: A growing and hidden epidemic among the elderly. *Counseling Today,* 19–26.

Frezza, M., DiPodova, C., Pozzato, G., Terpin, M. Baraona, E., & Lieber, D. S. (1990). High blood alcohol levels in women. *New England Journal of Medicine, 322,* 95–99.

Friere, P. (1989). *Pedagogy of the oppressed.* New York: Continuum.

Gambert, S. R. (1997). The elderly. In J. H. Lowinson, P. Ruiz, R. B. Millman, & J. G. Langrod (Eds.), *Substance abuse: A comprehensive textbook* (3rd ed.) (pp. 692–699). Baltimore: Williams & Wilkins.

Gary, L. E. (1986). Drinking, homicide, and the Black male. *Journal of Black Studies, 17,* 15–31.

Geller, A. (1991). The effects of drug use during pregnancy. In P. Roth (Ed.), *Alcohol and drugs are women's issues: A review of the issues (Volume One)* (pp. 101–106). Metuchen, NJ: Scarecrow.

Glass, E. J. (1980–81). Problem drinking among the blind and visually impaired. *Alcohol Health and Research World, 5,* 26–30.

Glow, B. A. (1989). Alcoholism, drugs, and the disabled. In G. W. Lawson & A. W. Lawson (Eds.), *Alcoholism and substance abuse in special populations* (pp. 65–93). Rockville, MD: Aspen.

Gordon, J. U. (1994). African American perspective. In J. U. Gordon (Ed.), *Managing multiculturalism in substance abuse services* (pp. 45–71). Thousand Oaks, CA: Sage.

Graham, K., Saunders, S. J., Flower, M. C., Timney, C. B., White-Campbell, M., & Pietropaolo, A. Z. (1995). *Addictions treatment for older adults: Evaluation of an innovative client-centered approach.* New York: Haworth.

Guthmann, D. (1994, November). *Counseling deaf and hard of hearing persons with substance abuse and/or mental health issues: Is cross cultural counseling possible?* Paper presented at the meeting of the Innovative Partnerships in Recovery, Overland Park, KS.

Guthmann, D., Swan, K., & Gendreau, C. (1994, November). *Placement, treatment, transition and ethical issues when serving chemically dependent deaf and hard-of-hearing clients.* Paper presented at the meeting of the Innovative Partnerships in Recovery, Overland Park, KS.

Harvey, W. B. (1985). Alcohol abuse and the Black community: A contemporary analysis. *Journal of Drug Issues, 15,* 81–91.

Hayes, L. L. (1997, June). Comprehensive services required when helping pregnant women overcome addiction. *Counseling Today,* 1, 20.

Hazelden. (1996). *How to talk to an older person who has a problem with alcohol or medications.* Center City, MN: Author.

Heinemann, A. W. (1997). Persons with disabilities. In J. H. Lowinson, P. Ruiz, R. B. Millman, & J. G. Langrod (Eds.), *Substance abuse: A comprehensive textbook* (3rd ed.) (pp. 716–725). Baltimore: Williams & Wilkins.

Herd, D. (1985). Migration, cultural transformation, and the rise of Black liver cirrhosis. *British Journal of Addiction, 80,* 397–410.

Hill, A. (1989). Treatment and prevention of alcoholism in the Native American family. In G. W. Lawson & A. W. Lawson (Eds.), *Alcoholism and substance abuse in special populations* (pp. 247–272). Rockville, MD: Aspen.

Hill, S. Y. (1981). A vulnerability model for alcoholism in women. *Journal of Addictions and Health-Focus on Women, 2,* 68–91.

Hill, S. Y. (1984). Vulnerability to the biomedical consequences of alcoholism and alcohol-related problems among women. In S. C. Wilsnack & L. J. Beckman (Eds.), *Alcohol problems in women* (pp. 121–154). New York: Guilford.

Hird, S., Khuri, E. T., Dusenbury, L., & Millman, R. B. (1997). Adolescents. In J. H. Lowinson, P. Ruiz, R. B. Millman, & J. G. Langrod (Eds.), *Substance abuse: A comprehensive textbook* (3rd ed.) (pp. 683–692). Baltimore: Williams & Wilkins.

Ho, M. K. (1994). Asian American perspective. In J. U. Gordon (Ed.), *Managing multiculturalism in substance abuse services* (pp. 72–98). Thousand Oaks, CA: Sage.

Hudson, H. L. (1986). How and why Alcoholics Anonymous works for blacks. *Alcoholism Treatment Quarterly, 2,* 31–43.

Hurley, D. L. (1991). Women, alcohol and incest: An analytical review. *Journal of Studies on Alcohol, 52,* 253–268.

Inaba, D. S., & Cohen, W. E. (1991). *Uppers, downers, all arounders.* Ashland, OR: CNS Productions.

John, S., Brown, L. S., & Primm, B. J. (1997). African Americans: Epidemiologic, prevention, and treatment issues. In J. H. Lowinson, P. Ruiz, R. B. Millman, & J. G. Langrod (Eds.), *Substance abuse: A comprehensive textbook* (3rd ed.) (pp. 699–705). Baltimore: Williams & Wilkins.

Johnson, S. (1991). Recent research: Alcohol and women's bodies. In P. Roth (Ed.), *Alcohol and drugs are women's issues (Volume One)* (pp. 32–42) Metuchen, NJ: Scarecrow.

Jones, B. M., & Jones, M. K. (1976). Alcohol effects in women during the menstrual cycle. *Annals of the New York Academy of Science, 273,* 576–587.

Jones, M. K., & Jones, B. M. (1984). Ethanol metabolism in women taking oral contraceptives. *Alcoholism: Clinical and Experimental Research, 8,* 24–28.

Jones, R. L. (1990). Evaluation of drug use in the adolescent. In L. M. Haddad & J. F. Winchester (Eds.), *Clinical management of poisoning and drug overdoses* (2nd ed.). Philadelphia: W. B. Saunders.

Joseph, H., & Paone, D. (1997). The homeless. In J. H. Lowinson, P. Ruiz, R. B. Millman, & J. G. Langrod (Eds.), *Substance abuse: A comprehensive textbook* (3rd ed.) (pp. 733–743). Baltimore: Williams & Wilkins.

Knox, D. H. (1986). Spirituality: A tool in the assessment and treatment of black alcoholics and their families. *Alcoholism Treatment Quarterly, 2,* 31–43.

Koegel, P., Burnam, M. A., & Baumohl, J. (1996). The causes of homelessness. In J. Baumohl (Ed.), *Homelessness in America* (pp. 24–33). Phoenix, AZ: Oryx.

Koss-Chioino, J. D., & Vargas, L. A. (1992). Through the cultural looking glass: A model for understanding culturally responsive psychotherapies. In L. A. Vargas & J. D. Koss-Chioino (Eds.), *Working with culture* (pp. 1–22). San Francisco: Jossey-Bass.

Lawson, G. W., Ellis, D. C., & Rivres, P. C. (1984). *Essentials of chemical dependency counseling.* Rockville, MD: Aspen.

Lawson, A. (1989). Substance abuse problems of the elderly: Considerations for treatment and prevention. In G. W. Lawson & A. W. Lawson (Eds.), *Alcoholism and substance abuse in special populations* (pp. 95–113). Rockville, MD: Aspen.

Madsen, W., & Madsen, C. (1969). The cultural structure of Mexican drinking behavior. *Quarterly Journal of Studies on Alcohol, 30,* 701–718.

Margolis, R. (1995). Adolescent chemical dependence: Assessment, treatment, and management. *Psychotherapy, 32,* 172–179.

May, P. A. (1986). Alcohol and drug misuse prevention programs for American Indians: Needs and opportunities. *Journal of Studies on Alcohol, 47,* 187–195.

McClelland, D. (1979). *Power: The inner experience.* New York: Irvington.

McCrone, W. P. (1982). Serving the deaf substance abuser. *Journal of Psychoactive Drugs, 14,* 199–203.

Miller, J. B. (1976). *Toward a new psychology of women.* Boston: Beacon.

Miller, L. J. (1995, October). *Addiction in women.* Paper presented at the National Dual Disorder Conference, Las Vegas, NV.

Miller, N. S., & Gold, M. S. (1990). Organic solvents and aerosols: An overview of abuse and dependence. *Annals of Clinical Psychiatry, 2,* 85–92.

Miller, G. A., & Peele, T. (1995). Inhalant abuse: An overview. *Focus on Later Childhood/ Early Adolescence, 8,* 1–3.

Minnesota Chemical Dependency Program for Deaf and Hard of Hearing Individuals. (1994, November). *Barriers to treatment and recovery.* Handout presented at the meeting of the Innovative Partnerships in Recovery, Overland Park, KS.

Mitchell, J. L. (1993). *Pregnant, substance-abusing women* (DHHS Publication No. (SMA) 93-1998). Rockville, MD: U.S. Department of Health and Human Services.

Mook, D. G. (1987). *Motivation: The organization of action.* New York: Norton.

Murphy, C. (1995). Scapegroup. *The Atlantic Monthly, 275,* 22–24.

National Institute on Alcohol Abuse and Alcoholism. (1990). *Alcohol alert.* Rockville, MD: Author.

Nelipovich, M., & Buss, E. (1989). Alcohol abuse and persons who are blind. *Alcohol Health Research World, 13,* 128–131.

Nelipovich, M., & Buss, E. (1991). Investigating alcohol abuse among persons who are blind. *Journal of Visual Impairment & Blindness, 85,* 343–345.

Oakeshott, M. (1991). *Rationalism in politics and other essays.* Indianapolis, IN: Liberty Press.

Oakley, D., & Dennis, D. L. (1996). Responding to the needs of the homeless people with alcohol, drug, and/or mental disorders. In J. Baumohl (Ed.), *Homelessness in America* (pp. 179–186). Phoenix, AZ: Oryx.

Orrok, B. (1992). Diverse presentations of substance abuse and posttraumatic stress disorder in incest survivors. In S. Shapiro & G. Dominiak (Eds.), *Sexual trauma and psychopathology* (pp. 113–142). New York: Lexington Books.

Pape, P. A. (1993). Issues in assessment and intervention with alcohol- and drug-abusing women. In S. L. A. Straussner (Ed.), *Clinical work with substance-abusing clients* (pp. 251–269). New York: Guilford.

Peluso, E., & Peluso, L. S. (1989). Alcohol and the elderly. *Professional Counselor, 4,* 44–46.

Rathbone-McCuan, E. (1982). Health and social intervention issues with the older alcoholic and alcohol abuser. In W. G. Wood, M. F. Elias, R. C. Adelman, & G. S. Roth (Eds.), *Alcoholism and aging: Advances in research.* Boca Raton, FL: CRC Press.

Rathbone-McCuan, E., & Bland, J. (1975). A treatment typology for the elderly alcohol abuser. *Journal of the American Geriatrics Society, 23,* 553–557.

Rebach, H. (1992). *Ethnic and multicultural drug abuse: Perspectives on current research.* New York: Haworth.

Reed, T. E. (1985). Ethnic differences in alcohol use. *Social Biology, 32,* 195–209.

Rendon, V. (1992). Deaf culture and alcohol and substance abuse. *Journal of Substance Abuse Treatment, 9,* 103–110.

Richardson, T. M., & Williams, B. A. (1990). *African-Americans in treatment: Dealing with cultural differences.* [Brochure]. Center City, MN: Hazelden.

Rogers, C. R. (1987). The underlying theory: Drawn from experiences with individuals and groups. *Counseling and Values, 32,* 38–45.

Ross, G. R. (1994). *Treating adolescent substance abuse: Understanding the fundamental elements.* Boston: Allyn and Bacon.

Ruiz, P., & Langrod, J. G. (1997). Hispanic Americans. In J. H. Lowinson, P. Ruiz, R. B. Millman, & J. G. Langrod (Eds.), *Substance abuse: A comprehensive textbook* (3rd ed.) (pp. 705–711). Baltimore: Williams & Wilkins.

Sandberg, K. A. (November, 1994). *Rehabilitation and substance abuse treatment working together to serve deaf clients.* Paper presented at the meeting of Innovative Partnerships in Recovery, Overland Park, KS.

Schonberg, S. K. (1993). *Guidelines for the treatment of alcohol- and other drug-abusing adolescents* (DHHS Publication No. (SMA) 95-3059). Rockville, MD: U.S. Department of Health and Human Services.

Schonfeld, L., & Dupree, L. W. (1991). Antecedents of drinking for early- and late- onset-elderly alcohol abusers. *Journal of Studies on Alcohol, 52,* 587–592.

Schutt, R. K., & Garrett, G. R. (1988). Social background, residential experiences and health problems of the homeless. *Psychosocial Rehabilitation Journal, 12,* 67–70.

Schutt, R. K., & Garrett, G. R. (1992). *Responding to the homeless: Policy and practices.* New York: Plenum.

Schwarz, B. (1995). The diversity myth: America's leading export. *Atlantic Monthly, 275,* 57–67.

Seed, The. (1987). Summer, pp. 4–5.

Sharp, C. W., & Rosenberg, N. L. (1997). Inhalants. In J. H. Lowinson, P. Ruiz, R. B. Millman, & J. G. Langrod (Eds.), *Substance abuse: A comprehensive textbook* (3rd ed.) (pp. 246–264). Baltimore: Williams & Wilkins.

Spelman, E. V. (1988). *Inessential woman: Problems of exclusion in feminist thought.* Boston: Beacon.

Stahler, G. J. (1995). Social interventions for homeless substance abusers: Evaluating treatment outcomes. In G. J. Stahler & B. Stimmel (Eds.), *The effectiveness of social interventions for homeless substance abusers* (pp. xiii–xxiv). Binghamton, NY: Haworth.

Stahler, G. J., and Stimmel, B. (1995). *The effectiveness of social interventions for homeless substance abusers.* Binghamton, NY: Haworth.

Straussner, S. L. A. (1985). Alcoholism in women: Current knowledge and implications for treatment. In D. Cook, S. L. A. Straussner, & C. Fewell (Eds.), *Psychosocial issues in the treatment of alcoholism* (pp. 61–74). New York: Haworth.

Sue, D. (1987). Use and abuse of alcohol by Asian Americans. *Journal of Psychoactive Drugs, 19,* 57–66.

Sue, D., & Sue, D. M. (1995). Asian Americans. In N. A. Vacc, S. B. DeVaney, & J. Wittmer (Eds.), *Experiencing and counseling multicultural and diverse populations* (pp. 63–89). Bristol, PA: Accelerated Development.

Sue, D., & Sue, S. (1987). Cultural factors in the clinical assessment of Asian-Americans. *Journal of Clinical and Consulting Psychology, 55,* 479–487.

Surry, J. (1985). The "self-in-relation": A theory of women's development. *Work in Progress, No. 13.* Wellesley, MA: Stone Center Working Papers Series.

Sutker, P. B., Goist, K. C., & King, A. R. (1987). Acute alcohol intoxication in women: Relationship to dose and menstrual cycle phase. *Alcoholism: Clinical and Experimental Research, 11,* 74–79.

Tyas, S., & Rush, B. (1993). The treatment of disabled persons with alcohol and drug problems: Results of a survey of addiction services. *Journal of Studies on Alcohol, 54,* 275–282.

Vandeputte, C. (1989). Why bother to treat older adults? The answer is compelling. *Professional Counselor, 4,* 34–38.

Vacc, N. A., DeVaney, S. B., & Wittmer, J. (1995). Introduction. In N. A. Vacc, S. B. DeVaney, & J. Wittmer (Eds.), *Experiencing and counseling multicultural and diverse populations* (pp. 1–8). Bristol, PA: Accelerated Development.

Vernon, M. (1990). *The psychology of deafness.* Reading, MA: Addison Wesley.

Weisner, T. S., Weibel-Orlando, J. C., & Long, J. (1984). "Serious drinking," "white man's drinking" and "teetotaling": Drinking levels and styles in an urban Indian population. *Journal of Studies on Alcohol, 45,* 237–249.

Westermeyer, J. (1997). Native Americans, Asians, and new immigrants. In J. H. Lowinson, P. Ruiz, R. B. Millman, & J. G. Langrod (Eds.), *Substance abuse: A comprehensive textbook* (3rd ed.) (pp. 712–716). Baltimore: Williams & Wilkins.

Westermeyer, J., & Peake, E. (1983). A ten-year follow-up of alcoholic Native Americans in Minnesota. *American Journal of Psychiatry, 140,* 189–194.

Wilsnack, S. C. (1973). Sex-role identity in female alcoholism. *Journal of Abnormal Psychology, 82,* 25–26.

Wilsnack, S. C. (1990). Alcohol abuse and alcoholism: Extent of the problem. In R. C. Engs (Ed.), *Women: Alcohol and other drugs* (pp. 17–30). Dubuque, IA: Kendall/Hunt.

Yee, B. W. K., & Thu, N. D. (1987). Correlates of drug use and abuse among Indo-chinese refugees: Mental health implications. *Journal of Psychoactive Drugs, 19,* 77–83.

Young, T. J. (1988). Substance abuse among Native Americans. *Clinical Psychology Review, 8,* 125–138.

Zimberg, S. (1978). Psychosocial treatment of elderly alcoholics. In S. Zimberg, J. Wallace, & S. B. Blume (Eds.), *Practical approaches to alcoholism psychotherapy* (pp. 347–362). New York: Plenum.

C H A P T E R

10 Personal and Professional Development of the Counselor

PRETEST

1. What are some common ethical dilemmas facing addiction counselors?
2. How can a counselor avoid ethical dilemmas?
3. What questions can counselors ask themselves to clarify their relationships with clients?
4. What are some basic documentation guidelines?
5. What are common addiction-related testimonies?
6. What are some general guidelines for testifying in court? Specific guidelines for substance abuse cases?
7. What are the components of a wounded healer theoretical framework?
8. What process can a counselor use in order to decide whether to stay or leave an agency?
9. What are some guidelines for realistic counselor self-care?
10. What are some ways for counselors to address their own issues?
11. What are danger spots for addicted counselors? Nonaddicted counselors?

Ethical Issues

Overall, counselors need to remember the importance of doing no harm to clients, and yet it is also important to remember that harm can be done by inaction as well as action (Bissell & Royce, 1994). The definitions of ethics, morals, and laws needs to be briefly addressed. *Ethical principles* act as a rudder that guides the behavior of counselors; they are the principles that direct the moral- and value-based decisions that affect the counseling process. *Moral decisions* are the concrete decisions counselors make in a situation based on the values (beliefs, attitudes, and behaviors) that have important personal meaning. *Laws* are the formalized moral decisions of a culture. Ethical principles for counselors, then, are highly intertwined with the laws of culture; at the same time, because an action is legal does not mean that it is ethical (Bissell & Royce, 1994). Ethical issues are explored in this section along with some of the laws with which they intertwine.

Counselors working with addicted clients should contact their respective professional organization(s) for copies of their ethical guidelines. Because of their work with addicted clients, counselors should also contact their state addiction licensing or credentialing agencies for copies of their ethical guidelines. Supervisors of addiction counselors as well as agencies employing addiction counselors would be well served to have a copy of pertinent ethical principles on hand for reference.

Common Ethical Dilemmas

Ethical standards guide the behaviors of counselors, and ethical dilemmas involve decisions about situations that are not explicitly prohibited or allowed by law (Anderson, 1996). Although numerous ethical dilemmas can arise for counselors, three main ones will be explored in this section: confidentiality issues, dual relationship issues, and the crossover area between legal and ethical concerns. Some ethical dilemmas can be avoided or reduced by awareness of the issues in these three areas.

Prior to discussion of confidentiality issues, some distinctions must be drawn between confidentiality and disclosure. *Confidentiality* means that the information obtained in a counseling session is not shared with others unless written permission has been given by the client. *Privileged communication* is legal protection given to certain professionals under state law, which prohibits information being given without the consent of the client. Therefore, while a counselor has a professional, ethical commitment to confidentiality, this commitment may or may not be held up under privileged communication laws in the state where the counselor works.

Anderson (1996) discusses two exceptions to privilege: duty to report and duty to warn. *Duty to report* means that the counselor has an ethical obligation to break confidentiality by contacting authorities when the client or a third person can be harmed. Counselors are mandated reporters of suspected child abuse, so they are legally required to report suspected abuse to the authorities. *Duty to warn* means that the counselor needs to determine if the client is seriously dangerous, and in some states, that the potential victim can be identified. Anderson (1996) suggests that counselors in this situation consult with a professional colleague or supervisor, make necessary referrals, contact the police and the potential victim, and think about possible commitment for the client. Excellent additional reading in the areas of confidentiality and privileged communication and exceptions to these areas are in the *ACA Legal Series,* volumes 6 and 8, respectively. Also, for a specific focus on addiction, "Ethical and Legal Aspects of Confidentiality" (Brooks, 1997) covers a variety of external and internal disclosures related to areas such as medical, legal, and criminal; research, audit, and evaluation; child abuse and neglect; duty to warn; HIV and AIDS; and modern technology issues.

In the early 1970s, the statute on substance abuse treatment patient disclosure information was passed (42 U.S.C. 290dd-2 and 42 Code of Federal Regulations, Part 2) and was clarified in 1975 regulations ("Confidentiality of Alcohol and Drug Abuse Patient Records"), which were amended in 1987 and 1995 (Brooks, 1997). In the area of confidentiality and disclosure, the *Federal Register* (1987) stipulates the regulations for all federally funded drug treatment programs. These federal regulations supercede less protective state and local laws (Brooks, 1997). Because the client's involvement with an addiction treatment program states the client's diagnosis, the individual's presence or absence at the facility cannot be told without a signed release of information (Bissell & Royce, 1994). All patient records are considered confidential. Programs cannot disclose patient information except in certain situations. These exceptions include a client's proper consent, a medical emergency, a court order, a crime committed against agency personnel or on the agency's premises, and research and/or auditing requests.

Proper consent means that the patient has been informed of the need for and the extent of the disclosure. It also requires that the consent form has the names of the program, disclosure recipient, and patient; the signature of the patient; the date of the signature; the right of the patient to revoke the disclosure; and written notification to the disclosure recipient of the prohibition to redisclosure the information to another agency. For example, a consent form for a client may include the following information: The Rural Addictions Treatment Center in Alexandria, South Carolina (name of program) releases information specifically to the Rural Halfway House in Alexandria, South Carolina (disclosure recipient who cannot redisclose the information) regarding the treatment of Rod Hoop (patient) who has the right to revoke this disclosure within one year of the signed date (patient signature and date of signature is on the form). Disclosure is allowed for the purposes of diagnosis, treatment, or rehabilitation; central registry, which prevents the client from being enrolled in more than one program concurrently; funding; employment; contacts with legal counsel, family, significant others, and the criminal justice system; and other situations where consent is given and no harm is anticipated to the patient or the relationship between the patient and the program.

It is important to note that some communications are not viewed as disclosures in the *Federal Register* (1987). These include communications within a program or between a program and the agency that has administrative control over the program, the qualified service organization that provides services to the program, and communications that do not involve any patient-identifying information.

Minors have basically the same rights as adults—they must be informed before disclosure occurs and be involved in and updated about decisions made (Remley, 1985). In order to have information released about him or her—even if the information is to be given to his or her parents—the minor has to sign the consent form (Brooks, 1997). If state law requires parental permission to treat the minor, a parent's signature is also necessary (Brooks, 1997). When counseling minors, issues regarding parents and schools often arise. Once again, the counselor needs to focus on the welfare of the client (adolescent) in a decision based on the client's age and education, the client's relationship with parents or guardians, and the extent of potential for harm of disclosing or not disclosing (Anderson, 1996). With regard to schools, Salo and Shumate (1993) state that the parent or guardian should be consulted before releasing information to school personnel, since the parent or guardian technically "owns" the privacy rights of the adolescent. Anderson (1996) also suggests that school personnel be told only that information that they need to know within the context of the educational setting.

CASE STUDY: JULIAN

Julian is a 16-year-old male who recently completed inpatient/outpatient addiction treatment and has come in for counseling regarding recovery issues. His parents have come with him to the first session and make some demands: (1) they want a weekly summary of what issues are discussed in counseling, (2) they want this summary to be specific and written, and (3) they want copies of the written summary to go to them and the principal of Julian's school. Julian appears quiet and sullen while his parents make their demands. Discuss how you would handle this situation in light of the following questions:

1. What information would you need to have about Julian and his parents to make clinical decisions regarding confidentiality that are in Julian's best interests?
2. What limits would you set with his parents regarding information sent to them? To the school?
3. How would you structure sessions with Julian and his parents (e.g., who would be present)?

A counselor may be required to go to court, due to a subpoena or a verbal order from a judge, but may be prohibited from giving the court information regarding the client based on the regulations of the *Federal Register* (1987). A subpoena does not give the counselor the right to testify, but it can result in the counselor being charged with contempt of court if it is ignored. This is an ethical dilemma in that the counselor has a responsibility to go to court, has limits on information that can be given in court, and faces contempt of court charges if not viewed as being compliant with the court's demands. The counselor has three options in this ethical dilemma. He or she can testify, refuse to testify (and possibly face contempt of court charges), or explore some limited recourse strategies when receiving a subpoena or a court order. Three limited recourse strategies are appealing for privileged communication, testifying in the judge's chambers, or cooperating with the client's lawyer (Herlihy & Sheeley, 1986). When a counselor receives a subpoena or a court order, it is wise to consult either a supervisor, the agency director, and/or a colleague experienced in legal matters.

Prior to discussing other ethical dilemmas, a final note is necessary. Addiction counselors who are following *Federal Register* (1987) guidelines need to communicate the limitations of their disclosure to others in a respectful way. For example, when other professionals request information, a thoughtful explanation of the guidelines and resulting limitations of disclosure cooperation can communicate professional respect, which can facilitate ongoing collaboration.

A common source of ethical dilemmas in counseling practice is found in the area of dual relationships. Dual relationship issues are sometimes relatively clear. For example, it is clearly prohibited for counselors to be sexual with their clients. However, other types of dual relationships are less clear, particularly regarding those addiction counselors who are in some type of recovery process that involves self-help groups. The counselor may be in recovery from addictions or be involved in a related organization such as Al-Anon. The 1994 membership of the National Association of Alcoholism and Drug Abuse Counselors (NAADAC) showed that 58 percent of its members were recovering addicts (NAADAC Education and Research Foundation, 1995). Issues of dual relationships may emerge around self-help meeting attendance, sponsorship, or general recovery support. As Doyle (1997) points out, risks exist when client and counselor attend the same self-help group in terms of anonymity (for the counselor) and confidentiality (for the client). Although the counselor may have the best intentions, a dual relationship with a client can be very confusing and potentially damaging for the client. The counselor is recommended to ask himself or herself the following questions:

1. What are the different roles I have with regard to this client?
2. Are these roles conflictual with one another or potentially confusing or damaging for my client?
3. What is the least number of roles I can feasibly have with this client?
4. What is the most important role I can have with my client?
5. Are there personal needs of my own that I am trying to have met with my client?
6. Is there anyone else in the recovering community who can meet these needs with my client?
7. Is a referral to another addictions counselor necessary in order to clarify my role and responsibility to my client?
8. Should I consult with another professional regarding the roles I carry with my client?
9. Am I trying to treat someone with whom I have a strong personal relationship (or with one of their family members)?

Using questions such as these may assist the counselor in clarifying the roles held with a client. A motto of "The fewer the roles, the better" may be a solid rule for a counselor to follow. Other colleagues or supervisors may be helpful in determining the extent of the dual relationship if they have a sensitivity to dual relationship issues. Doyle (1997) makes the following recommendations to addiction counselors: examine applicable ethical codes and regulations, seek out experienced colleagues for advice, minimize potential dual relationships, carefully self-disclose with regard to personal recovery, and advocate within the profession regarding clarity of dual relationship issues.

CASE STUDY: SHELLY

You have a client named Shelly who is the same age as you and is in a similar life situation as you in terms of partner, children, and living situation. Shelly is a recovering alcoholic. You have started to attend Al-Anon as a way of educating yourself about addiction and as you attend, you discover some family issues that you had previously overlooked and been in denial about. You have attended one Al-Anon group for about three months and you feel very comfortable talking with the members about your personal issues. After three months of being in the group and two weeks of counseling Shelly, she shows up at your Al-Anon group. Discuss your reactions to her presence with the following questions as a guide:

1. How would you greet Shelly?
2. How would you interact with her in the group?
3. How would you change your sharing in the group?
4. Would you give up this group so Shelly could go to it, would you insist Shelly not join the group, or would you continue to attend even though she is there?
5. How would Shelly's presence at the meeting affect the focus of your next counseling session with her?

In some areas, ethics and the law cross over extensively. Two areas that may involve the addictions counselor are documentation (making progress notes) and consultation. Documenting requires a safe balance between giving the facts as reported and giving too much information on the client. Some basic guidelines include:

1. Write in black ink so that copies can be made easily.
2. Write clearly (or have notes typed) so that it is easy to read the notes, thereby reducing misunderstandings of the notes.
3. Use a note-writing format approved by the agency.
4. Carefully choose words that place the emphasis on the self-report aspects of the information (e.g., "Client said," "Client stated," "Client reported," etc.).
5. Write enough so critical information is captured, but not so much as to increase one's liability.
6. Keep in mind who may be reading the chart notes, including the courts.
7. Remember: If it is not written down, it did not happen.

When in doubt of what action to take regarding a client, it is commonly good protection to consult with a colleague. The courts will generally respect a professional who acted in good conscience and with the consultation of a colleague. The consultation effort should also be charted.

Until a counselor or a colleague of a counselor is sued, the concern regarding legal matters may seem academic or overreactionary. Once a counselor has been sued or has watched a colleague be sued, the serious reality of the following ethical and legal principles cannot be ignored. The anxiety, frustration, confusion, and apprehension involved in a lawsuit as well as the time, energy, and money it requires can be overwhelming for the counselor. The following case study is included in an attempt to facilitate the legal reality of being sued.

C A S E S T U D Y

You are an addictions counselor at a mental health agency. Your client is a single, 33-year-old female who comes for addiction treatment on her own. It is discovered during treatment for her addiction that she also struggles with depression. She sees a psychiatrist affiliated with the agency and is prescribed antidepressants. After two weeks of addictions and mental health treatment, she overdoses on the antidepressants and kills herself. Even though you have seen her weekly, you did not pick up any indicators of suicidal tendencies; however, you did not chart that she stated she was not suicidal. Also, you did not consult directly with the psychiatrist or a colleague when she was diagnosed as depressed. Your chart notes make it appear that you talked with her only about attending self-help meetings and that she reported being sober. One week after her suicide, the family contacts the director of your agency and states that they will be suing you for malpractice.

1. What mistakes did you make in working with this client?
2. What actions could you have taken to protect yourself better?
3. What is your best course of action now?
4. How will you cope with your fears regarding the lawsuit?

Ethical dilemmas for the addictions counselor are complex, multifaceted situations that resist a simplistic approach. To avoid ethical dilemmas, the counselor can use the following guidelines (Hubert, 1996):

1. Inform the client of limitations on the counseling relationship before beginning counseling.
2. Always act in the best interest of the client.
3. Work within professional competency boundaries.
4. When needed, be able to explain the rationale for your professional decisions and behaviors.
5. Consult with other professionals regarding ethical dilemmas and consult with an attorney if necessary.
6. Stay current with professional and legal guidelines.

Testifying in Court

Addictions counselors, as other counselors, must use ethical principles to guide their behavior (Swenson, 1993). However, for the counselor in a different setting (e.g., a courtroom), the ethical principles may be too vague to guide behavior (Swenson, 1993). This section will discuss some basic tenets regarding courtroom testimony prior to discussing common areas of testimony for addictions counselors and how to increase their effectiveness.

First, the addictions counselor must qualify as an expert witness: having access to more than common knowledge in an area, demonstrating that knowledge, and using reliable information from the scientific (addictions) community (Haugaard & Reppucci, 1988; Swenson, 1993). Second, the addictions counselor must work closely with the attorney using his or her testimony (Bossin, 1992). Third, the addictions counselor needs to be aware of how differently counseling and the law look at issues in order to speak an understandable, ethical "language" in the courtroom. Fourth, documented consultation may include a review of ethical guidelines, contact with an attorney, and contact with an addictions counselor.

Typical Addiction-Related Testimony

Three main areas of testimony involving the addictions counselor are the DUI (driving under the influence)/DWI (driving while impaired), process of addiction, and custody hearings. In the DUI/DWI assessment (the label used depends on the state's legislation regarding using alcohol/drugs and driving), the addictions counselor is generally being asked to testify if the person is or is not addicted. The blood alcohol concentration (BAC) is also set by state legislation to determine if a person is legally intoxicated. As Shaffer and Kauffman (1985) suggest, the counselor determining the level of addiction enhances the assessment by drawing from a number of sources. These sources include interviews with clients and their significant others, measurements (self-report, psychometric, and physiological), case histories, and behavioral observations. The more thorough and broad the assessment, the more likely the counselor will be viewed as an expert and have his or her testimony taken seriously. Although a counselor may not always be able to obtain information from all of the previously mentioned areas, the more information obtained from each area, the stronger the testimony. One notation is important for the counselor. It is critical to know the assessment instruments typically used in the state in which the counselor is testifying. In addition, in order to enhance testimony, it is helpful for the counselor to have some basic knowledge of how the psychometric and physiological tests operate.

When testifying with regard to the process of addiction, two areas emerge: the development of addiction and the recovery from addiction. There are different theories as to the cause of addiction. McHugh, Beckman, and Frieze (1979) organized these theories into four models: moral, psychological, sociocultural, and medical. *Moral* theories view the alcoholic as a degenerate who is morally weak and should be treated with punishment. *Psychological* models focus on psychodynamic issues (personal pathology caused by unconscious conflicts that must be changed), personality trait issues (personality traits that cause the problems must be changed), and behavior learning (alcohol and the environment reinforcers must be changed). *Sociocultural* models view the alcoholic in a problem situation containing social forces and contexts that need to be addressed. *Medical* models view the alcoholic as the patient and the cause of the addiction as a physiological dysfunction. Also, more recent biopsychosocial models of addiction account for both biogenetic traits and psychosocial factors.

There is no firm agreement in the field of addictions as to the cause of addiction and the one proven method of recovery. In some parts of the country, the disease model of addiction (Jellinek, 1960) is the most widely used and respected. This model, which fits under the medical model discussed in Chapter 1, views alcoholism as a disease with symptoms that are progressive. The two key elements in this model are loss of control over drinking and progression of the disease, which ends in death. Counselors typically using this model will refer to a Jellinek symptomology sheet. It is important to remember, however, that although the disease model is popular in some parts of the country, in other areas of the country, other models, such as the harm-reduction model (Sorge, 1991), which encourages reduction from drug use harm to self and others, are more widely used.

The best approach for the addictions counselor is to determine the model he or she is most comfortable using in the assessment and treatment process, the one(s) his or her organization recommends, and the one(s) used by the state in which the counselor is testifying. In spite of the theoretical disagreements in the field of addictions, the counselor can rest his or her testimony in specific behaviors, a history of drinking/using related consequences (i.e., drinking on the job, unable to quit drinking, etc.), and reports by significant others.

Maintenance of the recovery process is also a type of testimony for the addictions counselor. This classification of testimony involves areas such as general relapse concerns, drug testing, and support group attendance. Regarding general relapse concerns, the counselor may need to educate the court as to the danger of relapse. Marlatt and Gordon (1985) and Prochaski, DiClemente, and Norcross (1992) do an excellent job of describing the difficulties in making a behavior change and would be a good reference for the addictions counselor. Court testimony that focuses on behavioral indicators of recovery maintenance (no legal problems, apparent attendance at self-help groups, contact with addictions counselor, etc.) is more beneficial than testimony that focuses on the individual client's motivations or intentions to remain drug free (Miller & Kaplan, 1996).

Drug testing is one avenue for determining if the client is free from the use of drugs. Inaba and Cohen (1989) describe approximately two dozen drug-testing methods involving samples of urine, blood, saliva, hair, and tissue. The authors also caution that no method is absolutely accurate because of problems that can occur with the technology, handling, or manipulation of the samples. If the counselor testifies regarding drug testing, it is important for the counselor to know the quality of the laboratory working with the specimens, the strengths and limitations of the type of drug testings used, as well as the informed consent of the client being tested (Miller & Kaplan, 1996).

In terms of support group attendance, courts have frequently referred clients with drug/alcohol problems to attend such groups. Often, courts will ask clients to have attendance slips signed by the group leader to acknowledge that they went to the meeting. The counselor needs to keep in mind that these slips can be easily forged by clients (only the first name and last initial is required for the signature) and that some groups, particularly 12-step groups, do not want to sign them because they believe it violates their group traditions. Finally, clients have often been referred to Alcoholics Anonymous (AA) by the courts; however, due to an increase of different types of self-help groups (see Chapter 7) and concerns regarding religious freedom (Trimpey, 1989), counselors may need to provide clients with alternative self-help group information as well as 12-step group information. Counselors must remember that the ease of forgery, group resistance to signing attendance slips, and the right to choose a self-help group that fits their values may shape the clients' behaviors regarding recovery and limit the soundness of counselor testimony.

Child custody testimony may arise for the addictions counselor when one or both parents is actively using alcohol/drugs or in the recovery process. Once again, the capacity to inform the court regarding the addiction and recovery process is important. The additional information that the counselor needs to incorporate at this stage is that which specifically addresses child custody. Bossin (1992) recommends that counselors (1) evaluate the family to determine the child's best interest, (2) demonstrate psychological deficiency in one parent and the mental health in the other, and (3) educate the court about the psychological problems. The addictions counselor will need to use these guidelines within the context of addictions and probably in conjunction with another mental health professional making the child custody assessment. Poirier (1991) encourages counselors to do very thorough evaluations in order to predict future behavior, and other authors (Howell, 1990; Remley & Miranti, 1991) encourage breadth and depth to the evaluations in order to improve the quality of evaluations. As stated previously, the counselor needs to acknowledge the limits to predicting parental behavior and use multiple data-gathering methods to make such predictions.

Miller and Kaplan (1996) offer these suggestions for expert testimony:

1. Upon receiving a subpoena or verbal order, either testify, risk contempt of court by refusing to testify, or explore limited recourse strategies (appeal for privileged communication, testify in camera [chambers], or cooperate with the client's lawyer).
2. When testifying regarding a diagnosis of substance abuse/dependency, be thorough and use psychometric assessment instruments approved by the state in which testimony is made.
3. When testifying about drug test results, know the strengths and limitations of the drug-testing method used.
4. In response to questions regarding a client's potential relapse, respond by commenting on behavioral indicators of abstinence.

When child custody is involved in a substance abuse case, make sure a thorough evaluation is done and know the limits of being able to predict relapse in a recovering individual.

Miller and Kaplan (1996) also provide 16 general guidelines for court testimony:

1. Watch other individuals testify.
2. Find out what the court expects from the testimony.
3. Be knowledgeable of current professional literature on the relevant mental health topic(s).
4. Obtain informed consent from the client.
5. Talk with the attorney representing the counselor prior to the court appearance.
6. Prepare testimony with the representing attorney and/or an experienced colleague.
7. Dress professionally for the court appearance.
8. Look confident in court, but do not appear overprepared.
9. Relax while testifying.
10. Listen carefully to the attorneys and the judge when on the stand, then take time to formulate a clear response.
11. Do not take notes to the stand.
12. Take a contact sheet with general dates and descriptions to the stand.
13. Provide testimony based on therapeutic knowledge:
    a. Characteristics observed in the client
    b. Conversations with the client and significant others
14. Admit not knowing an answer.
15. Be brief at cross-examination.
16. Avoid arguments with opposing counsel. (p. 28)

Working with Difficult Others

Wounded Healer Theoretical Framework

Remen, May, Young, and Berland (1985) present the polarized relationship between being wounded and being healed. Often, this view, when applied to counselors, holds the expectation that the counselor is and will be immune to psychological, spiritual, and emotional vulnerabilities. Remen and colleagues (1985), Jourard (1971), and Frankl (1963) describe the wounded healer more along a continuum than a dichotomy where the wounded healer bridges the worlds of wellness and illness: "Rather than concealing their wounds, shamanic healers often display them as marks of the authenticity of their skills" (Remen et al., 1985, p. 84). This section is an expansion of the article by Miller, Wagner, Britton, and Gridley (1998).

The counselor who is able to transcend painful, tragic life experiences can bridge the mental illness and mental health worlds, bringing compassion to the therapeutic relationship (Hollis, 1989; Holmes, 1991; Miller & Baldwin, 1987). One example of this bridging is addiction counseling where counselors, who are recovering addicts or who have lived in addicted systems, have learned from and transcended their pain, thereby becoming wounded healers. However, untreated wounds can be destructive to counselors' lives and the lives of their clients (Miller, 1981). It is important, then, for counselors to understand their own wounds so that they can do more effective work with their clients.

In this framework, the individual *counselor's history of emotional pain* is the first area addressed. These areas can be considered vulnerabilities. Due to different life experiences, these vulnerabilities will vary in frequency and depth for each counselor. They may emerge most readily in counseling with regard to countertransference issues—when the counselor projects his or her own issues on the client. For example, an addicted female client may be difficult for a counselor to work with in therapy because she reminds the counselor of his or her addicted mother. The client may then unknowingly elicit critical, defensive, self-protective attitudes, comments, and behaviors from the counselor, simply by the interaction. These projections can also occur with co-workers, supervisors, or administrators with whom the counselor has difficulty working at the agency.

The second level of the framework is at the *system entry level.* Two concepts important to discuss prior to system entry discussion are chance encounters and empty self. Bandura (1982) defines a *chance encounter* as "an unintended meeting of persons unfamiliar with each other" (p. 748), which has an impact on one's life because of liking the other person or obtaining satisfaction from him or her. The vulnerability of the individual to such encounters is enhanced by the loss of internal behavior guides and potential social rewards. Cushman (1990) discusses this vulnerability in a cultural sense: An individual has an *empty self* due to a lack of family, community, and tradition. In this experience of emptiness, one may be vulnerable to addictive tendencies and having systems define who one is and what one does. Chance encounters with individuals and an empty sense of self can be powerfully healing or crippling experiences for the unprepared counselor: The counselor can learn from and transcend the pain or become lost in it.

When entering a system, three aspects are operating: power differential, losses, and discrepancy. Upon entering the system, those with the least power will be new and lower-status individuals. As a counselor becomes more involved in the mental health system, he or she becomes more aware of the amount of power and influence he or she holds in the system. Also affecting the influence of the system on the individual is the amount of losses experienced. Any change involves both gains and losses. The types and extremes of loses experienced in joining a new agency depend on the individual counselor. Greater losses result in greater uprootedness and vulnerability to the influence of the system. The impaired counselor may reflect the malfunctions of the work system (Stadler, Willing, Eberhage, & Ward, 1988).

Finally, the greater the discrepancy between the counselor's expectations of the job and the reality of the job, the greater the cognitive dissonance experienced by the counselor. Forsyth (1983) reports that individuals who invest in a group with high costs will emphasize the rewards, minimize the costs, and become more favorable to the group. Minimizing the costs of being involved in a system may make the counselor more vulnerable to being abused by the system: The denial about the abuse may keep the counselor from protecting himself or herself. The greater the discrepancy between the expectations and the reality of working in a mental health system, the more potential for abuse to the counselor by the system. A counselor may be abused by a system in many ways. For example, he or she may be given the least desired on-call schedule, be asked to take on additional responsibilities without adequate compensation, and/or be harassed openly or subtly by other staff members. By contrast, counselors who aware of manipulations they experienced as a child will be better able to protect themselves, because they are less likely to idealize others or the system, to feel helpless, or to allow themselves to be manipulated.

It is at the third level, *continuance in the system,* that critical incidents occur for the counselor. Because environments, like people, have personalities, they can affect an individual's potential, initiative, and coping (Insel & Moos, 1974). The struggle with being at a particular mental health agency may hinge on the match between the agency's values and the individual's values. A counselor new to a mental health system may neglect his or her own self-care in order to impress others, and veterans of the mental health system may feel "dethroned" by the new counselor. The critical incident is a painful, transitional point that combines vulnerabilities and current authority figure interactions. The system authority response to a critical incident can have an impact on future interactions of the counselor within the system and the individual's feelings toward the system.

Following a critical incident, there will be a critical authority response or a compassionate authority response. The occurrence of and ramifications of the incident are blamed on the counselor in a *critical authority* response, resulting in more pain for the counselor and possibly an increase in isolation, vulnerability, self-neglect, and competitiveness within the counselor and among other counselors at the agency. In a *compassionate authority* response, the painful incident is compassionately discussed with the counselor, resulting in a reduction of pain and an increase of trust. In this response, the issue of "who started it" is not relevant; it is more important that the counselor be heard and the issue addressed. The latter response recognizes that the counselor may be responding to behavior settings in the environment (Barker & Wright, 1955)—that is, a system environment that encourages certain behaviors in individuals. In such a case, the counselor is not behaving solely out of individual characteristics, but is being shaped by the system to act in a certain manner. The latter response encourages a compassionate dialogue between the counselor and the system.

Recognition of Problems: Leaving versus Staying

The counselor needs to be able to recognize critical incidents at his or her agency and develop a strategy for approaching such problems. Generally, such an approach involves recognition of the difficult encounter (critical incident), use of coping strategies that include stress management, and a decision to stay at or leave the agency.

Most counselors will not have difficulty recognizing the critical incident for them at an agency. As described previously, it is an incident that is uncomfortable and emotionally painful for the counselor. It is during such incidents that the counselor may reexamine his or her commitment to the field of counseling, particularly with regard to the agency. Probably the best indicator of a critical incident is when the counselor experiences intense emotions regarding a work-related incident. These critical incidents may underscore an unknown or known difference in values between the counselor and the agency. The incident may also highlight the degree of the match and/or mismatch between the counselor and the agency.

While the incident itself may be difficult for the counselor, it may be even more difficult if the authority response is critical in nature. The counselor may ask himself or herself: Can I continue to do the type of counseling I value and remain at this agency? Can I survive personally in such an environment? There are a number of avenues the counselor can explore in the process of addressing these questions.

Because both individual and situational factors are related to the impact of stress on one's health (Levi, 1990), the counselor may want to obtain a therapist to determine how much of the struggle is the counselor's and how much is the agency's. If a counselor chooses this approach, it is wise to select a therapist the counselor does not know personally or professionally. Another approach to self-reflection is to obtain a supervisor with whom the counselor can process the difficulties of the system. This supervisor would preferably be someone outside the agency who is either familiar with the dynamics of the agency or willing to learn about the dynamics. The danger of talking with only colleagues in the system is that the counselor may not be encouraged to examine thoroughly his or her own involvement in the process.

The process of determining whether to stay or leave involves self-care. The counselor needs to determine if he or she needs to stay in the system and, if so, how to survive within the difficulties of the system. Although it is preferable to operate in healthy systems, creating support groups may enhance the counselor's ability to cope with the stresses of the system. French and Raven (1959) discuss the importance of referent power with a group: When individuals identify with a group, their behavior will be consistent with that group. If a counselor has a referent power group outside the mental health system, the counselor may be able to use the referent group as an anchor, a way of surviving the upheaval of being involved in the abusive system. The referent group may provide the counselor with a model of behavior that is self-respectful as well as provide support to the counselor during times of critical incidents.

Common stress management strategies include individual and organizational reactions (Cherniss & Dantzig, 1986). Individual techniques include relaxation (yoga, biofeedback, meditation, relaxation training, etc.) and cognitive-behavioral approaches (addressing irrational thoughts) (Lazarus & Folkman, 1984). Organizational approaches such as changing jobs, providing supervision, and building in problem-solving processes may also be helpful. Although the counselor cannot rely on the agency to provide stress management strategies, the counselor can develop a support system that assists in the self-care of the counselor. Ross, Altmaier, and Russell (1989) found among doctoral-level counseling center staff that although higher job stress was associated with higher burnout, support from supervisors and colleagues was related to lower burnout. In addition, the counselor may attempt to have an impact on the system by respectfully educating influential individuals within the organization about the importance of creating a community of wellness. Witmer and Young (1996) suggest the following components be present in a wellness community: compassion, commitment, leadership, involvement, creative problem solving and conflict resolution, communication, and autonomy.

Self-Care

Guidelines to Realistic Self-Care

Counselors are rarely taught about self-care in their academic preparation, yet they work in a field that consistently exposes them to the dysfunctional behavior of humans. In order to prevent relapse or dysfunctional behavior in the counselor, each counselor must develop an individualized approach as well as a commitment to self-care. Sowa, May, and Niles (1994) underscore the importance of self-care for counselors by reporting studies that demonstrate a negative correlation between burnout and coping strategies/self-care: The more coping strategies, the less burnout. If a counselor does not develop effective coping strategies, he or she may leave the field of counseling (Cherniss, 1991) or continue to practice counseling when impaired (Emerson & Markos, 1996).

In some agencies, the highly respected counselor is one who may have difficulty setting limits in giving to others, perhaps too idealistic and dedicated (Emerson & Markos, 1996). This counselor may be willing to fill in whenever someone is needed, or will work overtime without pay, or will drop his or her schedule to meet the needs of others. Although this counselor may be appreciated and valued, if he or she does not practice self-care, this individual will likely burn out on the job. Gladding (1991) reports that counselors may abuse themselves by acting in dysfunctional ways on the job and by not setting necessary boundaries between themselves and their clients or colleagues. Wearing oneself out at a job appears related to negative perceptions about oneself, one's job, and one's clients (Cummings & Nall, 1983), which also seem related to the amount of daily struggles outside of work the counselor has.

One way to prevent job burnout is to examine one's counseling philosophy. Some self-help phrases such as "Progress, not perfection" and "Be responsible for the effort, not the outcome" may help counselors realize the limits of what they can do. A counselor is only responsible for making the best effort he or she can. This does not mean that the client will be able to stay sober, nor does it mean that others may not hold the counselor accountable for his or her counseling efforts. The philosophy, though, may help the counselor realize that he or she has limits on what can be provided to the client. The counselor is metaphorically standing in a river and needs to work with who or what floats their way on the river: Some objects may be missed, some may only be able to be worked with for a short time, some may stay until they are more in balance.

The areas for self-care include mind, body, emotions, and spirit. In terms of the *mind*, counselors are often aware of the need for challenges and positive thinking to encourage oneself. There is also a need to be aware of leisure activities where one "loses oneself" in manners that are not harmful to oneself. Losing oneself requires a sense of timelessness and playfulness where one forgets one's problems. In terms of the *body*, counselors are also aware of the need for eating, sleeping, and exercising correctly. Counselors need to learn to listen to their bodies because their bodies will not lie: The body will not say it is relaxed when it feels stress. Counselors are also aware of the need to express thoughts and feelings in "I" statements and to respond to their *emotional* needs. Possibly the area counselors are least familiar with is the *spirit*. This area does not necessarily mean religious, but it is the basis for answering the questions: What keeps my spirit alive? What makes me glad to be alive, interested in living, and want to face the day? It is this area, these interests, that must be incorporated into the lives of therapists to keep them alive and healthy.

One block to self-care for counselors seems to be the illusion that self-care takes another chunk of time from the counselor. The approach to self-care being advocated here is self-care "on the run." Most counselors have very demanding work schedules and personal lives. They need to learn to practice self-care in spurts as time and opportunity allow themselves rather than wait for a significant period of time off work. In small, regular ways, the counselor must fuse his or her life with activities that keep the spirit alive and nurture the interest in work. For example, during a stressful workday, a counselor may need to find brief breaks and do something enjoyable, such as take a short walk, listen to some music, or talk with a friend.

It is also important for the counselor to practice on-going self-compassion and forgiveness. The counselor must learn to aim for his or her best, both personally and professionally, and then let it go. Although these may sound like lofty goals, the counselor also needs to prepare for a sense of failure and/or helplessness. It is at these times that the process of self-forgiveness may be helpful. Smedes (1984) presents a forgiveness model of four stages: hurt, hate, heal, and coming together. The focus of the stages are as their labels imply. Counselors may feel wronged by their clients, their clients' families, the organization for which they work, or their own powerlessness in helping their clients. They may need to practice forgiveness with others as well as themselves in order to continue working as counselors.

In the hurt stage, the counselor needs to feel the hurt and the wrong that has occurred. In the hate stage, the counselor needs to allow himself or herself to experience the hatred and the urge for revenge to "right the wrong." In the heal stage, the counselor begins to feel free of the hurt and hatred and look at the wrongdoer in a different light. Finally, in the coming together stage, the counselor begins to invite the other into his or her life. This process cannot be hurried, nor, as Smedes (1984) suggests, can stages be skipped. Therapists must learn to acknowledge and learn from their own mistakes and forgive themselves for their humanness, even though others may continue to hold them accountable for their behavior.

Importance of Commitment to Self-Care

Frequently in working with addicted clients, counselors talk with them about taking care of their own needs. These words will appear more meaningful and have more basis if the clients can look to the therapists to see how the therapists take care of themselves. If counselors do not set limits or care for their bodies, minds, emotions, and spirits, their words may look empty for their clients.

Families, loved ones, employers, and clients cannot be expected to know all of the demands put on therapists. A commitment to self-care is critical if counselors plan to stay "alive" professionally.

CASE STUDY: CLYDE

Clyde is an addictions counselor at a local mental health center and has worked in the field for the last 15 years. He has been married, for the second time, for the past five years. Clyde has worked a 12-step recovery program for 17 years. At work, he believes he is increasingly asked to "do more with less" and feels frustrated with how he is asked to know more about the field of addictions (working with specific issues of sexual abuse and domestic violence) and working with special populations (women and racial minorities). Clyde is also upset that his agency may be having cutbacks, which will mean more responsibility for him. In particular, the new director of his agency called Clyde into her office and yelled at him for being "too independent" on the job and compared him with recent graduates from programs working at the agency, who she views as more open to teamwork and new ideas. Since that incident, he has spoken very little to others at work except to say that he feels burned out and overwhelmed by stress. He has lost interest in activities he used to enjoy, such as car racing and watching sports.

1. What type of authority response did Charlie experience and how did it affect him?
2. What recommendations would you make to Clyde regarding staying or leaving the agency? The field of counseling?
3. What recommendations would you make to him regarding self-care?

Working with Addicts

Examination of Own Use History

Addicts can be a difficult group of clients to counsel. They may be very challenging and rebellious with regard to authority figures, such as counselors, and they may have a difficult time changing their habits and behaviors. They can be trying for any counselor, even one who has no negative history with an alcoholic/addict.

For the counselor who grew up in a home with an alcoholic parent, sibling, or relative, or who has a spouse or child who is addicted, working with addicts and alcoholics can be even more difficult. Although the chemicals used and the type of relationship may differ, the dynamics and the pain of the relationship are the same. Counselors may find themselves trying to reason with clients in the same manner they tried to reason with the addicted significant other in their lives. They may feel the same feelings of frustration and helplessness. For this type of counselor, the addict/alcoholic holds the promise for uncomfortable countertransference, which may affect the professional abilities of the counselor.

There are a number of ways in which the counselor may address such unresolved issues. First, a counselor wanting to work with addicted individuals will need to have a clear understanding of his or her current and past drug usage. This process may require an assessment from an addictions specialist. At the very least, the counselor needs to be sure no chemical abuse is presently occurring that would interfere with his or her professional abilities. A counselor who does determine that there is an addictions problem, be it through personal or professional assessment, needs to obtain treatment for the addiction as any addicted individual needs. This treatment could be through a formalized addictions program, through therapy with an addictions specialist, and/or through a self-help group.

The counselor who does not have an addictions problem, but has lived with or currently lives with someone who does, may also want to join a self-help organization. Groups such as Al-Anon, Nar-Anon, and SOS were discussed in Chapters 4 and 7. The questions used in Chapter 7 to assist a counselor in helping a client find a good match with a self-help group can also be used by the counselor who needs a self-help group to cope with their own or a loved one's addiction. There are some special concerns, however, that arise when a counselor joins a self-help group.

When members of self-help groups find out that a counselor is in the group, the members may be tempted to try to obtain "free counseling" from the counselor. They may also have difficulty imagining counselors having problems, and as a result, not respect the counselor for joining the group or not take the counselor's issues as seriously as those of other group members. Although anonymity is encouraged in different self-help groups, members might accidently let others know that the counselor has joined the group. Such a break of anonymity may have an impact on the counselor's professional life. Therefore, a counselor joining a self-help group needs to answer some specific of questions:

1. In what type of group am I comfortable letting members know I am a counselor?
2. What type of negative impact might I experience professionally if the self-help group members were to let others in the community know that I have joined the group?
3. What types of limits must I put on the sharing I do in the group, given my profession?
4. How will I set limits on the time I will listen to others and how can I make sure that my own needs are being met?

Some counselors cope with this situation by attending meetings away from the area in which they live or work. Other counselors attend meetings specifically designed for professionals or professional counselors. Also, some counselors choose not to attend meetings, but spend time reading the literature from the self-help organizations in order to obtain support. There is a fine line between running from one's own issues and making oneself vulnerable professionally. Although surgeons are never expected to have the objectivity to operate on themselves, counselors are often expected by lay people not to have any personal problems if they are "good" counselors.

A third approach to addressing one's own issues is to obtain therapy to address these unresolved issues. Therapy will be most beneficial if the counselor chosen as the therapist is knowledgeable in addictions counseling. He or she can understand some of the difficulties inherent in working with addicted individuals and can perceive how these interactions have an impact on the counselor-as-client with regard to his or her personal history.

Self-help group attendance, self-help group literature, and therapy can be used in whatever mix-and-match fashion that seems most beneficial to the counselor and his or her situation. Certain factors, such as living in a small town, may influence the treatment selected by the counselor. As with any client, the counselor who is in the client role must be respected for the values he or she holds.

Knowledge of Own Limitations

Counselors who work with addicts need to be aware of their own limitations as they apply to the use of chemicals/drugs, "soft spots" for the counselor, and danger spots for counselors who are in recovery and those who are not. Sometimes, it almost seems assumed that one needs to be addicted to work with addicts effectively. However, both addicted and nonaddicted counselors have issues they need to address in the counseling context with the addicted individual. The face of the issue may change, but the existence of the issue does not.

Both addicted and nonaddicted counselors must look at their own chemical usage. Addicted counselors need to remain chemically free, and nonaddicted counselors need to determine if they want to use. The following questions must be addressed by the nonaddicted counselor:

1. Should I give up the use of mood-altering substances in order to work with addicted clients?
2. Can I understand the addictive issues with mood-altering substances if I continue to use them?
3. If I continue to use mood-altering substances, how will I respond in situations where I meet addicted clients and I am under the influence of the substances?

These types of questions need to be addressed by the counselor who is planning to work with addicted clients. At the very least, the nonaddicted counselor may need to work on changing a habit/addiction that they have struggled with in order to understand and have compassion for the addicted client's struggle with change. Addicted clients will frequently ask nonaddicted counselors how they can counsel them when they themselves are not addicted. Counselors need to be prepared to answer such a question based on limits they have set on their own chemical usage and habits they have tried to change. Many addicted clients will be satisfied with a thoughtful, genuine answer by a nonaddicted counselor.

Both addicted and nonaddicted counselors will have "soft spots" in certain areas that will make them less comfortable in working with clients on their issues. It is important for the counselor to know these limitations and then work within them. For example, a counselor may work more effectively with same-gender clients if the alcoholic/addict in his or her background was the opposite gender, or may work more effectively with certain types of addicts (based on their drug of choice) or with addicts from a certain socioeconomic status level. A counselor may want to reduce these limitations by dealing with personal countertransference issues in his or her own therapy, or the counselor may simply state that he or she is unable to work with that population due to personal values or life experiences. If the counselor works at a mental health agency, these limitations must be stated from the start so that any intake process will take the counselor's preferences into account. If the counselor works privately, it is helpful to state these limitations in a manner most respectful to clients and to let possible referral sources know of these limitations. Experiences in working with different addicted individuals with good supervision and self-examination of one's own issues can allow for the counselor to "stretch" himself or herself and yet learn the limitations that are not negotiable.

Danger Spots (Addicted Counselors)

Addicted counselors have some areas they need to be aware of in their work with addicted clients. It is often assumed that addicted counselors have some time in their own recovery process before they begin counseling others. This minimum is often established by addictions counselor certification or licensure boards and is typically in the range of one to two years. Due to being addicted, these counselors may experience a relapse. When a relapse occurs, it is best for the counselor to be evaluated by someone who works outside the system or organization for whom the counselor works.

Another option is to contact the state certification or licensure board and determine its process for ethically handling such a situation. If the counselor is certified or licensed in the state, he or she must inform the board of the relapse and follow the board's recommendations. If the counselor works with addicted individuals in some capacity, but is not licensed, the organization for whom he or she works will determine the best way to address the situation. For example, in larger organizations, the counselor could be transferred to a no-patient-contact job (Bissell & Royce, 1994). However, whatever the situation, when an addicted person relapses, it is best to consult with someone outside the organization in order to be sure that the addicted employee will not be enabled by the organization.

Another common issue for addicted counselors centers on the actual treatment of addicts. Recovering addicted counselors may be tempted to treat clients in the same manner in which they were treated. This may be especially true for the counselor who views a client (and the client's usage) as very similar to himself or herself. Recovering addicted counselors need to remember that each client is an individual and each recovery path is unique. The most important concern is to assist the client in becoming sober; the path to obtaining that goal may be less important. In addition, the counselor needs to avoid the temptation of competing with the client as to who had the worse addiction problem.

A final issue for the recovering addicted counselor may be in regard to attendance of self-help groups. A counselor will need to determine how comfortable he or she is being at meetings with their clients and how to handle such dual relationships. This crossover may be more common in small towns or with certain populations (e.g., gays and lesbians). A counselor may need to consider attending the same meetings, but being cautious of what he or she discusses, or attend meetings specifically for professional counselors.

CASE STUDY: JAKE

Jake is a recovering addict who has worked as a licensed addictions counselor in a small town for 8 years. He was sober 10 years, until a relapse a month ago following the sudden death of his mother. Jake is well respected in the local community and at the treatment center where he works. He has not told anyone (including his sponsor and his NA group) of his relapse with cocaine. He is afraid he will lose his job, his wife, and his reputation if he speaks of his relapse. Many of his former clients attend the same self-help groups he attends.

1. If Jake came to you as a colleague for advice, what recommendations would you make him, regarding the action he should take?
2. What are your professional responsibilities as a counselor if you are aware that Jake has relapsed?
3. What action would you take professionally and personally to be of assistance to Jake?

Danger Spots (Nonaddicted Counselors)

Nonaddicted counselors may have some issues particular to their work with addicted clients, such as difficulty understanding the struggles clients experience in making a behavior change. As stated previously, it may help with their compassion for addicts if these counselors attempt to change a habit with which they struggle. These counselors may want to obtain supervision and/or therapy to address unresolved issues they have regarding addicts they have known, which promotes countertransference. This countertransference may be overly critical, enabling, or fluctuate between the extremes, depending on the clients with whom these counselors work.

A second problem can be the bias held against nonaddicts working in the addictions field. When a nonaddicted counselor is attempting to understand recovery-related issues and struggles, it may be best to approach clients in a manner that encourages dialogue. A nonaddicted counselor who acknowledges his or her own ignorance about addiction is more likely to be educated by both clients and addicted counselors regarding the recovery concerns. If nonaddicted counselors seek self-help group assistance, they will likely run into similar struggles as the addicted counselors. Thus, they will need to be prepared as to how to address these same concerns.

CASE STUDY: RUTH

Ruth is a new addictions counselor who just began facilitating a DUI group at her work. She is not a recovering addict, but she is the daughter of an alcoholic. Her childhood was very traumatic for her in terms of physical, psychological, and emotional abuse from her alcoholic father. She has had some short-term therapy for these issues and has felt relatively resolved about them for the last year. She has been facilitating the group for a couple of months and overall has enjoyed the challenges. Recently, a member came into the group who looks, acts, and talks like her father. Although she has felt very comfortable with group members in the past, when this group member speaks or even sits quietly in the group, she experiences a range of emotions: fear, anger, and hurt. Ruth is confused and overwhelmed with the intensity of her feelings. She is afraid to talk with her supervisor or colleagues about her reactions to this member because she is concerned that they will view her as unprofessional. She has rationalized that it is okay to not say anything to anyone because the DUI group is just about over, she has never had another client who elicited such a reaction from her, and she is sure it will not be an issue in the future.

1. If you believe that Ruth's course of action is wrong, what specifically is she doing wrong?
2. If you could intervene on the situation with Ruth, what action would you take?
3. If possible, what advice would you give Ruth about action she needs to take

with regard to the situation in terms of both herself and the welfare of her client?

Same Support

The issue of attending the same support group has been discussed previously for both addicted and nonaddicted counselors. Another related issue is having a mentor or sponsor in a self-help group who also serves as a mentor or sponsor to a client. Sometimes this situation occurs by accident and sometimes it is due to small-town meetings or minority-population meetings. The sponsor in this situation may be the critical component. The sponsor needs to make sure that he or she has good boundaries regarding the confidence of the sponsee. The counselor needs to reinforce these boundaries in the counseling session by limiting conversations about the sponsor as much as possible or providing minimal self-disclosure with the client. It may be easiest for all concerned if the counselor obtains a different sponsor while working with the client on therapy issues.

Summary

This chapter has highlighted significant personal and professional issues in the arenas of ethics, law, agency, and self-care. Counselors are encouraged to stay current with these issues by joining professional organizations; reading current theoretical and research articles in journals and books; attending workshops, courses, and conventions; and working closely with other colleagues in the field of addictions counseling. Given the current, rapid changes in the mental health service delivery system, a counselor needs to work within a network of other professionals in order to be both self-protective and appropriately concerned with the welfare of the client. All counselors need to be concerned with these personal and professional issues in order to provide the highest quality of addictions counseling possible.

SUGGESTED READINGS

Anderson, B. S. (1996). *The counselor and the law* (4th ed.). Alexandria, VA: American Counseling Association.

Bissell, L. C., & Royce, J. E. (1994). *Ethics for addiction professionals.* Center City, MN: Hazelden.

Brodsky, S. L. (1991). *Testifying in court: Guidelines and maxims for the expert witness.* Washington, DC: American Psychological Association.

Brooks, M. K. (1997). Ethical and legal aspects of confidentiality. In J. H. Lowinson, P. Ruiz, R. B. Millman, & J. G. Langrod (Eds.), *Substance abuse: A comprehensive textbook* (3rd ed.) (pp. 884–899). Baltimore: Williams & Wilkins.

Federal Register. (1987, June 9). *Part II Department of Health and Human Services,* 42 CFR Part 2, Vol. 52, No. 110, 21796-21814.

Marlatt, G. A., & Gordon, J. R. (Ed.). (1985). *Relapse prevention.* New York: Guilford.

Prochaska, J. O., DiClemente, C. C., & Norcross, J. C. (1992). In search of how people change. *American Psychologist, 47,* 1102–1114.

Remley, T. P. (Ed.). (1993). *ACA Legal Series* (Volumes 1–12). Alexandria, VA: American Counseling Association.

REFERENCES

Anderson, B. S. (1996). *The counselor and the law* (4th ed.). Alexandria, VA: American Counseling Association.

Bandura, A. (1982). The psychology of chance encounters and life paths. *American Psychologist, 33,* 334–358.

Barker, R. G., & Wright, H. F. (1955). *Midwest and its children: The psychological ecology of an American town.* New York: Harper and Row.

Bissell, L. C., & Royce, J. E. (1994). *Ethics for addiction professionals.* Center City, MN: Hazelden.

Bossin, P. G. (1992). How to handle custody cases. *Trial, 28,* 24–26, 28.

Brooks, M. K. (1997). Ethical and legal aspects of confidentiality. In J. H. Lowinson, P. Ruiz, R. B. Millman, & J. G. Langrod (Eds.), *Substance abuse: A comprehensive textbook* (3rd ed.) (pp. 884–899). Baltimore: Williams & Wilkins.

Cherniss, C. (1991). Career commitment in human service professionals: A biographical study. *Human Relations, 44,* 419–437.

Cherniss, C., & Dantzig, S. A. (1986). In R. Kilburg, P. E. Nathan, & R. W. Thoreson (Eds.), *Professionals in distress: Issues, syndromes, and solutions in psychology* (pp. 255–273). Washington, DC: American Psychological Association.

Cummings, O. W., & Nall, R. L. (1983). Relationships of leadership style and burnout to counselors' perceptions of their jobs, themselves, and their clients. *Counselor Education and Supervision, 22,* 227–234.

Cushman, P. (1990). Why the self is empty. *American Psychologist, 45,* 599–611.

Doyle, K. (1997). Substance abuse counselors in recovery: Implications for the ethical issue of dual relationships. *Journal of Counseling and Development, 75,* 428–432.

Emerson, S., & Markos, P. A. (1996). Signs and symptoms of the impaired counselor. *Journal of Humanistic Education and Development, 34,* 108–117.

Federal Register. (1987, June 9). *Part II Department of Health and Human Services, 42* CFR Part 2, Vol. 52, No. 110, 21796–21814.

Forsyth, D. R. (1983). *An introduction to group dynamics.* Monterey, CA: Brooks/Cole.

Frankl, V. E. (1963). *Man's search for meaning.* New York: Simon & Schuster.

French, J., & Raven, B. (1959). The basis of social power. In D. D. Cartwright (Ed.), *Studies on Social Power* (pp. 150–167). Ann Arbor: University of Michigan, Institute for Social Research.

Gladding, S. (1991). Counselor self-abuse. *Journal of Mental Health Counseling, 13,* 414–419.

Haugaard, J. J., & Reppucci, N. D. (1988). *The sexual abuse of children.* San Francisco: Jossey-Bass.

Herlihy, B., & Sheeley, V. L. (1986, April). *Privileged communication: Legal status & ethical issues.* Paper presented at the Annual Convention of the American Association for Counseling and Development, Los Angeles.

Hollis, J. (1989). The wounded vision: The myth of the tragic flaw. *Quadrant, 22,* 25–36.

Holmes, C. (1991). The wounded healer. *Society for Psychoanalytic Psychotherapy Bulletin, 6,* 33–36.

Howell, R. J. (1990). Professional standards of practice in child custody examinations. *Psychotherapy in Private Practice, 8,* 15–23.

Hubert, M. (1996, February). Guidelines for

avoiding ethical pitfalls. *Counseling Today,* 10, 14.

Inaba, D. S., & Cohen, W. E. (1989). *Uppers, downers, all arounders.* Ashland, OR: CNS Productions.

Insel, P. M., & Moos, R. H. (1974). Psychological environments: Expanding the scope of human ecology. *American Psychologist,* 29, 179–187.

Jellinek, E. M. (1960). *The disease concept of alcoholism.* New Haven, CT: College and University Press.

Jourard, S. M. (1971). *The transparent self.* New York: D. Van Nostrand.

Lazarus, R. S., & Folkman, S. (1984). *Stress, appraisal, and coping.* New York: Springer.

Levi, L. (1990). Occupational stress: Spice of life or kiss of death? *American Psychologist,* 45, 1142–1145.

Marlatt, G. A., & Gordon, J. R. (Ed.). (1985). *Relapse prevention.* New York: Guilford.

McHugh, M., Beckman, L., & Frieze, I. H. (1979). Analyzing alcoholism. In I. H. Frieze, D. Bar-Tal, & J. S. Carroll (Eds.), *New approaches to social problems* (pp. 168–208). San Francisco: Jossey-Bass.

Miller, A. (1981). *The drama of the gifted child.* New York: Basic Books.

Miller, G., & Kaplan, B. (1996). Testifying in court. *Psychotherapy in Private Practice,* 15, 15–32.

Miller, G., Wagner, A. U., Gridley, B., & Britton, T. (1998). A framework for understanding the wounding of healers. *Counseling and Values, 42,* 124–132.

Miller, G. D., & Baldwin, D. C. (1987). Implications of the wounded-healer paradigm for the use of the self in therapy. *Journal of Psychotherapy and the Family, 3,* 139–151.

National Association of Alcoholism and Drug Abuse Counselors Education and Research Foundation. (1995). *Income and compensation study of alcohol and drug counseling professionals.* Arlington, VA: Author.

Poirier, J. G. (1991). Disputed custody and concerns of parental violence. *Psychotherapy in Private Practice, 9,* 7–23.

Price, L., & Spence, S. H. (1994). Burnout symptoms amongst drug and alcohol service employees: Gender differences in the interaction between work and home stressors. *Anxiety, Stress, and Coping: An International Journal, 7,* 67–84.

Prochaska, J. O., DiClemente, C. C., & Norcross, J. C. (1992). In search of how people change. *American Psychologist, 47,* 1102–1114.

Remen, N., May, R., Young, D., & Berland, W. (1985). The wounded healer. *Saybrook Review, 5,* 84–93.

Remley, T. P., Jr. (1985). The law and ethical practices in elementary and middle schools. *Elementary School Guidance and Counseling, 19,* 181–189.

Remley, T. P., & Miranti, J. G. (1991). Child custody evaluator: A new role for mental health counselors. *Journal of Mental Health Counseling, 13,* 334–342.

Ross, R. R., Altmaier, E. M., & Russell, D. W. (1989). Job stress, social support, and burnout among counseling center staff. *Journal of Counseling Psychology, 36,* 464–470.

Salo, M. M., & Shumate, S. G. (1993). *Counseling minor clients* (ACA Legal Series, Vol. 9). Alexandria, VA: American Counseling Association.

Shaffer, H., & Kauffman, J. (1985). The clinical assessment and diagnosis of addiction. In T. E. Bratter & G. G. Forrest (Eds.), *Alcoholism and substance abuse: Strategies for intervention* (pp. 225–258). New York: Free Press.

Smedes, L. B. (1984). *Forgive & forget: Healing the hurts we don't deserve.* San Francisco: Harper and Row.

Sorge, R. (1991). Harm reduction: A new approach to drug services. *Health/PAC Bulletin, Winter,* 22–27.

Sowa, C. J., May, K. M., & Niles, S. G. (1994). Occupational stress within the counseling profession: Implication for counselor training. *Counselor Education, 34,* 19–29.

Stadler, H. A., Willing, K. L., Eberhage, M. G., & Ward, W. H. (1988). Impairment: Implications for the counseling profession. *Journal of Counseling and Development, 66,* 258–260.

Swenson, L. C. (1993). *Psychology and the law for the helping professions.* Pacific Grove, CA: Brooks/Cole.

Trimpey, J. (1989). *The small book.* New York: Delacorte.

Witmer, J. M., & Young, M. E. (1996). Preventing counselor impairment: A wellness approach. *Journal of Humanistic Education and Development, 34,* 141–155.

INDEX